Byzantine Studies
Essays on the Slavic World
and the Eleventh Century

Published under the Auspices of
the Speros Basil Vryonis Center for the Study of Hellenism
Sacramento, California

This work is the ninth volume in the series
Hellenism
Ancient, Mediæval, Modern

General Editors
Christos P. Ioannides, Stylianos Spyridakis, Speros Vryonis, Jr.

Byzantine Studies

Essays on the Slavic World and the Eleventh Century

Edited by Speros Vryonis, Jr.
with contributions by
*Henrik Birnbaum, Michael S. Flier
Michael Hendy, Alexander Kazhdan, Bariša Krekić
Ja. Ljubarskij, Gerhard Podskalsky, Peter F. Sugar
Speros Vryonis, Jr., John J. Yiannias*

Aristide D. Caratzas, Publisher
New Rochelle, New York

To the Memories of

Fredi Chiapelli

Will Mathews

Gustave von Grunebaum

Lynn White

Byzantine Studies: Essays on the Slavic World and the Eleventh Century

Copyright © 1992 by Aristide D. Caratzas, Publisher

No part of this book may be reproduced in any form without the permission in writing of the publisher.

Aristide D. Caratzas, Publisher
30 Church Street, P.O. Box 210
New Rochelle, NY 10802

ISBN: 0-89241-517-7

Printed in the United States of America
Bound by Hoster Bindery, Ivyland, Pennsylvania

Articles in part 1 of *Byzantine Studies: Essays on the Slavic World and the Eleventh Century* originated in the January 1990 conference at UCLA "Byzantine Civilization and the Slavic World," sponsored by the Alexander S. Onassis Center for Hellenic Studies, New York University, The Speros Basil Vryonis Center for the Study of Hellenism, Sacramento, California, The Center for Medieval and Renaissance Studies, UCLA, and the Department of Slavic Languages and Literatures, UCLA.

Articles in part 2 originated in the March 1991 conference at UCLA "Byzantine Society and Civilization in the Eleventh Century," sponsored by the Alexander S. Onassis Center for Hellenic Studies, New York University, The Speros Basil Vryonis Center for the Study of Hellenism, Sacramento, California, and The Center for Medieval and Renaissance Studies, UCLA.

Contents

Preface   vii

PART 1 BYZANTIUM AND THE SLAVIC WORLD

1 *Henrik Birnbaum*   1
The Slavic Settlements in the Balkans and the Eastern Alps

2 *Speros Vryonis, Jr.*   15
The Slavic Pottery (Jars) from Olympia, Greece

3 *Bariša Krekić*   43
Medieval Serbia: The Nemanyids and Byzantium

4 *Michael S. Flier*   53
The Iconology of Royal Ritual in Sixteenth-Century Muscovy

5 *Peter F. Sugar*   77
The Least Affected Social Group
in the Ottoman Balkans: the Peasantry

6 *John J. Yiannias*   87
The Byzantine Artistic Tradition under Ottoman Rule

PART 2 BYZANTIUM AND THE ELEVENTH CENTURY

7 *Alexander Kazhdan*   111
Russian Pre-Revolutionary Studies on Eleventh-Century Byzantium

8 *Speros Vryonis, Jr.*   125
The Greek and Arabic Sources
on the Battle of Mantzikert, 1071 A.D.

9 *Michael Hendy*   141
The Economy: A Brief Survey

10 *Gerhard Podskalsky*   153
Religion and Religious Life in Eleventh-Century Byzantium

11 *Ja. Ljubarskij*   175
The Fall of an Intellectual: The Intellectual and
Moral Atmosphere in Eleventh-Century Byzantium

Index   183

Preface

The presentation of this collection of conference papers by a group of distinguished scholars marks the inauguration of a series of joint conferences that involve the U.C.L.A. Center for Medieval and Renaissance Studies (with the important contribution of the UCLA Department of Slavic Languages and Literatures for the first conference), the Speros Basil Vryonis Center for the Study of Hellenism of Sacramento, and the Alexander S. Onassis Center for Hellenic Studies of New York University. The occasion for the beginning of this ambitious enterprise was the millennial celebration of the conversion of Kievan Rus' to Christianity and the subsequent development of civilizational relations between Kiev and Constantinople. The Onassis Center and the Vryonis Center of Sacramento, in making the decision to organize such a scholarly meeting, very naturally turned to the UCLA Center for Medieval and Renaissance Studies because of its long and distinguished history as a great institution in the field of medieval studies, and of medieval studies conceived of in the broadest manner. The organizer of the center, the late Lynn White, had early structured medieval studies on the UCLA campus according to a vision which included not only western Europe, but also Byzantium, Slavdom, Islam and Judaic Studies. Further, the Department of Slavic Languages and Literatures at U.C.L.A. has been one of the most distinguished in the world, with specialization in the medieval and early modern period. In broaching the subject with the director of the Center for Medieval and Renaissance Studies, Professor Michael Allen, we were most generously received and encouraged. The result was the conference, and then a second conference, the proceedings of which bear witness to the richness and fruition of the conferences and cooperation. Thus we owe great thanks to Professor Allen and to his assistant Suzanne Kahle, as well as to Professor Henrik Birnbaum then chairman of the Slavic Department. Further we must thank Dr. Christos Ioannides, Director of the Speros Basil Vryonis Center, for his encouragement and support as well. Finally I wish to thank Dr. Athena Coronis, Director of the Onassis Center Outreach Program who, along with Suzanne Kahle and Dr. Ioannides, carried out the organization and execution of the conferences.

The papers from the conference "Byzantine Civilization and the Slavic World" held at UCLA in January 1990 include six pieces and attempt to deal with a wide chronological and thematic spectrum from the world of Byzantino-Slavica, beginning as they do with the question of the Urheimat of the Slavs and the chronological, linguistic and toponymic framework of their appearance in the Balkans, as well as their earliest certifiable material remains in the Peloponnese, going through the Byzantine period into that of Muscovite Russia and the Ottoman Balkans. Henrik Birnbaum gives an invaluable survey-analysis on the new literature that deals with the nature of Slavic appearance in the Balkans and then goes on to analyze the thorny historico-linguistic-archaeological problem of the paths and manners by which they entered the peninsula. Vryonis makes the first presentation of a comparatively large body of very early Slavic pottery, which constitutes the first such major archaeological evidence for the Slavs in the Peloponnese. He tackles the problem of dating and concludes that under the present circumstances this pottery is coeval with the earliest Slavic pottery found extensively by Bulgarian archaeologists in Bulgaria. Barisa Krekić analyzes the intensification of political and cultural contacts of the medieval Serbian dynasty of the Nemanyids with Byzantium and its civilization. Michael Flier combines cultural history and Russian political history in an effort to locate Russian ecclesiastical ritual (the rituals of Epiphany and Palm Sunday) within Muscovite political ritual in the sixteenth and seventeenth centuries. His analysis revolves about the interpretation of the iconographies of these two religious/political ceremonies. He moves away from the "submissive thesis" of earlier interpretations of these rituals, a thesis which had previously assumed the subordination of the ruler to the metropolitan. Flier shows clearly that the ceremonies were manipulated by the Muscovite ruler to show his Christian humility only, and did not apply at all to the relations of church and state. Indeed in the latter the ruler did not relinquish his authority over the church.

With the papers of Peter Sugar and of John Yiannias we return to the Balkans where the descendants of the Byzantine and Balkan Slavs continued to live, but under the rule of Muslim conquerors. Sugar focuses on one social class among the Balkan Christian subjects of the Ottoman Turks, the Greek and Slavic peasants, saying of them that they were the "least affected social group in the Ottoman Balkans." His analysis is simple, highly structured and absolutely convincing, bringing to bear the historical facts that the Ottomans by and large centered their control and demographic impact in the towns and along the strategic arteries of movement and conquest. The rural areas were brought under the economic and political control of the warrior class who were not nearly so numerous as their subjects. Thus the countryside most often remained Christian, and when the merchant-enlightened classes of Serbs, Greeks, and Bulgars returned from the West with its ideas of enlightenment, progress, revolution and nationalism they found their military support in this peasant class. The permeation of Byzantine civilization had been decisive for the descendants of the Byzantines and Slavs in the Balkans. Finally, Yiannias turns our attention to the discussion, long overdue, of the fate of Byzantine art in its competition not with the art of Islam but with that of Gothic-Renaissance-Baroque Europe. He differentiates between the art "impulse" amid leadership of Constantinople and the other Turkish held Balkan lands, which were destroyed with the Ottoman conquests, and the leadership of Crete-Ionian Islands under Venetian, Christian control. For the sixteenth and seventeenth centuries this was decisive and set the modes and styles of Christian art throughout the Orthodox Balkans, constituting thus a pan-Orthodox style. Gradually however these same painters began to learn the western styles in Italy and finally, after the conquest of Crete, a type of crude western art, western in iconography and rough style, replaced the older Byzantine style.

Such are the contents of these highly complex studies which though very specialized are nevertheless keyed into the broad historical sweep and understanding of Byzantine civilization and the Slavic world. A careful reading of these texts constitutes a rich and enjoyable journey through the world of this second or eastern Europe, with which we are so concerned today. Their relevance is immediately apparent.

The papers making up part 2 of *Byzantine Studies: Essays on the Slavic World and the Eleventh Century* emerged from the conference "Byzantine Civilization in the Eleventh Century," also held at U.C.L.A. (March 8, 1991), and also organized by the Alexander S. Onassis Center for Hellenic Studies, New York University, the Speros Basil Vryonis Center for the Study of Hellenism, Sacramento, California, the Center for Medieval and Renaissance Studies, UCLA. We again thank the two directors, Michael Allen and Christos Ioannides, as well as Suzanne Kahle and Athena Coronis. This was conceived as an introductory or mini-symposium that would lead to a larger symposium in the near future to probe and reconsider Byzantine civilization in this crucial period of change and fall from high political and military power. Many scholars have noted the spectacular military and political collapse of the empire at the end of the eleventh century, at the time of the appearance of new and powerful forces: from the Islamic side the appearance of the Seljuk sultans, their Turkish nomads and the traditional forces of Islam; from the Western side the appearance of the militant Crusaders, the voracious Italian commercial and maritime powers, and the ambitious Normans of southern Italy. When the emperor Alexius I Comnenus ascended the imperial throne he was assailed on all sides by these potent military and commercial forces, and for a while his writ hardly ran outside the imperial city itself. Little over a century later the empire was to be shattered by the Fourth Crusade. This combination of facts has led many scholars to look at the century, a century of cosmic change in many other parts of the world, to ascertain the causes of what some consider decline.

In the five papers presented in part 2 we have very specific analyses of discrete themes and problems through which we can come to terms with the broader issues. Alexander Kazhdan analyzes Russian pre-Revolutionary (pre-Marxist that is) Byzantinists and their labors. Though substantial it was a branch of Byzantinology that was, and is, not well known to the rest of Byzantine scholars because of the linguistic barrier. Beginning with Basil Vasil'evsky, Kazhdan gradually filters out the strand of socio-economic history through which he and his successors attempted to explain the greatness and decline of Byzantium. Because the towering figure of the late George Ostrogorsky was a descendant of this school a refined and brilliantly analyzed version of the socio-economic explanation of the Russian school has become well known in the West. Kazhdan indicates that it is this tradition which has condemned the eleventh century as one of decisive decline and he ends with the rhetorical question: "Should the eleventh century be accursed, with Fedor Uspenskij and George Ostrogorsky, as a period of westernization and feudalization, as a period of greedy and egotistic officialdom? Or does it deserve a rehabilitation? This is probably one of the most challenging goals that modern Byzantine studies envisages."

Vryonis examines in minute detail the Greek and Arabic sources for the spectacular battle of Mantzikert where the Seljuk Sultan Kilidj Arslan defeated, captured, and then released the emperor Romanus IV. Long a central "battle" in Byzantium's long list of battles, the prevailing reconstruction and interpretation has been that of the Islamic historian Claude Cahen. The latter had relied almost exclusively on the Muslim historians, rejecting the testimony of the Byzantine sources. Vryonis shows that there was only one surviving eyewitness account, that of Michael Attaleiates, and from internal and comparative evidence he proceeds to the rehabilitation of Attaleiates and the rejection of practically all the Arab historians.

Michael Hendy gives a revisionist interpretation of an economy which traditionally had been depicted as an economy in a state of precipitous decline or as a stagnant economy. He does this by reinterpreting the significance of coinage, its debasement, and by pointing to a kind of reciprocity of losses and gains that Byzantium experienced in the use of her land holdings at one time in the Balkans and at another in Asia Minor. In this his views of the eleventh century tend to respond to Kazhdan's rhetorical question in the negative. The same is true of the study of Gerhard Podskalsky on the state of religion and religious life in the eleventh century. He begins with an in-depth examination of aspects of the studies which have been carried out on Byzantine religious life in the previous twenty years, thus touching upon a disparate array of important themes: the "Great Schism," the relation of classical education to the Christian faith, heresies, Islam, internal tensions within the church, the conversion of Rus' to Christianity and finally monasticism. It is monasticism that particularly concerns him for in it he sees a positive development in the eleventh century in the proliferation of monastic institutions, and it is against this background that he analyzes the doctrine of knowledge and the mystical doctrine of the "Light" of the famous mystic Symeon the New Theologian. Knowledge is thus not simply the product of the physical senses of sight and hearing, but also of the divine "Light." His student Nicetas Stethatos, who was also his "biographer," stated that those who have only pagan Greek education, but not this inspiration by the divine "Light," cannot understand the scriptures and should not be allowed to teach dogma. Indeed he begins his biography of Symeon by proudly announcing that Symeon had no need for pagan Greek learning. Though Podskalsky does not render a judgement on this view of the relation of secular and religious knowledge, it is obviously related to Kazhdan's rhetorical question, and it is in the last essay that we get a positive answer to Kazhdan's question.

Jakov Ljubarskij, an acknowledged specialist on Michael Psellus, the famous polymath and reviver of interest in Plato in the eleventh century, ends this collection with a short but tantalizing study on what he terms "The Fall of an Intellectual," the intellectual of course being none other than Psellus himself. He picks a set of Psellus's writings, two to the famous patriarch Michael Cerularius and one to his own former friend John Xiphilenus. On first reading of some of these Ljubarski describes Psellus as "liberal," "secular," and "tolerant," in other words, the opposite of his hierarchical correspondents, and also versed in the "outside education," i.e., that of pagan Greece. And yet in a second writing addressed to Cerularius (a legal condemnation) and in the end of his encomium on his former friend Xiphilenus, he attacks them both as guilty of "asebeia" or addiction to pagan learning, and Cerularius as guilty of murder and the like. What had happened was that Psellus was obliged by the rulers to attack these men, and so he became the instrument of the state attacking his own beliefs. Ljubarskij uses this instructive episode to depict the changing moral and intellectual climate in Byzantium during the century. For a restricted few it had been "free" and "liberal," but gradually this changed at the behest of the rulers for reasons of state. By the early reign of Alexius I, the recent emergence of free thinking and secular philosophy was tried in the courts and condemned. They were thus banished from Byzantine society for some three centuries. Ljubarskij has placed this episode within his own view of recent Soviet society. It is, further a positive answer to Kazhdan's question. Yes, in this area, the late eleventh century was one of decline.

But the details are before you in the published essays. Read them and derive knowledge, delight, and assurance.

SPEROS VRYONIS, JR.

1
The Slavic Settlements in the Balkans and the Eastern Alps

Henrik Birnbaum

University of California, Los Angeles

UNTIL QUITE RECENTLY, and mostly also today, it has been, or still is, common to assume that the Slavs invaded, and soon enough indeed literally inundated, large parts of the Balkan Peninsula beginning with the rule of Emperor Justinian I (527–65). The first appearance of Slavs north of the Danube is recorded in the fifth century. At that time, they seemed to have been divided into many separate tribes that, however, were grouped—at least according to contemporary sources—into two larger ethnic entities, the Sclaveni (or Slaveni) and the Antes. The historian Procopius, writing in the early 550s, stated that the two groups spoke the same language and looked alike. A half-century later, a military manual, "Strategikon," attributed to Emperor Maurice (582–602), corroborated Procopius's claim, mentioning that the Sclaveni and the Antes—the latter ethnonym possibly betraying Iranian origin—shared a common life-style. Though Slavic incursions across the Danube-Sava line, forming the border of the Byzantine Empire, had occurred earlier, the number of raids increased dramatically in the second half of Justinian's reign or, at the latest, by 550. In fact, Procopius and other sources report that such raids had virtually become an annual occurrence. Also, Procopius lists a number of Slavic placenames in present-day Yugoslavia (primarily in the Morava and Timok valleys, the two rivers being right-bank tributaries of the Danube) and in northern Bulgaria, which suggests an early, permanent settlement of some Slavic elements in Byzantine territory. It is also known that there were Slavs in the ranks of Justinian's armies fighting in Italy. On the whole, however, up to the late 560s, raiding mobile bands penetrating deep into the heartlands of the Empire constituted the basic pattern of Slavic moves and activities in the Balkans. The fairly numerous but, in general, small-sized Slavic settlements on Byzantine soil therefore did not yet amount to anything that actually could be called a veritable Slavic land taking.

However, as indicated above, these migratory moves toward the south have been viewed, at least until quite recently, as part, or rather, the beginning of a far-flung, massive expansion of the Slavs from their original homeland (located somewhere beyond the Carpathians) which soon—or, at any rate, within a matter of a few centuries—took them all the way to the shores of the Adriatic and as far south as the Peloponnesus. According to some scholars, the Slavs reached the southern tip of Greece as early as 587 while others believe that they did not come into that region until sometime after 746. The very fact of the arrival of the Slavs in the Balkans, originating in their assumed erstwhile protohome, their invasions in several waves, and eventual land taking of large portions of the peninsula have so far basically not been in doubt. It is only the details of their initial migrations toward and into the Balkans—in other words, the question of which main routes they may have taken—that have been the subject of scholarly debate (cf., e.g., Ivić 1971: 7–14; 1972: 66–72; 1981; Birnbaum 1984/1985: 78–79; Kovačević 1981; Fine 1983: 25–73). However, as of late, this whole question has come into a somewhat different light as new theories concerning the location of the original habitat of the Slavs were advanced. Furthermore, doubts have even been expressed by some scholars as to the justification for operating with the concept of a single protohome (or original homeland) of the Slavs. This applies, in particular, to contributions toward resolving this issue by the Soviet linguist O.N. Trubačev (1982/1985) and the German Slavist H. Kunstmann (esp. 1987).

Concerned with a number of theoretical and methodological issues, including a critique of the very notions of protohome and land taking (which we need not be concerned with here), Trubačev places the earliest ascertainable area of Slavic settlements not north, but south of the Carpathian Mountains. Trubačev bases his hypothesis primarily on onomastic and etymological evidence and, in so doing, vindicates, as it were, the claim of the Old Russian chronicler, that is, the early twelfth-century compiler of the "Primary Chronicle," written in Kiev, who had located the cradle of the Slavs on the Danube, "where nowadays are the lands of the Hungarians and the Bulgarians." To be sure, Trubačev's theory carries certain unmistakable Slavocentric overtones. For he locates the presumed, earliest known habitat of the Slavs in what he, along with several other scholars, considers one of the core regions of settlement of the ancestors of the Slavs—the as yet largely undifferentiated Proto-Indo-Europeans. If we were to accept the basic tenet of Trubačev's bold, yet impressively argued hypothesis, the Slavic advances into the heartlands of the Balkans, across the Danube and Sava rivers, would therefore amount to only relatively short-range migratory moves whereas the Slavs' resettlement in the Danubian basin could actually be viewed as a recovery, or reconquest, of previously held territories. Thus, Trubačev himself writes (1982/85: 4:11 and 5:7, 205 and 227): "Perhaps then this famous Danubian-Balkanic migration of the Slavs did prove to be a *Reconquista* that ran somewhat out of control owing to favorable circumstances and to the eagerness of the Slavs. The South Slavs are newcomers in the

Balkans, but they probably came from whence they could also penetrate by early infiltration to the East and to the North."

However, it should be noted here that Trubačev's view has by no means met with general approval. For example, the German onomastician J. Udolph (1987) has assessed Trubačev's various arguments and in a paper titled "Kamen die Slaven aus Pannonien?" concluded that neither historical Pannonia's toponymy, the relationship of Slavic with other languages (Indo-European as well as non-Indo-European), ancient tradition, archeological data nor the assumption of a Slavic center of linguistic innovations south of the Carpathians were viable arguments for a Proto-Slavic settlement of that region. Udolph, therefore, stands by his own previously expressed and thoroughly substantiated view that the linguistic, archeological, and historical evidence still points to an area beyond the Carpathian Mountains or, to be exact, to the region north of that mountain range somewhere between the Tatra Mountains in the west and the Bukovina in the east—in other words, roughly to historical Calicia. According to Udolph, the Slavs consequently did not originate in Pannonia, that is, today's western Hungary and adjacent territories.

In this context, it is worth noting, however, that the Slovak linguist L'udovit Novák (1984), echoing his earlier opinion (1939/40), again recently expressed views fairly close to those of Trubačev. Thus, Novák, like Trubačev, considers the Carpathian basin and the adjacent mid-Danube region the last compact protohome of the Slavs. From this core area, the Slavs would have subsequently moved in various directions, thus creating new conditions at somewhat different periods for the gradual differentiation of the separate Slavic languages, among them those of the Southern Slavs. According to Novác the crystallization of an autonomous Slavic ethnolinguistic entity can be viewed as a result of the Altaization—or, in his less fortunate phrasing, "Mongolization"—of the southeastern branch of the Indo-European group of the "Balto-Slavs" or rather of their ancestors, once settled on and near the Dnieper River. The effect of this Altaic (Turkic) superstratum would have begun with the appearance of the Huns in the Pontic Steppe region (c. 375 A.D.). That splinter group of the larger Indo-European complex would thus have been drawn into the Eurasian language alliance, or *Sprachbund*, once assumed by Roman Jakobson on purely phonological grounds, a line of reasoning that is today, however, considered largely obsolete. In Novák's view, it was the defeat and annihilation by Charlemagne's campaigns in the 790s of the Avar state—or rather perhaps, of the loosely organized political-military entity centered in the Carpathian-Danubian region that included a fairly large number of Slavic tribes under Avar sway or possibly allied with that Turkic people—that prompted what amounted to a remigration (primarily from today's Transylvania) of Slavic groups settling and, in part, rejoining local residual Slavic elements in the mid-Dnieper region.

In my own opinion, the assumption of a superstratum-type Altaization of part of the ancestors of the subsequent Balts and Slavs is far from convincing. Rather, I would suggest, we can conceive of the Slavs as having emerged from a larger late Indo-European subgroup (which included also the forebears of the Baltic and Germanic peoples) as a consequence of the invasion by Iranian, namely, Scytho-Sarmatian, tribes of the steppe region in southeastern Europe. While the ancestors of the Balts and of Germanic ethnic groups managed to escape Iranian domination, the precursors of the Slavs were not so fortunate. But it was only later that various Slavic tribes encountered and were partly subdued by Turkic peoples of the steppe, among them in particular the Avars. It is also Turkic groups that may have been instrumental in forcing the Slavs out of their earlier areas of settlement and in making them move into the mid- and lower-Danube region, only to subsequently impose themselves on them there as well. The latter obviously is true of the Bulgars, or Proto-Bulgarians, in the lower Danube valley and of the Avars in the mid-Danube and Sava basin.

In this connection it should further be noted that according to Pavle Ivić (1972: 67), the ranking Yugoslav dialectologist, the "Slavic dialects in most of Transylvania belong to the eastern group," that is, to the eastern branch of the forebears of the Southern Slavs. While the eastern portion of the subsequent South Slavic tribes for some time seems to have dwelled in the Dacian plains of present-day Romania, the western group previously inhabited the Pannonian plain (now, usually referred to as the Great Hungarian Plain or, in Hungarian, *Alföld*) with the Carpathians north of the Iron Gate and probably also the smaller Apuseni mountain range separating these two Slavic groups. The mountainous districts themselves were presumably not settled by Slavs but rather by Proto-Romanian, or Vlach, and Albanian ethnic groups adapted to the pastoralist life-style of transhumance, or seasonal migration.

Concerning the potential role of the Avars as a formative and unifying force in the crystallization of the Slavs and their common language, remaining or reintegrated into a relatively homogeneous whole, the American Slavist Horace C. Lunt, following an idea of his Harvard colleague Omeljan Pritsak, has seriously considered such a possibility. Thus, Lunt (1985: 203) wrote: "The historical intervention of steppe-peoples, principally the Avars, between about 500 and 750, created a Slavic lingua franca which spread throughout Slavic territory and well beyond into new areas, obliterating older dialects and languages. This new uniform language remained fairly stable through the 9th century with a small number of new isoglosses that began to form before O[ld] C[hurch] S[lavonic] was written down."

An even more unorthodox view as to the early migrations of the Slavs has been voiced since the beginning of the 1980s by the German scholar Heinrich Kunstmann. In a number of articles now collected in a volume on the history of the alleged settlement of northern and central Germany by Balkan Slavs (1987), he has argued that a large number of Slavic ethno-, topo-, and hydronyms, that is, designations of peoples, places, and bodies of water, as well as names of certain regions in the Slavic north, that is, north of the Carpathian and the Sudeten Mountains, should be interpreted as brought there by various Slavic groups—tribes (in the sense of *gentes*) or perhaps merely smaller, clanlike formations—in the course of settling in these new, northern territories, arriving there from the Balkans sometime around or shortly after 800 A.D. Without insisting on—or, for that matter, being able to identify—the exact location of their earliest habitat, but presuming it to have been somewhere north of the Black Sea, the Slavs (or rather, a number of relatively small-sized, but as yet unconsolidated Slavic entities) would originally have been swept away by the Avars moving from the Pontic Steppe region into the Carpathian-Danubian basin; subsequently they settled in various—Thracian, Greek, Latin (or Early Romance), and Illyrian—parts of the Balkans. These relatively small Slavic groups, who took firm shape and achieved individual character only during their stay in the Balkans, would have subsequently moved north, carrying with them their ethnic and geographic names. These names are therefore said to echo their Balkan past, brought to an end by Byzantium's drive and counteroffensive initiated around 800 A.D.

While much in Kunstmann's conception needs further corroboration and clarification, its main thrust, underpinned by an impressive array of thoroughly verified linguistic, textual, historical, and archeological data, is certainly worth considering inasmuch as it would dramatically change our previous notions of the Slavic invasions and indeed land taking of the Balkans. This new conception, in one variety or another recently endorsed by such authorities as the Croatian historian Nada Klaić and the East German archeologist Joachim Herrmann, would imply that we no longer conceive of the Slavic invasion of the Balkans as momentous, massive events but rather view the arrival of the Slavs in these regions as a gradual, limited penetration and infiltration of initially relatively small and isolated groups whose clear-cut ethnolinguistic identity and self-consciousness may well have been fully formed only at that time, presumably under the pressure of the Avars. At any rate, according to this view, the Slavic tribal entities would not have conceived of themselves as forming part of some larger, unified ethnic whole prior to the Avar-Slavic symbiosis.

Nonetheless, the appearance of Slavic groups in the Balkans, as well as in the region of the Eastern Alps, particularly in the 600s and 700s, in ever-increasing numbers is a fact, even if we perhaps have to reassess the kind, extent, and force of these Slavic invasions. They may, therefore, at least in its earlier phase, indeed not qualify as a full-scale land taking. In particular, the fact that Slavs, in alliance with Avars as well as in part with Bulgars and the Germanic tribe of the Gepids, did militarily assail Byzantium should not lead us to believe that at that time vast regions of Byzantine territory—other than presumably the environs and hinterland of Salonica—were as yet solidly and permanently settled by a Slavic-speaking population only. In 614 the Slavs captured the Dalmatian provincial capital of Salona (near today's Split into whose Diocletian Palace the Romance population of Salona fled) and launched major, albeit unsuccessful, attacks on Salonica (Thessaloniki) in 614–616 and again in 618 and in 626 on the imperial capital, Constantinople, itself. As the American Balkan historian John V. A. Fine, Jr., (1983: 36) put it: "Since imperial control was lost from such a large area, we can assume that, though the Balkans were not evenly settled throughout, the Slavs must have had large numbers of settlements in every region of the Balkans lost to the empire." Also, some Slavs moved into territories that remained under Byzantine rule, notably Thrace.

Which then, were the routes by which the Slavs—or more precisely, the future Southern Slavs—arrived and settled in what is today Bulgaria and Yugoslavia as well as parts of Greece and Albania? To consider this question it is useful, I submit, to first take a look at the specific peoples and tribes involved. In doing so, it should be kept in mind, however, that these ethnic groups in all likelihood did not actually emerge, as previously indicated, until the various smaller Slavic entities had arrived and at least temporarily settled in the Balkans. Note particularly in this connection the fact that the Byzantine emperor Constantine VII Porphyrogenitus, writing in the mid-tenth century, in his famous work *De Administrando Imperio*, still singled out a number of individual tribes in addition to the ethnically controversial Serbs and Croats. More specifically, Constantine, to be sure, in a somewhat confused manner, refers to "Slavs . . . who were also called Avaas" (ch. 29) and later speaks again of "Slavs subject to the Church of Patras" (ch. 49) and of "the Slavs of the province of Peloponnesus," that is, the Milingoi and Ezeritai (ch. 50). (Parenthetically it may be added that these two Slavic tribes in the Peloponnesus, settling on the slopes of the Tayettos Mountain near Sparta, seem to have survived in that area up to Ottoman times; cf. Birnbaum [1986].) But, in addition he also singles out the Croats (chs. 13, 29–33, 35, 40–41), the Serbs (chs. 29, 31–33, 36), and further the Zachlumi (chs. 29, 30, 32–33, 35), the Telbouniotes (chs. 29 and 34), the Kanalites (chs. 29, 32, 34), the Diocletians (chs. 29 and 35), as well as the Arentani or Pagani (chs. 29–30, and 36). While the ethnic identity of the Croats and Serbs in Constantine's account is controversial, his designation of the Bulgarians, or Bulgars, (chs. 5, 8, 13, 22, 31–32, 40–41) refers in all likelihood still to the Turkic tribe, and his ethnonym Ragusians ("Rausians," ch. 29) presumably means the early Roman population of Ragusa-Dubrovnik.

As is well known, just as the Turkic Bulgars eventually—but possibly not as rapidly as sometimes assumed (cf. Fine 1983: 74–78 and 94–112)—were assimilated by the Slavs of the lower Danube valley whom they had conquered and then ruled, so the ethnonyms of both the Serbs and Croats mentioned by the Byzantine emperor, while not entirely clear as to their precise reference, seem to point to non-Slavic origins. It has been fairly common until recently to assume that both these ethnic designations can be traced to Iranian sources.

However, Trubačev (1982: 5:13–14 and 1985: 242–3) is inclined to ultimately assume Old Indic origin for the name of the Serbs, while for that of the Croats, rather than the traditional Iranian derivation, a Turkic—and, more specifically, Avar—etymology now seems more plausible (cf. Kronsteiner 1978:146–9; Gołąb 1982; Birnbaum and Merrill 1985: 82; Birnbaum 1987a: 339). As indicated, the question has so far not been settled whether Emperor Constantine Vll with Serbs and Croats had actually in mind Slavic ethnic groups, as would seem most likely, or whether he referred to some as yet non-Slavic leadership strata, merely in charge of the local Slavs, the latter obviously outnumbering the former just as the Slavs of the lower Danube region were more numerous than their Bulgar rulers. At any rate, there can be little doubt that these originally unequivocally non-Slavic ethnonyms fairly soon came to designate Slavs. Moreover, there is certainly no reason to distinguish between Slavic-speaking Bulgarians and Macedonians when we are dealing with the early Middle Ages (whereas today they are undoubtedly two distinct South Slavic peoples; cf. Fine [1983: 37 and 105]; Birnbaum [1987b: 378–379, 383, 393–394]). However, there are good grounds to assume the existence of two separate ethnic entities—Serbs and Croats—throughout the medieval period, once these two Slavic peoples had consolidated as distinct political entities. This national division is not contradicted by the fact that Serbs and Croats today still speak basically one and the same language.

This broad, general statement is in need of two qualifications, however. One concerns the ancestors of today's speakers of the Serbo-Croatian (historically, Serbian) Torlak dialects, also known as Prizren-Timok dialects; the other one applies to the Serbo-Croatian (historically, Croatian) dialect area of Kajkavian and the original settlers in this linguistically fairly compact territory.

As for Torlak, let me summarize here what I have earlier stated elsewhere (Birnbaum 1980: 168–170). While Bulgarian linguists of an older generation were inclined to consider the transitional Torlak dialects regional varieties of Bulgarian, and also such unbiased an expert in South Slavic dialectology as the Polish Slavist Franciszek Sławski (1962: 115) would state that "from a contemporary point of view these are already dialects of the Bulgarian-Macedonian type, marked by virtually all the Balkanisms characteristic of the Bulgarian-Macedonian group," it is now the consensus of most scholars in the field that as far as their origin and earliest evolution is concerned these were Serbian dialects. Thus, already the Dutch Slavist Nicolaas van Wijk (1956: 104), when discussing the transitional status between Serbian and Bulgarian—Macedonian then not yet having been acknowledged as an independent language—stated in a lecture originally delivered at the Sorbonne in the 1930s: "Cette répartition des particularités linguistiques des deux langues n'admet qu'une seule conclusion, à savoir: que le dialecte de transition etait serbe à l'origine, mais que dans la suite, il a traversé avec le bulgare une periode d'évolution commune." The two Yugoslav linguists Aleksandar Belić and Milan Rešetar had counted Torlak among the Serbo-Croatian dialects (though Belić, contrary to Rešetar, would not recognize its autonomous status, separate from Štokavian). But it was only Pavle Ivić who, as far as the status of Torlak goes, shifted from Belić's to Rešetar's point of view (1958: 88–9) and provided a modern theoretical justification for the proper classification of these regional varieties of Serbo-Croatian. Thus, Ivić (1956: 121) pointed out that the main isoglosses that link the Prizren-Timok dialects with Macedo-Bulgarian are all chronologically secondary in relation to those that mark their closeness with Serbo-Croatian and notably its Štokavian dialect group. When speaking of the ancient Serbs (and their forebears) we should therefore also include here the ancestors of the speakers of Torlak.

This situation appears to be the opposite, as it were, when it comes to the origin of the Kajkavian dialect of Serbo-Croatian, notwithstanding the fact that the capital city of Croatia, Zagreb, is located in the heart of the Kajkavian-speaking territory. Personally, I share the opinion of those linguists who believe that Kajkavian and Slovenian go back to a common dialectal base. As is well known, Slovenian is among those Slavic languages whose territory shrank considerably in early historical times. The Late Common Slavic dialect group that, with some qualification, we may call Proto-Slovenian, or more accurately perhaps, Early Alpine Slavic, once extended across all of today's Slovenia, the Kajkavian portion of the Serbo-Croatian linguistic territory: western Hungary, that is, Transdanubia up to Lake Balaton, if not beyond, and deep into present-day Austria, namely, Carinthia, Styria, and parts of the provinces of Lower and Upper Austria as well as Salzburg/Salzkammergut, Tyrol, and Burgenland . (The Croatian-speaking population of the latter region consists of immigrants of more recent times.) In addition, Alpine Slavs penetrated also into northeastern Italy—the region of Friuli (cf. Katičić 1980 and, in general, Birnbaum 1977). Most of the major characteristics that today separate Kajkavian from Slovenian can be traced to the period of the tenth through the fifteenth century while some of the shared features of Slovenian and Kajkavian may well antedate the arrival of the ancestors of the speakers of those languages and dialects in their present-day sites. Having previously noted (Ivić 1961: 21) that the region of Croatia bordering on Slovenia is among the most differentiated dialect areas of the Serbo-Croatian language tertitory, Ivić (1972: 71) had this to say on the subject: "Since there was no specific political link between Slovenia and the Kajkavian area in northern Croatia before the 16th century, and since the geographic conditions in the present habitat of Slovenians and Kajkavians did not favor their common linguistic development distinct from that of their eastern and southern neighbors, it seems likely that their common linguistic features stem from the propinquity of their ancestors in the period preceding their settlement in what is now Yugoslavia." Needless to say, while Kajkavian can thus be considered a secondarily Croatized form of the language once shared with the subsequent speakers of Slovenian, there can be no doubt, of course, that Kajkavian today is—and, as a matter of fact, for the last five hundred years or so has been—part of the Croatian speech community into which it has been firmly integrated.

Summing up, we can thus posit four major subgroups of the Slavs settling south of the Danube, Sava, and Drava, as well as in the Eastern Alps and their foothills. In this context we disregard various smaller Slavic tribes and clans that originally invaded and subsequently penetrated deep into the Balkans and the East Alpine–Adriatic region, but who later may in part have remigrated to the north. These four major groupings were thus (1) the Bulgarians (once they had absorbed and fully assimilated the non-Slavic Turkic Bulgars), including the forebears of today's Slavic-speaking Macedonians of southernmost Yugoslavia, (2) the Serbs, and (3) the Croats (both of them at an early time having assimilated the respective non-Slavic ethnic element that originally presumably dominated them, as echoed in their ethnonyms); here we also subsume the various Slavic groups in the area mentioned by Emperor Constantine VII Porphyrogenitus; and (4) the Slovenes (including the ancestors of the subsequent speakers of the Kajkavian dialect of Serbo-Croatian), once spread over a fairly large territory extending all the way to Lake Balaton, present-day central Austria, and Italian Friuli. However, it should also be kept in mind in this connection that, although representing several separate ethnic groups (and originally, obviously, even many more tribal divisions and clanlike clusters), all of these various Slavs must still have spoken a language that in the second half of the first millennium A.D. was only minimally differentiated. For, as clearly attested by the effective supra-ethnic—if not yet truly supranational—function of Old Church Slavonic, devised and introduced in the second half of the ninth century by SS. Cyril and Methodius, and on the whole only insignificantly adapted to regional needs and speech habits, this largely uniform language was understood throughout not only the Slavic south, but indeed in all or most of the Slavic-settled lands.

It is possible that modern, largely (though not entirely) homogeneous Serbo-Croatian may well be the result of a secondary process of language and dialect mixing, or convergence, that could have taken place in the Balkans only after the Southern Slavs had settled there. Thus, the forebears of that portion of the Serbs that had originally migrated south (as opposed to the subsequently West Slavic Sorbs, or Lusatian Sorbians) could have split off from the Slavic ancestors of the Bulgarians, moving west- and southwestward into their historical heartlands of Raška (around the city of Niš) and Zeta/Duklja, that is, today's Crna Gora, or Montenegro. By the same token, the Proto-Croats could have separated from the Proto-Slovenes and, on the one hand, advanced into Slavonia between the Sava and Drava Rivers while, on the other, pushing toward the

Adriatic and occupying large parts of Dalmatia in the process. Even more likely, though, it would appear that the main thrust of the Slavic invasions across the Danube-Sava line (and, along with the Avars, already earlier across the Drava and into East Alpine regions) proceeded along three—and not only two—main routes once these moves had swelled to more than a mere trickle of isolated settlers or occasional raiders. Therefore, one of them would have been the Black Sea–lower Danube track, circumventing the Carpathian in the east (and south) and migrating through and settling in the Dacian plains. Another one would have led through passes and valleys of the Western Carpathians and Eastern Alps, or through natural "gates" separating these two major mountain ranges.

While both these routes could be viewed as geographically more restricted, essentially not reaching beyond the territories now and in the recorded past occupied by Slovenes and Kajkavian Croats or their immediate ancestors, they are those traditionally assumed (with the western one further extended). The unresolved issue, given this hypothesis, amounts essentially to the question of whether the east versus west track division closely matches the established subgrouping of the South Slavic languages into a (south)eastern and a (north)western branch, that is, Macedo-Bulgarian versus Sloveno-Serbo-Croatian. For the gradual emergence of largely unified (though not fully uniform) Serbo-Croatian as the shared language of two peoples—the Serbs and the Croats (in which context we can disregard the subsequent further national divisions and identifications of Bosnian Muslims and Montenegrins)—we could thus hypothesize a secondary linguistic merger shortly before recorded and during early historical times. Some of the speakers of Serbo-Croatian (namely, the Proto-Serbs) would thus have arrived from the east and northeast after having separated from the Slavs of the lower Danube valley (and northern Greece, as well as, possibly, some districts in Albania), that is, the forebears of the Slavic-speaking Bulgarians. Alternatively, and more likely perhaps, an additional—that is, third—main route could conceivably have followed the central course of the Danube and the Tisza rivers, through the Pannonian plain and leading straight into what are now the Ijekavian-Štokavian and Čakavian-speaking regions of Yugoslavia. These, therefore, would be the ancestors of the present-day Croats, while the predecessors of today's Serbs (speaking Ekavian-Štokavian) would have come from the east after having separated from the Bulgarians.

In conclusion, let us take a somewhat closer look at the two wings—the southeasten and the northwestern—of the migratory moves of the prehistoric and early historic Slavs invading and at least temporarily settling in the Southern Balkans (notably Greece) and in the Eastern Alps, respectively.

As for the Slavic advances into Greece, and the onomastic evidence af the Slavic presence on Greek soil previously studied thoroughly by the German Slavists Max Vasmer (1941/70) and in more recent years critically reexamined particularly by the Greek scholar Phaedon Malingoudis (1981, 1983, 1987; cf.

also Birnbaum 1986), it should be noted that the Romanian Slavist Ion Pătruţ (1972) was able to demonstrate, primarily on the strength of toponymic data, that the first wave of Slavic penetration, up to the eighth century, was linguistically still essentially Common Slavic. Only the second wave of Slavic influence and settlement, now limited largely to northern Greece—Macedonia, Thrace, and, to a lesser extent, Epirus and Thessaly—shows unequivocally Bulgarian linguistic characteristics.

Turning to the other end of the advancing Slavs in Southeastern Europe, the Austrian Slavist Otto Kronsteiner (1975) concluded primarily on the basis of Slavic anthroponymic data—that is, personal names—in the East Alpine region that the term "Alpine Slavic," designating a Late Common Slavic dialect group, is applicable to the period up to the eleventh century, but not later. After that, the Slavic evidence from Carinthia and Styria (south of the ridge of the Alps) also exhibits unambiguously Slovenian features. While Alpine Slavic displays phonological, morphological, and onomastic peculiarities unique to that area, markedly South Slavic characteristics cannot be found in the onomastic material north of the Alpine ridge. Characteristics otherwise encountered in West Slavic (historically, Moravian) did occasionally reach south of that line and their traces can thus be found throughout today's central and eastern Austria, in other words, not only in Upper and Lower Austria but also in Carinthia, Styria, and East Tyrol. Some early recorded names of Carinthian nobles are further proof of the linguistic ties that once existed between the Alpine Slavic region and the Slavic west, notably Moravia. The Slavic area of the Eastern Alps was thus linguistically somewhat heterogeneous, with West Slavic elements playing a larger role than previously thought. Superseding his earlier assumption of some minor Old Croatian splinter groups in the Eastern Alps, Kronsteiner has subsequently (1978) identified the earliest attestation of Croats with the Avar military echelon among the Alpine Slavs. In this connection, it ought to be mentioned here that Constantine Porphyrogenitus's erroneous placing of "Great Moravia" south of the Danube, accepted as correct by some scholars, notably Imre Boba (1971) and Charles R. Bowlus (1986*a*, 1986*b*, 1987*a*, 1987*b*, 1988), has recently again been refuted by the Austrian medievalist Herwig Wolfram (1989).

In closing, we may state that, while there was eventually what amounts to a genuine Slavic land taking of the Balkans (and at least temporarily also of parts of the East Alpine region), it occurred only gradually, with increasing force and in ever-larger numbers. Yet, by around 800 A.D., it was slowed down and, in part, reversed as a result of a large-scale Slavic withdrawal from Greece (and Albania) and a certain thinning out and possible remigration of Balkan Slavic groups toward northerly territories, in Central and Eastern Europe. The full extent of this advance and conquest, if only in terms of approximate numbers of people involved, is not easy to estimate. As far as the routes of the Slavic southward moves from north of the Carpathians and, by a somewhat later date, from the

Carpathian-Danubian basin are concerned, it now seems most likely that the advancing Slavs proceeded along three major tracts—an eastern one, into and through Moldavia and Wallachia; a western one, through the Moravian Gate west of the Carpathians and along the foothills and valleys of the Eastern Alps; and an additional, central one, through the Pannonian plain, along the Danube and Tisza Rivers and farther into the south.

Bibliography

Birnbaum, H. 1977. "Der österreichische Jasomirgott und die frühe Verbreitung der Alpenslaven (Urslovenen)," *Anzeiger für slavische Philologie 9, 33-48.*

——. 1980. "Language, Ethnicity, and Nationalism: On the Linguistic Foundations of a Unified Yugoslavia," in: *Th e Creation of Yugoslavia 1914-1918,* D. Djordjevic, ed., Santa Barbara-Oxford, 157-182.

——. 1984/85. "A Typological View of Serbo-Croatian: Some Preliminary Considerations," *Zbornik Matice srpske za filologiju i lingvistiku* 27/28 (FS M. and P. Ivić), 77-84.

——. 1986. "Noch einmal zu den slavischen Milingen auf der Peloponnes," in: *Festschrift für H. Bräuer zum 65. Geburtstag. . .,* R. Olesch and H. Rothe, eds., Cologne-Vienna, 15-26.

——. 1987a. *Praslavjanskij jazyk. Dostiženija i problemy v ego rekonstukcii,* V.A. Dybo and V.K. Žuravlev, ed. and tr., Moscow.

——. 1987b. "On the Genealogical and Typological Classification of Old Church Slavonic and its Textual Evidence," *Die Welt der Slaven* 32, 362-407.

Birnbaum, H. and P.T. Merrill. 1985. *Recent Advances in the Reconstruction of Common Slavic (1971-1982),* Columbus, Ohio.

Boba, I. 1971. *Moravia's History Reconsidered: A Reinterpretation of Medieval Sources,* The Hague.

Bowlus, C. R. 1986a. "Krieg und Kirche in den Südost-Grenzgrafschaften: Zusammenhänge zwischen militärischen Auseinandersetzungen in den Marken und der Slawenmission," in: *Mitteilungen der Gesellschaft für Salzburger Landeskunde,* 126, 71-91.

——. 1986b. "Where was Ninth-Century Moravia?" *Die Slawischen Sprachen,* 10, pp. 5-35.

——. 1987a. "Imre Boba's Reconsiderations of Moravia's Early History and Arnulf of Carinthia's *Ostpolitik* (887-892)," *Speculum,* 62, 552-574.

——. 1987b. "Die geographische Lage des Mährischen Reiches anhand fränkischer Quellen," *Bohemia,* 28, 1-24.

——. 1988. "The Military Organization of Carinthia and Pannonia (818-846)," in: *Gesellschaftsgeschichte* (FS Karl Bösl), F. Seibt, ed., Munich, 168-178.

Fine, J. V. A., Jr. 1983. *The Early Medieval Balkans: A Critical Survey from the Sixth to the Late Twelfth Century.* Ann Arbor.

Gołab, Z. 1982. "About the Connection Between Kinship Terms and Some Ethnica in Slavic (The Case of Sĭrbi and Slověne)," *International Journal of Slavic Linguistics and Poetics* 25/26 (FS E. Stankiewicz), 165-171.

Ivić, P. 1956. *Dijalektologija srpskohrvatskog jezika. Uvod i štokavsko narečje,* Novi Sad.

——. 1958. *Die Serbokroatischen Dialekte, ihre Struktur und Entwicklung,* Vol. I: *Allgemeines und die štokavische Dialektgruppe,* The Hague.

——. 1961. "Prilozi poznavanju dijalekatske slike zapadne Hrvatske" (with English summary), in: *Godišnjak Filozofskog fakulteta u Novom Sadu*, Vol. VI, 191–212.

———. 1971. *Srpski narod i njegov jezik*, Belgrade.

———. 1972. "Balkan Slavic Migrations in the Light of South Slavic Dialectology," in: *Aspects of the Balkans: Continuity and Change*, H. Birnbaum and S. Vryonis, Jr., eds., The Hague-Paris, 66–86.

———. 1981. "Jezik i njegov razvoj do druge polovine XII veka," in: *Istorija srpskog naroda*, Vol. I: *Od najstarijih vremena do Maričke bitke (1371)*, S. Ćirković, ed., Belgrade, 125–140.

Katičić, R. 1980. "Slavica Foroiuliensia," *Wiener Slavistisches Jahrbuch* 26, 28–32.

Kovačević, J. 1981. "Doseljenje Slovena na Balkansko poluostrovo," in: *Istorija srpskog naroda*, Vol. I: *Od najstarijih vremena do Maričke bitke (1371)*, S. Ćirković, ed., Belgrade, 109–124.

Kronsteiner, O. 1975. *Die alpenslawischen Personennamen*, Vienna.

Kunstmann, H. 1987. *Beiträge zur Geschichte der Besiedlung Nord-und Mitteldeutschlands mit Balkanslaven*. Munich (*Slavistische Beiträge*, 217).

Lunt, H. G. 1985. "Slavs, Common Slavic, and Old Church Slavonic," in: *Litterae Slavicae Medii Aevii* (FS F. V. Mareš), J. Reinhart, ed., Munich, 185–204.

Malingoudis, P. 1981. *Studien zu den slavischen Ortsnamen Griechenlands*, Vol. I: *Slavische Flurnamen aus der messenischen Mani*, Wiesbaden.

———. 1983. "Toponymy and History. Observations Concerning the Slavonic Toponymy of the Peloponnese," *Cyrillomethodianum* 7, 99–111.

———. 1987. "Frühe slawische Elemente im Namengut Griechenlands," in: *Die Völker Südosteuropas im 6. bis 8. Jahrhundert*, B. Hänsel, ed., Munich-Berlin, 53–68.

Novák, L. 1939/40. "Slovenské a podkarpatoruské nárečia vo svetle europske fonetické geografie. Synchronické a diachronické poznámky k porovnávacej jazykovede stredoeuropskej," *Linguistica Slovaca* 1/2, 85–105.

———. 1984. "Vznik Slovanov a ich jazyka (Základy etnogenézy Slovanov)," *Slavica Slovaca* 19, 219–232.

Slawski, F. 1982. *Zarys dialektologii jezykow poludniowo-slowiańskich (z wyborem tekstów gwarowych)*, Warsaw.

Trubačev, O. N. 1982/85. "Jazykoznanie i ètnogenez slavjan. Drevnie slavjane po dannym ètimologii i onomastiki," *Voprosy jazykoznanija* 1982: 4, 10–26; 5, 3–17. English version: "Linguistics and Ethnogenesis of the Slavs: The Ancient Slavs as Evidenced by Etymology and Onomastics," *The Journal of Indo-European Studies* 13: 1–2, 203–256.

Udolph, J. 1987. "Kamen die Slaven aus Pannonien?" in: *Studia nad etnogeneza Slowian i kultura Europy wczesnośredniowiecznej. Praca zbiorowa*, G. Labuda and S. Tabaczyński, eds., Wroclaw, 167–73.

Vasmer, M. 1941/70. *Die Slaven in Griechenland*, Berlin-Leipzig.

Wijk, N. van. 1956. *Les langues slaves: De l'unité à la pluralité (Serie de leçons faites à la Sorbonne)*, 2nd corr. ed., The Hague.

Wolfram, H. 1989. "The Image of Central Europe in Constantine VII Porphyrogenitus," in: *Constantine VII Porphyrogenitus and His Age. The Second International Byzantine Conference*, Athens, 5–14.

2
The Slavic Pottery (Jars) from Olympia, Greece

Speros Vryonis, Jr.
Alexander S. Onassis Center for Hellenic Studies
New York University

The Slavic Pottery (Jars) from Olympia

When the digging for the foundations of the new archaeological museum at Olympia commenced in the late 1950s, the site was, unfortunately, virgin archaeological ground. The result was that the builders stumbled on a rich and as yet unexplored portion of ancient Olympia, and materials going back at least to the Middle Helladic were uncovered. The latest or most recent stratum that the builders encountered, only 50 to 65 cm below the surface, consisted of a number of very crude jars with ashes. Below followed the early Byzantine-Roman stratum. More precisely these vases, and others like them, were uncovered from 1959 to at least 1966, were briefly recorded and announced in the annual reports of the then ephor of Olympia, Dr. Nicholas Yalouris, in the Archaiologikon Deltion.[1] From the brief records available we are informed that they were found in the area presently directly below the central hall of the new museum, under the wing housing the Hermes of Praxiteles, and in the adjacent areas to the north, east, and southeast. This site is very close to the small stream bed of the Kladeos, with its high banks, that flows down into the Alpheios River. Yalouris identified the vases as Slavic, handmade, and used for the burial of the dead after their cremation. Yalouris had stumbled onto, and identified, the first Slavic necropolis in medieval Greece, but it is difficult to know the size of this necropolis. Since the announcement of their discovery in the Archaiologikon Deltion, their existence has received very brief notice and attention here and there, but as yet there has not appeared any detailed analysis of them, and certainly no published catalog.[2]

In August of 1981, by kind permission of Dr. Nicholas Yalouris, then the General Ephor of Antiquities, I was allowed to examine the materials that were unearthed at Olympia, to study and measure them, and was given photographs (duplicates) from the photographic archives of the Olympia Museum. Unfortunately there were no archaeological day books or diaries to be found at the Museum which recorded the details of their uncovering, and so there is

Type I A$_1$

31

29

38

28a

Type I A_1

35

4

14

13

Type I A$_1$

11

Type II A$_1$

34

37

Type II A$_1$

30

21

3

18

Type II A$_1$

19

Type I A$_4$

22

9

V 20

20

V 16, 36

16

36

nowhere at the moment a complete account of the circumstances and stratification of their finding. Thus I had very little with which to work. Further my efforts to examine the area archaeologically proved futile as the bulldozers had completely mixed the earth and destroyed the stratigraphy. Thus the material at hand included:

1. The vases, fragments, sherds, and the other meager finds, namely, small iron knives, some rings, glass and beads, all stored in the basement of the museum.

2. The photographs of this material in the photographic archives of the museum that often, though not always, have the date and place of discovery inscribed on them.

3. The accession catalogs.

4. A very rough, small sketch drawn by the superintendent of the work, Mr. Liangouras of Olympia, indicating where a number of these grave-jars were found.[3]

The Vases

During my visit to the site of Olympia in 1981, I proceeded to match, to the degree possible, the vase photographs in the photographic archive with their partial identifications, sometimes to be found on the back of the photo, sometimes not, and with whatever could be matched from the acquisitions catalogs, and finally with the few photographs in the Archaiologikon Deltion. Though this did not serve to complete all identifications, locations, and so forth, it was largely successful in the museum. The sum total of about forty vases, fragments, and groups of sherds emerged, a significant number, many of which were either complete, or at least sufficiently substantial in surviving form, to allow a study of the form and type.

Here I shall describe, very briefly, six types:

Type I Variant A_1

Type I A_1 is characteristically tall, has a wide, open mouth and short outwardly stretched lips, and a very short neck with the shoulders coming very high up on the vase and close to the lips. Then the vase's sides slope downward and inward to the base. The maximum circumference is attained at the shoulders. The lips of the vase extend beyond the neck and far beyond the base but never reach the diameter extent of the shoulders. The vase is very rough, uneven, assymetrical, and the bottoms often uneven.

At least nine of our vases belong to this category (Vry. #35, 38, 14, 13, 31, 14, 11, 28a, 29, 4). Of these four are plain (V. #4, 14, 13, 35), and five have striated decorations (V. #38, 11, 29, 28a, 31).

Type II Variant A_1

Again this type has a long body, as in the above, and again the shoulders have the greatest diameter, the mouth is open and its diameter is larger than those of both the neck and base. The shoulders however are much further down on the body of the vase. Thus the slope of the vase from the neck to the shoulder extends outward farther down, displacing the shoulders considerably in the direction toward the base, somewhere near the middle of the body. This type too is coarse, asymmetrical, the base uneven. There are seven jars of this general shape in the Olympia material (V. #30, 19, 34, 3, 21, 37, 18), though they vary somewhat from those photographed in the work of Doncheva-Petkova.

Type I Variant A_4 (not included in the types of Doncheva-Petkova)
In this variant the neck is longer than in I A_1 and the shoulders slightly farther down than in I A_1, but not as far down as in II A_1. In other words this particular form is somewhere between the first two forms discussed above. It too is very crude, asymmetrical and unusually uneven at the bottom. Of the two examples from Olympia, one (V. #2) is plain, and the other (V. #9) has decorations on the surface.

Vryonis #20 (not in Doncheva-Petkova)
Yet a fourth form is represented by one vase in which the base is slightly larger than the mouthlips, but the greatest diameter is still reached in the main part of the jar's body slightly below the middle. It is very rough, asymmetrical, without any decoration whatever.

Vryonis #16, #36 (not in Doncheva-Petkova)
In these two vases the shoulder, which sits at the half way point of the jar, is of the same diameter as the base, but the neck and mouth are much narrower. One of these two pieces is very crude, is not symmetrical, but has some decoration (striated lines). The other is similar to the type of I A1 but is shorter and its shoulder is a little farther down from the neck, with wavy lines in batches crossing at right angles. This is better made, though it is not even or symmetrical, and has been made, perhaps, on a crude handwheel.

Measurements and Proportions

I shall not go into the matter of the measurements of height, various diameters of the parts of these vases, and the appropriate proportions that determine their various shapes. The tallest of these vases is 24.5 cm, and many are of a height between 17 and 24.5 cm. The thickness of the coarse pottery varies between 0.5 and 1.0 cm.

Conclusions as to the Form and Physical State of the Pottery

1. It is of a characteristic shape, namely, long, with very high shoulders, or shoulders fixed at the quarterway mark toward the bottom of the vase, at the half-way mark, and even in some cases sagging below the half-way mark. In most cases the greatest diameter is reached by the shoulders, next by the lips/mouth, and finally by the base.
2. Certainly its most striking characteristic is its coarseness, one would even say

its crudity. It is completely asymmetrical to the degree that it pains the eye. It is a pottery of which all examples, with perhaps but one exception, were made completely by hand and without the assistance of a potter's wheel. The one exception may have been the product of a crude handwheel, but it too is asymmetrical.

3. Its consistency is uneven, the clay breaks and crumbles easily, giving proof of very poor or incomplete baking, a fact which had caused Yalouris to describe it as unbaked.

4. The color is very dull, mostly reddish brown, with a shading off to dull tomato-grey, weak brown, brownish grey, and grey. This dull coloring is also a striking characteristic. It looks dirty, whatever the weak color.

5. As for decoration there are two types: Those vases without any decoration whatever (about half of the items), and the others with simple striated decorational patterns. At times the striations are horizontal, at other times they are perpendicular, at still other times they are made up of undulating lines in or out of combination with one of the other incised types.

Function of the Pottery

From the brief descriptions given by Yalouris and Themelis, by no means complete, we see the following. Vases #11 and #29 were found on top of ashes and coals; #30 and #32 had some bones in them, and most of them seem to have contained ashes. Further, a few of them contained trinkets of a personal nature: small knives, beads, glass, and a few coarse rings. The obvious function of many of these jars was that of funeral urns. The finding of two of the jars in situ, atop the coals, indicates that after the cremation of the dead, the ashes were placed in the jar and placed in the burned-out ashes and coals.

Dating

Because of the disturbance of the stratification and the hurried nature of the uncovering of this area of the Olympian archaeological grounds, we have been deprived of an essential tool in the establishment of the chronology. On first sight this seems an irreparable loss. Yet upon the examination of the great number of early Slavic cemeteries carried out by Vyzharova, and from the conclusions of Doncheva-Petkova, we learn that the early Slavic strata of these cemeteries did not permit them to date the pottery exactly either. Indeed, Doncheva-Petkova had to use the entirety of the mass body of early Slavic pottery to establish general but very inexact guidelines for the dating of the material. So it is probable that the settlement at Olympia, so obviously poor from the lack of rich grace adornments, would have told us nothing more in any case.

Yalouris had, generally, dated the cemetery to the sixth century since it came atop the early Byzantine and late Roman strata. I. Nestor dates these vases (what little he had seen of them in the Archaiologikon Deltion) to the late seventh century on the basis of style. Whereas he had the enormous advantage of having excavated the great cemetery of Sarata Monteoru with its 1,500 or so graves, nevertheless Slavic pottery was not sufficiently well known then to dare such a method of dating.[4]

Typology of Pottery in the Greater Slavic Area in the Sixth Century

The Czech archaeologist Z. Vana, in his succinct and important book, summarizes the vast body of archaeological material and studies dealing with the end of the common Slav life and the beginning of the migrations. As to the pottery types, he distinguishes three which are of interest here: the Korchak, the Penkovka, and the Prague types. The Korchak ceramic type spreads out between the east Carpathians and the Dnieper in the fifth-seventh centuries. The Penkovka type is found along the south Dnieper along its right and left tributaries, along the south Bug and to the lower Dniester. The Prague type (the more westerly equivalent of the Korchak type) covers a large area from the Pripiati, along its tributaries on the right and upper Dniester toward the southwest and the territory in between as well, as well as to the Vysil and Elbe, as far as the middle course of the Danube.

Of the three general types of pottery associated with these broad archaeological areas, the early pottery associated with the Balkan Slavs is often, though not always, associated with the third broad division, the Prague type, in regard to its form and other characteristics.[5] Rusanova, who has studied this particular aspect in detail, has seen part of Romania as the land where pottery types are to be found intermixed because of the variety of tribes, Slavic and otherwise, that converged there by the sixth century. It is on this ground that she explains the mixture of certain ceramic types found in the great cemetery of Sarata Monteoru. As for the material culture of the Balkan Slavs at the earliest time, insofar as it is archaeologically discernable, she finds it associated more generally with the broad picture of Slavic material culture throughout the vast European area that the Slavs occupied by that time: the polyzemljani, that is, crude small houses built half under the ground and half above, with their stone ovens, burials that include large scale cremation and burial in urns, and a type of pottery that is of the Prague type. This early unified Slavic culture, common to the larger Slavic area in Europe by the sixth century, is not to be found south of the Danube until the seventh century, according to Rusanova. There the Slavic pottery, a later form of the Prague type, developed local varieties because of interaction with local peoples and conditions. Vana finds Russia as the area of interaction of all these ceramic types. Thus the ceramic types were already spread among the Slavs at the time of their settlement in the Balkans.[6]

Thus, according to the students of this early Slavic culture in Europe, the early

Balkan ceramics attributed to the presence of the first Slavs in Romania and south of the Danube are related to, and are later versions of, the Prague and other pottery types. There is no doubt that the jars of Olympia share some of the features of the earlier Prague, Penkovka, and Korchak pottery in that they are made by hand and have some similarity of form. Nevertheless there are differences of size and quality, the Balkan examples being quite crude in the beginning. M. Čorović-Ljubinković observed that Slavic ceramics had its own specific development and thus one cannot simply apply systems of dating pottery utilized in Czechoslovakia, Poland, and Russia. Even within the Balkans one needs to look at the accumulating finds in both Bulgaria and Romania with care in their dating, for portions of the indigenous populations survived and so influenced differently the evolution of the ceramic art in various parts of the Balkans. Thus according to the perception of that scholar the development of Slavic ceramics in the Balkans could have varied from area to area according to local conditions and their strength or weakness in influencing this craft among the newly settled Slavs. Finally he notes the almost total absence of other grave/domestic material finds in the excavations during the early period of the arrival of the Slavs so as to be unable to date the pottery on this basis.[7] Irma Čremošnik emphasizes the difference between what she calls the older Prague type of pottery (i.e., found outside the Balkans by the sixth century, but not within) and the later Balkan version. The latter is not as sleek or slender, or as finely made in texture, and does not have the slip of fine clean earth, and the younger or later version of Prague pottery that she is examining and that was found at Musici and Batkovici in Bosnia-Herzegovena, is shorter, more crudely made. The first of the later so-called Prague type of the Balkans is made completely by hand and only at a later stage is there evidence of a primitive wheel. It has a thick base and sides and is coarsely made.[8]

Greece and its archaeology have come into the discussion of the Slavic archaeological remains in the Balkans relatively late. Though the discussion of the Slavic invasions and settlements has been heated and the output prolific, the discussion has centered about the reliability, or not, of the few written sources, the coins, and the buildings of given sites. Also, the ever-elusive belt buckles have drawn their share of attention. But there was no assurance that we had positive material evidence that could be associated with the Slavs. There are the Slavic placenames and the chronicles, but since the Slavs were so completely absorbed in most of Greece, their medieval presence constituted the enigmatic phantom of both Slavists and Byzantinists. Yalouris first identified the crude pottery known by some as a later version of the Prague type, at Olympia. Then he identified a burial urn studied much earlier by Davidson at Corinth.[9] Since then, the French excavations at Argos have turned up an interesting group of sherds of this type of pottery in the destroyed Bath A, and this has been dated, at the time of their study, to 585/586 A.D. This would have been an excellent starting point for the dating of the pottery from Olympia, for the sherds seem to be similar in texture to the pottery from Olympia, and there is a certain chronological coincidence with the Byzantine literary sources for the settlement of the Slavs in the Peloponnese.[10] Prof. Timothy Gregory of the University of Ohio showed me photographs of a restricted number of pot sherds, found in the region of the Isthmus of Corinth, and which also seem to belong to this small body of ceramic evidence from Olympia and Argos. Still, for Greece we have no systematic study of an extensive Slavic necropolis or village settlement as there is for Bulgaria, Yugoslavia, and Romania, and so we must await the archaeologist's pick and spade in the coming decades to provide us with this necessary evidence.

Typology and Chronology of Early Slavic Pottery
Found in Bulgaria (Vyzharova, Doncheva-Petkova)

It is to the extensive and systematic labors of Bulgarian archaeologists that we must look for more specific information that will help us to place the pottery found at Olympia. In the post–World War II era, Bulgarian archaeologists have devoted serious efforts and attention to the study of the early Slavic and Proto-Bulgar material remains in their excavations. The accumulated results are to be seen in the two important books of Vyzharova and Doncheva-Petkova.[11]

The publication of Vyzharova's book in 1976 revealed for the first time to the greater scholarly public the extent and richness of the Bulgarian archaeological efforts. By this time enough medieval sites had been systematically excavated so as to enable Vyzharova to undertake a study of twenty necropolis's excavated throughout Bulgaria, to inventory the finds in the graves, and to make a systematic analysis of the types of burial practices, the vases, and the other material objects. Beyond this she made a systematic effort, seemingly successful, to establish links between ethnic groups within one level of analysis, and between religious groups within another level of analysis. Then she proceeded to the difficult problem of establishing chronologies and chronological frameworks. Proceeding from a careful cataloging of the types of burial and the contents of each grave, the richness of the material enabled her to associate ethnic and religious groups with specific burial rites and to a certain degree with material objects. In the first part of her work she cataloged and examined cemeteries that were characterized by the burial rite of the cremation of the dead; in the second part, she examined cemeteries characterized by both cremation and by the laying out of the dead (inhumation) according to pagan rite; in part three she studied cemeteries that bore witness to both cremation and to Christian inhumation (which have been found in northern Bulgaria); in part four, she turned to the analysis of cemeteries, throughout Bulgaria, characterized by Christian burial rites. In part five, Vyzharova turned to the material finds in the graves, particularly the pottery, which she then related to particular types of funeral rites. At the same time she included all the other material objects, that is, the jewelry and so forth, as indications of the material culture of the medieval "inhabitants" of these cemeteries.

Of special importance, in chapter six of her book, are her conclusions as to the types of burial. She observed that cremation is the only manner of burial in a number of cemeteries, whereas in others there is simultaneously inhumation (according to pagan as also to Christian rite). Later the Christian burial replaced the others. The inhumation of bodies in certain cemeteries is chronologically simultaneous with the cremation practiced in other cemeteries, but it is spread over much smaller areas and for restricted periods of time. Christian burial, which begins in 865, continues for a long time alongside burial by cremation, and certain elements of cremation penetrate the Christian rite as do certain pagan rites of inhumation.

In chapter seven Vyzharova brings all the evidence together in an effort to establish periods and rough dates of the material. The results: a) Some cemeteries with cremation stretch from the end of the sixth to the eighth century, whereas other cemeteries with cremation belong to the eighth–tenth century period. b) Cemeteries with cremation and inhumation belong to the beginning of the eighth and ninth centuries. c) Cemeteries with cremation and the Christian rite belong to the ninth–eleventh centuries. d) Cemeteries with only Christian style burial date to the ninth–eleventh centuries (Vyzharova's survey stops with the eleventh century).

Vyzharova then attempts to link ethnic/religious groups living in medieval Bulgaria with these various types of burials in the cemeteries, between the late sixth to the eleventh century.

1. The cemeteries with cremation, both those of the sixth–eighth centuries, and those of the eighth–tenth centuries, are attributed to Slavs.

2. Cemeteries with both inhumation and cremation according to pagan rite are attributed to the Proto-Bulgars (I do not here go into her reasons and the evidence except to say that the evidence for all this exists).

3. The graves with inhumation according to pagan rite are unconditionally ascribed to the Proto-Bulgars.

4. Cemeteries with Christian burial are an evidence of Slavic particularity, for only in a few of these in north Bulgaria are some Proto-Bulgarian traditions to be seen.

Thus Vyzharova has created a massive set of guidelines for the disentanglement of various ethnic and religious groups in medieval Bulgaria. Further, and this is of great interest in the light of the efforts of current Bulgarian scholarship to find traces of the Thracians as a dynamic element, along with the Proto-Bulgarian and Slavic, in the ethnogenesis of the Bulgarian people in the Middle Ages, she concludes that traces of the population that had previously existed in the Balkans are hardly to be found.[12] As for many of the Olympia jars, found in ashes and often on the very coals, occasionally with remnants of bones and with some personal effects, they obviously fit well into the cremation according to pagan rite which Vyzharova has found present exclusively in many of the early cemeteries in Bulgaria, which she attributes to the Slavs exclusively, and which she dates to either of two periods: late seventh–eighth century, or eighth–tenth century.

Doncheva-Petkova in her study has composed the first systematic book on early Slavic pottery in the Balkans and one that is based on a comparatively numerous and rich collection of excavated, whole vases, vases in a fragmentary state, and on sherds, and so builds on the work of Vyzharova as well as on that of other Bulgarian scholars. Hers is a holistic approach to the subject, for not only does she essay a descriptive illustrated catalog of 378 vases of the early medieval period, with several pages of illustrations of the various types and variants, but she goes into the problem of the technology of this craft and finally of course attempts to broadly date these various types and variants. Obviously this is an immensely important labor and one which is relevant for the Slavic jars of Olympia. The author describes the nature and chemical consistence of the clays, the resultant colors produced therein, the manner of the working of the clay, either by hand or by primitive handwheel, or finally by a more sophisticated footwheel, the manner of firing and the effects of different types of firing, and the development of decoration of the ceramic surface. It would prolong the discussion to go into any one of these details here except to say that she has made very acute observations on all this from an on-hand study of the sites and materials. It would, perhaps, be relevant to say something about two matters of this technological aspect: formation of the actual pot and its baking. The most primitive of this early Slavic pottery from Bulgaria was made by hand, without the aid of even a primitive handwheel. The potter began with the base and then built up the sides toward the lip, evidently in sections, then joining the sections in such a manner, always by hand, that the juncture lines were effaced. At the end of the process the surface and the inside were smoothed by the fingers, telltale trace lines indicating all this, or else with smooth pieces of wood or seashell (evidence from Djedjevi-Lozja): the lines are vertical or slighting slanting, obviously not the sign of the horizontal circular lines left by wheels. The end result is of course extremely crude and the pottery sides are thick. The first improvement, she relates, comes with the use of the primitive handwheel at some time in the seventh century. The earliest of these vases are usually plain and without decoration. Later, linear and wavy-line decorations are introduced sometimes through the action of the wheel. The very poor quality, both as to brittle, thick texture (crumbles easily) and as to dullness and unevenness of color, indicates shoddy baking. This early pottery must have been baked over an open flame or else in a crude domestic oven, so that it baked unevenly, and both the texture and color were affected, sometime the color gradually changing from one to another color on one and the same vase. All of this is very relevant to the Olympia pottery, as we shall see.[13]

I wish now to turn to the description and dating that she gives to two sets of vases in her catalogue: Type I Variant A_1, and Type II Variant A_1.

Type I Variant A_1

These jars are classic representatives of early Slavic ceramics in the Balkans. They are characterized by the following particulars:

a) The shoulders are weakly rounded and are situated directly under the wide, barely hinted-at neck, or a very little lower down toward the middle of the vase's body;

b) The mouth is large, uneven, and weakly turned outwardly;

c) The crown of the mouth is ordinarily round with gradually outward-sloping lips;

d) The bottom of the vase is flat and nearly always uneven;

e) The places of the unions of the various parts of the sides are sometime round but at times constitute sharp beginnings of corners;

f) These vases are worked exclusively by hand, are very coarse, asymmetrical, thick-walled (between 0.005–0.01 m at slip), and slightly thicker in the body and base.

As mentioned above, Type I Variant A_1 is the earliest representative of the medieval ceramics uncovered in Bulgaria. They are close in type to jars excavated in other countries (Soviet Union, Romania, Yugoslavia, Czechoslovakia, Poland, Germany) and in the scholarly literature are known variously as Prague, Korchak-Zhitomirksi, Hlincha.

The question of dating, she continues, is not only important, but it is very difficult: "For exactly dated materials—coins, fibulae and other objects have not been found, up to this date, together with this pottery of Type I Variant A_1 in Bulgaria."[14] She finds the closest ceramic type to be that of the Prague dated to the fifth–sixth centuries and diffused over the broad area of central and western Europe to the Elbe and Zaale Rivers. Being closest to the Prague type it has a body that is like a truncated cone, has a short mouth, relatively clean clay, and an absence of ornament. Such fragments were found, indeed even an entire vase, at Kaleto together with late ancient ceramics. The excavators thus dated these pieces to the second half of the sixth century. Such early ceramic forms were also found elsewhere (Garvan-Staretsa). At Nova Cherna also the excavations uncovered fragments of early Slavic pottery together with late ancient vases and fibulae. This early Slavic pottery has thus been dated to the end of the sixth century and the seventh century. The pottery found in the earliest stratum at Djedjevi Lozja, as to color, coarse clay, and form is also an early development of the Prague and Zhitomirski type.[15] Thus this pottery was not produced earlier than the seventh century. Vyzharova, relying on the stratigraphy, has dated it to the end of the seventh century. Thus Doncheva-Petkova seems to conclude that Type I Variant A_1 is basically seventh century, and possibly late sixth century as well.

Type II Variant A_1

All these vases are of somewhat smaller proportion, though similar in many ways to Type I Variant A1. The widest expanse of the vessel comes much further down on the body, the base is thick and uneven. As in the case of the abovementioned type this too is made by hand of coarse clay with grains of sand. This type too is known elsewhere, that is, Soviet Union and Romania, and is to be dated to the end of the sixth–seventh century.[16]

The Slavic Pottery of Olympia

I wish now to return to the Slavic pottery of Olympia, of which I described and presented eighteen examples in the following categories:

Type I Variant A

Type II Variant A

Type I Variant A_4

Vryonis #20

Vryonis #16

The first two categories are typed according to the exact number and letter as in the catalog of Doncheva-Petkova, as in fact they are very close to these two types. The third category, Type I Variant A_4, is similar to both these first two categories, being somewhat between them. The last two categories, #20 and #16, while of the same type of pottery as to fabric, construction, and firing, are different sufficiently as to forms described in Doncheva-Petkova to note here. Only one, #16, may have been made on a crude handwheel. Thus the Olympia pottery is directly related to the earliest body of pottery studied by both Vyzharova and Doncheva-Petkova, materials that they have dated to the late sixth and seventh centuries, on the assumption that the plain, undecorated pottery precedes the decorated (though with the possibility that after the beginning of the decorative style the two could have coexisted). Proportions are similar, and coloration, due to poor firing, as well. The function of all this pottery, or at least the majority of it, is for the burial of the cremated dead, as witnessed by the presence of ashes in the urns, and by the few penurious personal effects in some of the jars, as well as of charred bones (these have not been examined by the necessary specialists to see if they are from humans).

It is of interest that the cemetery at Olympia is located on the hill overlooking the small tributary brook of the Kladeos that flows into the Alpheios River, a fact which reminds us of the Strategicon of the Pseudo-Maurice, which reports that Slavs tended to place their settlements along waterways.[17] Now, the dating of this pottery by Doncheva-Petkova to the late sixth, but mostly to the seventh century is possibly relevant here too, simply on the basis of the pottery. It is also of interest that we have the plain jars, as well as the incised or decorated jars, and it is assumed that the plain are the earlier of the two, though there is no guarantee that at Olympia the two did not co-exist inasmuch as the urns have been found in the same stratum, 50–65 cm from the surface. That it is a matter of Slavic pottery and burials admits, I think, of little doubt. First, there is the matter of cremation. Cremation, though practiced by the ancient Greeks, simultaneously with inhumation, by the late classical and Hellenistic periods, seems to have declined, though not disappeared, in the face of the increasing practice of inhumation of the dead. Though I have not studied the matter systematically, Christian burial in Byzantium by the sixth century seems to have been largely by inhumation and not by cremation, a fact which would tend to preclude that the burials at Olympia were Greek Christian. That the area was effectively Christian by this time is attested by the existence of the Christian basilica at Olympia.[18] There is also the written testimony, already brought to bear by Vyzharova, as to the fact that the Slavs were burning their dead in the third decade of the seventh century. After the failure of the Avaro-Slavic attack on Constantinople in 626, the attackers suffered very heavy losses of their soldiery. The slaughter of the Avaro-Slavs was very extensive, we are told by a sermon delivered on August 7, 627, by the syncellus Theodore:

Such a multitude of dead from among the enemy fell at every point near the wall and everywhere else that the barbarians were no longer able to drag away and to burn their fallen men.[19]

The story is repeated in an anonymous tract entitled Hymnus Acathistus, in the first half of the ninth century.[20]

A later text referring to the military victories of John Tzimisces over the Russian prince Svjatislav, outside the gates of the Danubian Durostolum, comments on this practice among what would seem to be Slavic (in contrast to Scandinavian) Russians. Tzimisces and the Byzantine armies had inflicted very heavy losses on the Russians on the plain before the walls of the town:

When night had fallen, and there being a full moon, they [the Russians] came out on the plain searching for their dead. Having gathered them before the wall and having lighted dense fires, they burned them. Then they slaughtered over the burned dead a great number of men and women according to their ancestral law. Having made offerings [to the dead], they brought suckling infants and roosters and having thrown them into the rushing river, drowned them.[21]

Vyzharova has observed that the cremation of the dead among the Balkan Slavs is observable well into the ninth century and even beyond, alongside the spreading Christian practice of inhumation. As late as the fourteenth century Dushan's Zakonik, in article 20, forbids the burning of the dead.[22]

While at Olympia studying the Slavic pottery, Dr. Kollwitz, then the director of the German Archaeological Institute in Athens, very kindly allowed me to consult the original journal/diary of the German excavations on the site of

Olympia in the beginning of the German activity there. The entries for December 20, 1877, mention and describe a hoard of Byzantine coins and a cache of Byzantine agricultural implements. The major portion of this find consisted of a great clay pithos filled with copper coins, hidden in the east wall of the so-called Slavenmauer not far from the northeast corner. There was a second urn nearby similarly filled. Further, there were five bronze vessels, and various metal tools closely stuffed into a secure hiding place in the wall. These tools and containers were agricultural in nature and included four picks, a hack, two spades, a sickle, a long spoon-like implement, and a rake. The coins in the large container are said, by the German recorder of the find, to have weighed five okas and 120 drams, and he gives a list of them, reaching from Constantine I to Justinian I.

I bring the evidence of this hoard of coins and tools to bear because the objects will furnish further supplementary evidence in the matter of dating. No coin after Justinian I (527–565) is present.

All the evidence, then, points to a very early date for the handmade and undecorated crude funeral jars of Olympia. If only the dates of the Slavic sherds from Argos can be fixed with incontrovertible precision we shall have a very helpful indication for the Slavic pottery of Olympia. I am inclined to place the date of the latter rather earlier than I. Nestor (who had spoken of the later seventh century). The probability of a late sixth or early seventh century presence of Slavic tribes in the Peloponnese is now seemingly considerably strengthened by the evidence of Olympia and strongly supports the conclusions of my late and dear friend Peter Charanis, a staunch supporter of the Chronicle of Monemvasia and of its historical importance.[23]

Notes

1. Yalouris in 'Αρχαιολογικὸν Δελτίον XVI (1960), 125–126; (1961–62), XVII, B 106, with photos on plate 117, a–d, and also mentioned in the *Bulletin de Correspondance Hellénique*, LXXXIV (1960), 720, and LXXV (1961), 722; 'Αρχαιολογικὸν Δελτίον XIX (1964), B', 174, 176; XX (1965), B'$_2$, 209; XXI (1966), B'$_1$, and plate 182.

2. Zh. N. Vyzharova, *Slaviani i Prabylgari po danni na nekropolite ot VI–XI v. na teritoriata na Bylagriia* (Sofia, 1976), p. 242, where in fn. 7, she remarks that the material was being studied by scholars in East Germany. I wish to express here my profound gratitude to this very great scholar both for her publications, from which I learned so much, but also for her very warm hospitality during the stay of my wife and me in Bulgaria during the spring and summer of 1987. She opened all the archaeological treasures in Bulgaria dealing with the early Slavs and the Proto-Bulgars, and she guided me through them patiently and wisely. Her recent death is a great loss to scholarship as well as to all those who knew her.

3. I wish to express my thanks for the kindness and help that Mr. Tzachas, then ephor of antiquities of Olympia, for the many kindnesses extended to me, and also to Mr. Liangouras for his knowledge of the finding of the graves and for his rough sketch map indicating where a number of the vases had been found.

4. For the varying views see the work of Vyzharova, as in n. 2 above, and also that of Lj. Doncheva-Petkova, *Bylgarska bitova keramika prez rannoto srednovekovie (vtorata*

polovina na VI-kraja na X v.) (Sofia, 1977). For other opinions see the references in S. Vryonis, "The Evolution of Slavic Society and the Slavic Invasions in Greece: The First Major Slavic Attack on Thesslaoniki, AD 597," in *Hesperia* L (1981), 380 and the footnotes.

5. Z. Vana, *The World of the Ancient Slavs* (Detroit, 1983), 21-24. V.D. Baran, "Slaviane v seredine I tysiacheletiia n.e.," in Baran, *Problemy etnogeneza slavian* (Kiev, 1978), 15-24.

6. I.P. Rusanova, *Slavianskie drevnosti VI-VII vv* (Moscow, 1976), 192-196. Vana, as in n. 5 above, 40-41.

7. M. Čorovič-Ljubinkovič, "Les Slaves du centre balkanique du VIe au IXe siecle," *Balcanoslavica* I (1972), 48-49.

8. I. Čremošnik, "Die altesten Ansiedlungen und Kultur der Slawen in Bosnien und der Herzegovina im Lichte der Untersuchungen in Musici und Batkovici," *Balcanoslavica* I (1972), 59. D. Jelovina, *Starohrvatske nekropole* (Split, 1976), 67. S. Dolinescu Ferche, "La culture 'Ipotešti-Ciurei-Cindešti' (Ve-VIIe siecles). La situation en Valachie," *Dacia* XXVIII (1984), 117-147, esp. pp. 144ff., on the handmade Slavic pottery.

9. For a listing of a wide sampling of this broad and profuse literature, Vryonis, loc. cit., fn. 3. Vryonis review article of M. Weithmann, *Die slavische Bevölkerung auf der griechischen Halbinsel. Ein Beitrag zur historischen Ethnographie Südosteuropas* (Munich, 1978), in *Balkan Studies*, XX-2 (1981), 405-439. P. Malingoudis, Σλαύοι στὴν μεσαιωνικὴ Ἑλλάδα, (Thessaloniki, 1988); and Ἡ Θεσσαλονίκη καὶ ὁ κόσμος τῶν Σλαύων (Thessaloniki, 1991).

10. The appropriate papers appeared in Supplement VI of the *Bulletin de Correspondance Hellenique, Etudes Argiennes* (1980): P. Aupert, "Ceramique slave à Argos (585 ap. JC)," 373-394; idem, "Objets de la vie quotidienne à Argos en 585 ap. JC," 295ff. Yannopoulos, "La penetration slave à Argos," 323-372.

11. For the full reference to the book of Vyzharova, see n. 2 above, and for the book of Doncheva-Petkova, n. 4 above.

12. Vyzharova as in n. 2 above, pp. 409-441, with a German summary on pp. 440-441. See also her *Srednovekovnoto selishte. S. Gavran, silistrenski okryg* (Sofia, 1986), on the Salvic villages. 13. Doncheva-Petkova, as in n. 4 above, pp. 15-32.

13. Doncheva-Petkova, as in n. 4 above, pp. 15-32.

14. Doncheva-Petkova, as in n. 4 above, pp. 37-40.

15. Doncheva-Petkova, as in n. 4 above, p. 39. A. Milcev and S. Angelova, "Razkopki i mouchovanie b. m. Kaleto krai s. Nova Cherna, Silistrenski okryg, prez 1968 g.," *Arkehologija* XII (1970), 24-34.

16. Doncheva-Petkova, as in n. 4 above, 49-50. For a different system of pottery dating, D. Dimitrov, *Prabulgarite po severnoto i zapadnoto chernomorie* (Varna, 1987).

17. Pseudo-Marucie, *Strategikon* XI, 4.

18. P. Velisariou, "Σχόλιον εἰς ἐπιγραφὴν τῆς ἀρχαίας Ὀλυμπίας. Ἡ χρονολόγησις τοῦ μνημείου," Πρακτικὰ τοῦ Αʹ. Συνεδρίου Ἐλειακῶν σπουδῶν (Athens, 1980), 159-166. D. Kurtz and J. Boardman, *Greek Burial Customs* (Ithaca, 1971), pp. 2140, 51-56, 71-76.

19. Edited with Bulgarian translation by G. Tsankova-Petkova, in *Izvori za bylgarskata istorija* (hereafter *IVI*) (Sofia, 1960), VI, 52.

20. *IVI*, vol. VI, 172. See also the poem of George Pisides, *IVI*, vol. VI, p. 65, where he implies that the bodies of the dead were so numerous that they acted as fertilizer for the trees that grew greatly, as a result, about the walls.

21. *IVI*, vol. IX, 269.

22. Cited in Vyzharova, as in n. 2 above, p. 415.

23. P. Charanis, "The Chronicle of Monemvasia and the Question of the Slavonic Settlements in Greece," *Dumbarton Oaks Papers*, V (1950), pp. 141ff.

Catalog

In the first rough catalog of the Slavic vases of Olympia it has been very difficult to devise a logical and systematic scheme because of the lack of systematic data and excavation diaries. I have, therefore, listed (1) first the arbitrary number I have assigned to the vases and sherds as I encountered them in the museum at Olympia, (2) then the museum acquisition number which is always preceded by the Greek letter π; (3) there follows the photographic number from the photographic archive of the museum, and (4) the date of the find or photo. (5) Wherever available I next place the number assigned to the tomb by Yalouris or Themelis, though on occasions the same number had been assigned to two different tombs. (6) There follow data (where available) of the place, and the depth at which the object was found (this is not always clear because the point of reference is not always mentioned in the sparse notes, and the suface of the area has been changed at least twice: first by the actual digging, and then secondly by the refilling of the area). There follow (7) a description of the vase, (8) measurements, and (9) any other data.

1. No acquisition number; no photographic number; 9/2/63; Tomb #4 (Themelis) (another tomb #4 is identified by photo 2598, 4/20/60, pediment chamber); the east embankment opposite the Hall of Hermes in the museum, at a depth of 0.4 m from the surface of filling, and at a depth of the surface of the water conduit. Sherds of a Slavic vase: about half of the base, 3 pieces from the lip, odd pieces. Clay has many small white bits on surface and inside. It is grey. No striations or lines. The sherds have a thickness of 0.7 cm. The entirety is in a deep, square, green cardboard box.

2. π 501; photo 7337, on left, 2498, 2499; 9/4/63; Tomb #9 (Themelis). Eastern slope opposite Hall of Hermes, at a depth of 0.5 m. Bottom half of vase, brownish color, vertical striations; height of restored portion 17.75 cm; diameter of base, 15 cm; thickness 0.7 cm. In it were also found three metal objects (M170 a, b, g, photo 10686.

a) M170a is iron knife, 0.075 m in length, 0.160.016 m in breadth

b) M170b-two long, thin iron pieces in semi-circular form.

γ M170-bronze wire

y 41-s crystal bead.

3. π 500; photo 7336 left, 4802, 4803, 4804; 7/24/64; Tomb XI (Themelis); east slope oppose Hall of Hermes. Vase, substantially remounted but is lacking the base and one-half of the lip and mouth. Red-brown in color. A cross section of sherds shows they are grey with white particles and red-brown on outside. The vase has a height of c. 21 cm, base with c. 7.5 cm diameter, shoulder 13.0 cm, neck 11.5 cm, and the thickness of the clay is 0.8 cm.

4. π 498; photo 7336 right, 2502, 2503, 2592; 9/4/63; Tomb VIII (Themelis); East slope opposite Hall of Hermes, at depth of 0.8 m. Vase, with one buckle or clasp of bronze, grey in color. Height (base to neck) 17.1 cm, base 8.7 cm diameter, shoulder 14.3 cm diameter, neck 11.7cm. Thickness of clay 0.8 cm.

5. π 504b; photo 7339 right, 6422, 6423, 6424, 6425; 4/28/65; Tomb XIV (Themelis); slope northeast of Hall of Hermes at depth of 1.2 m from original surface of earth. Sherds and ashes; bottom of vase has been restored. Is reddish brown in color, with vertical striations. (Is kept in green cardboard box.)

6. π 504a; photo 7331; date not given; Tomb II. Site of find not reported. Vase fragments, only base and bottom portion, base 8.5 cm in diameter, height 4.75 cm, and thickness of clay 0.75 cm. (Is kept in same box as #4 above).

7. No accession number, no photo, no date given, simply described as "ἀκατάγραφον." Reddish-brown sherds, striated, of 1 cm thickness. (In light cardboard box).

8. π 502; photo 7332 right; 4/1/59; Tomb III (Yalouris); 14th trench, basement of the museum at a depth of 1.0 m. Fragments and base of one vase, and other fragments from a different or from different vases, some with striations. Height (from base to tip of restored part) 6.3 cm, base 7.5 cm diameter, thickness of clay 0.27 cm. (Is in light brown cardboard box).

9. π 457; photo 7347; 10/28/63; found by drainage ditch south of the new museum, 4 meters from the fourth column from the east, at depth of 0.8 m. A vase, reddish brown in color, parallel striations at top, perpendicular striations on remainder of vase with beads of a necklace. Height (base to tip of reconstructed neck) 15.0 cm, base 9.5 cm diameter, shoulder 13.4 cm diameter, thickness of clay 0.8 cm. There are 11 glass beads. Of these:

a) 4 are heartshaped, deep blue.

b) 2 are spindleshaped, one of which was pierced, with traces of bronze.

c) 1 is cylindrical, blue.

d) 1 is spindleshaped, blue.

e) 3 are spherical, (2 are green and one blue). See photo.

10. π 1651a; no photo; 11/22/61; Found under present day central hall of the new museum. The base and bottom portions of a vase, reddish brown, vertical striations. Height (base to tip of reconstructed part) 8.5 cm, base 10 cm in diameter.

11. π 458; photo 7346; 7/20/1960; Found in Trench A at depth of 1.1 m. The vase, reddish brown with two bands of undulating striations toward the top, was found inside coals and ashes. It has a height (base to beginning of neck) 20.0 cm, base 9.6 cm diameter, shoulder 19.5 cm diameter, thickness of clay 0.6 cm.

12. π 1651B; no photo; 11/22/61; found under central hall of present-day new museum at a depth of 0.9 m. It seems to have been found with #10 above. Fragment of a vase (base and one side reconstructed), reddish brown, unstriated. Height (base to neck) 10.0 cm, base 8.0 cm diameter, thickness of clay 0.6 cm. This is kept in a square light brown cardboard box together with sherds, from another vase, that are striated and have a thickness of 0.45 cm also of a tomato brown color.

12a. π 502; photo 7332 right; no date; no mention of site; Vase (base, beginnings of sides) brown and dirty grey. Height 7.0 cm, base 8.4 cm in diameter, thickness 0.6 cm. It should be compared with the sherds from #8 above.

13. π 460; photo 7351 right; 3/24/59; Found in twelfth trench at site of new museum, at depth of 0.65 m. Vase (largely reconstucted and reglued), reddish brown, no striations. Height (complete) 20.0 cm, base 9.4 cm diameter, shoulder 17.9 cm, lip 17.0 cm diameter, thickness of clay 0.75 cm.

14. π 459; photo 7351 left; date, site confused; Vase, large, reddish brown, with parallel striations at the neck. Inside the vase I found sherds from a different, larger vase with striations. Also, composition and texture of clay of sherds differ from those of the vase, as the sherds are blacker on inside of clay and have white particles. I found two site/location identifications written on two slips of paper inside the vase, without any indication as to which identification belonged to the vase and which to the sherds:

a) 3/26/59, 13th trench of new museum, depth of 0.6 m.

b) 9/8/59, northeast corner of slope opposite Hall of Hermes.

I failed to record the dimensions of this vase.

15. No acquisition number; seems to be similar to photo 10682 (dated 3/6/59); 3/20/59; found in eleventh trench under new museum. Vase (base and lower section) reddish brown with perpendicular striations, and loose sherds. Height 6.2 cm, base 8.8 cm diameter, thickness 0.6 cm. (Is kept in a light brown cardboard box).

16. π 503; photo 7330, right; date of find unclear, 1959 or 1961; Tomb II. Vase, reddish brown with perpendicular striations. Height (reconstructed partially from lip down), c. 12.0 cm, shoulder 15.0 cm diameter, lip 11.0 cm diameter, thickness of clay 0.7 cm. There is a photograph of this vase in 'Αρχαιολογικὸν Δελτίον, XVII B' 1961-1962, pl. 117, top right. Sherds also were found with this vase.

17. π 454; photo 7350 left; no date. On back of the photo is written, Nr. 1 Od 5073, which seems to have no relevance to further identification of this object). This vase is much better baked than most, brown with perpendicular striations. height (complete) 15.0 cm, base 9.9 cm diameter, neck 14.2 cm diameter, lip 12.1 cm, thickness of clay 0.5 cm. Inside this vase was found an iron knife (M 117, photo 10685, top).

18. π 497; photo 7335 right, 2502, 2503, in situ with two other vases; 9/4/63; Tomb VIII (Themelis); Found on east slope opposite Hall of Hermes, at depth of 0.80 m. Vase (restored) is reddish-brown, unstriated, height (entire) 11.1 cm, base 7.2 cm diameter, shoulder 10.4 cm diameter, neck 8.4 cm diameter, lip 9.2 cm diameter, thickness of clay 0.5 cm.

19. π 491; photo 7332 left; 1/22/64; Tomb III (Themelis); found in trench of the air vent under the central hall of the new museum at a depth of 0.67 m. Vase, reddish brown with undulating striations and perpendicular striations. It had beads inside it (photograph 10 688, Y38). Height 17.7 cm, base 8.8 cm diameter, shoulder 18.0 cm diameter, neck 16.15 cm diameter, lip 17.4 cm diameter, thickness of clay 0.6 cm.

20. π 453; photo 7340; no date or site given. Vase, unstriated, light brown. Height (complete) 19.0 cm, base 12.2 cm diameter, shoulder 17.8 cm diameter, neck 12.2 cm diameter, lip 13.9 cm diameter, thickness 0.7 cm.

21. π 495; photo 7334; 2504 and 2505 are of the base in situ; 9/3/63; Tomb VII (Themelis); Found at slope opposite Hall of Hermes. Vase, reddish brown, unstriated, largely glued and reconstructed. Was found with piece of a small knife inside it—M167, photo 10686). Height (base to neck) 24.5 cm, base 11.9 cm diameter, shoulder 20.6 cm diameter, neck 13.7 cm diameter.

22. π 494; photo 7344; 10/28/63. Found at drainage pipe south of new museum, 4 m from fourth column from east, at depth of 0.8 m. Vase, reddish-brown, unstriated, has been glued and reconstructed. It contained the beads of a necklace inside it (Y39, photo 10688). Height (base to neck) 16.0 cm, base 10.5 cm diameter, shoulder 15.7 cm diameter, thickness of clay 0.6 cm.

23. No acquisition number, no photo; 9/3/63; Tomb VII (Themelis). Various sherds, some dirty grey, others tomato red. Thickness of clay 0.7 cm. (Are kept in a small paper sack.)

24. No acquistion number; no photo; no date; described as ajkatavgrafa. No location given. Vase (reconstructed and glued to one-half height), reddish-brown, unstriated; also sherds. Height (c. one-half) 15.0 cm, vase 11.6 cm diameter, thickness of clay 0.75 cm.

25. π 179; photo 7330 left; no date or location given. Vase, small, of different shape from the others, much rounder, grey on outside but broken sherds show red on inside. Height 5.0 cm, base 4.0 cm diameter, shoulder 6.5 cm diameter, thickness of clay 0.5 cm.

26. No acquisiton number; no photo; 11/22/61; found in trench at depth of 0.9 m (under new museum?). Sherds, dull reddish brown, dirty color, vertical striations, 0.6 cm in thickness. Also a base, but it does not seem to belong with the base (base is 7.5 cm diameter); also additional pieces which seem to come from a separate vase (kept in a brown cardboard box).

27. Wooden box containing:

a) A yellow cardboard box—no acquisition number, no photo; 1/22/64; Tomb IV (Themelis). Found in the trench of the air duct of the central hall of the new museum at a depth of 0.67 m. Vase (large) fragments, brownish-red and dirty grey, perpendicular and horizontal striations intersecting at right angles. Thickness 1.0 cm.

b) In wooden box; no acquisition number, no photo or date, and no location given. Vase fragment, reddish-brown and grey with little white particles, thickness of clay 0.7 cm.

c) A cigarette box with bones but no indication if they belong to (b).

28a. π 496; photo 7338, and 2500, 2501 in situ); 9/5/63; Tomb X (Themelis) burial 11; Found at east slope opposite Hall of Hermes, at depth of 0.8 m, north of Tomb IX (1.30 m).

Vase (found almost intact), only part of lip missing. Was cracked and has been reglued. Reddish-brown and dirty grey. Has a double row of horizontally and perpendicularly undulating striations. Height (entire) 23.0 cm, base 12.3 cm diameter, shoulder 21.2 cm diameter, neck 17.3 cm diameter, lip 19.9 cm diameter, thickness 0.8 cm.

28b Inside vase are sherds . . . no acquistion number.

29. π 451; photo 7348; 6/20/60? 6/7/60?. Found in coals and ashes in trench B under the lower hall of the new museum, at a depth of 0.52–0.63 m; 2.54 m in from Side A and 0.75 m in from side B (sic). Vase, glued together, is reddish-brown with perpendicular striations. Height (entire) 17.0 cm, base 5.5 cm diameter, shoulder 14.2 cm diameter, neck 10.7 cm diameter, lip 11.5 cm diameter, thickness of clay 0.9 cm. Is photographed in' Ἀρχαιολογικὸν Δελτίον XVII, 1961–1962, B', pl. 117, upper left, which is a different view from photo 7348.

30. π 456; photo 7350 right; 4/21/59; Found in the eighteenth trench, 11.8 m from west end of trench, at a depth of 1.6 m, under the site of the new museum. Vase (with a piece of bone inside it), reddish-brown, dirty grey. Height (entire) 21.5 cm, base 10.3 cm diameter, shoulder 18.0 cm diameter, neck 14.25 cm diameter, lip 16.5 cm diameter, thickness of clay 0.7 cm.

31. 450; photo 7349; no date; found in Trench E3, 2.7 m east of wall and 0.4 m north of wall of trench, at depth of 1.6 m. Vase, reddish-brown and dirty grey. Parallel striations around neck with a small undulating striation at bottom of parallel striations. Then four undulating, parallel striations below. Height (entire) 24.5 cm, base 10.1 cm diameter, shoulder 18.9 cm diameter, neck 15.5 cm diameter, lip 16.5 cm diameter, thickness of clay 0.8 cm.

32. No acquisition number; no photo; 8/30/63; Tomb I (Themelis); found at east slope, opposite Hall of Hermes, at a depth of 0.5 m. Vase (bottom half and one side), grey and tomato brown, unstriated. It is together with bones and sherds. Height (partial) 8.6 cm, base 10.75 cm, thickness 0.6 cm. (Is kept in a green cardboard box with wire around it.)

33. π 1650; no photo in museum archives, but is photographed in Ἀρχαιολογικὸν Δελτίον XXI, 1966, pl. 182, a, b; photos 7342, 7343 from photo archive of museum reproduce the metal and glass objects found in it. There are two contradictory dates given as to the find: (a) the acquisition card in the museum dates it to 2/5/67; (b) the journal reports the find date as 4/18/65. Vase, grey, tomato brown, unstriated. Inside the vase were found an iron knife, an iron bracelet, 2 glass beads (green and blue), and a fragment of another iron knife (M 169 in photo 10685).

34. π 499; photo 7341 shows vase before reconstruction; photo 10428 shows it in situ; 2/5/67; Burial XII; Found near peristyle of new museum. Vase, reddish-brown and dirty grey, with perpendicular striations and one undulating horizontal striation. Height 20.1 cm, base 10.8 cm diameter, shoulder 16.5 cm diameter, neck 13.0 cm diameter, lip 15.0 cm diameter, thickness 0.6 cm.

35. π 492; photo 7335 left, and photos 2502, 2503, 2592 which show the three vases in situ; 9/4/63; Tomb VIII (Themelis); found on east slope, opposite Hall of Hermes, at a depth of 0.90 m. Vase, grey, but when flaked it becomes reddish-brown. Height 12.1 cm, base, 7.3 cm

diameter, shoulder 10.7 cm diameter, neck 9.0 diameter, lip 9.8.

36. π 455; photo 7333; no date in inventory list. It is either 1959, 1960, or 1961, 'Αρχαιο–λογικὸν Δελτίον, 1961–1962, XVII, B pl. 117; Tomb VII? Found above first trench of the New Museum. Vase, grey at top, reddish brown at bottom, perpendicular and horizontal striations. Used for cremation of the dead. Height 24.0 cm, base 11.0 cm diameter, shoulder 21.2 cm diameter, neck 18.1 cm diameter, lip 20.1 cm diameter, thickness of clay 0.7 cm.

37. π 493; photo 7345; 7/25/63; found at south slope of drainage pipe of new museum laboratory, at a depth of 1.8 m. Vase, reddish-brown, with horizontal, undulating striations around neck. In it was found a small knife (M 166, photo 10685, at bottom) and coals.

38. π 449; photo 7329; 3/27/59; Tomb I (Yalouris); Found in fourteenth trench of basement of new museum, at a depth of 0.5 cm. Vase, reddish-brown, perpendicular striations. Found with iron knife and part of iron nail (116a, b, in photo 10687; also photographed in 'Αρχαιολογικὸν Δελτίον, 1961–1962, XVII B, plate 117e #4–6). Height of vase 23.5 cm, base 10.0 cm diameter, shoulder 19.6 cm diameter, neck 17.1 cm diameter, lip 19.1 cm diameter, thickness 0.8 cm.

Photograph Corpus

2   3   4

5   6   9

41

42

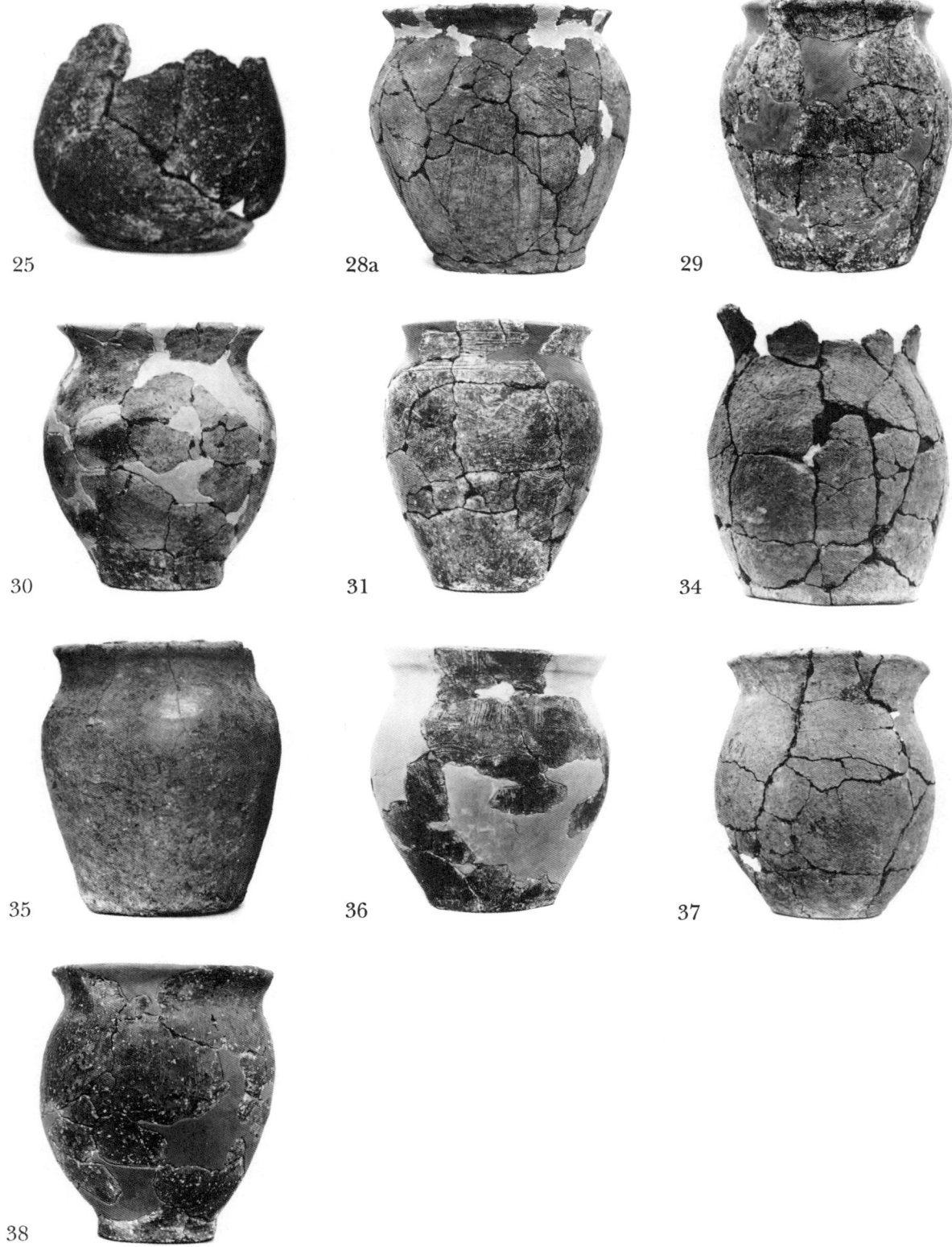

3
Medieval Serbia: The Nemanyids and Byzantium

Bariša Krekić

University of California, Los Angeles

THE RELATIONSHIP BETWEEN SERBIA AND BYZANTIUM during the rule of the Nemanyid dynasty in Serbia was marked by ambiguity throughout the 200 years of that dynasty's presence on the Serbian political scene. The ambiguity was exemplified already in the life of the founder of the dynasty, the Grand Zhupan Stevan Nemanya (1166–1196). Baptized first in a Roman Catholic church, he ended his life as an Eastern Orthodox monk in the Serbian monastery of Chilandar, founded by his youngest son, Sava, on Mount Athos. Having started his career as a vassal of the mighty Byzantine Emperor Manuel I Comnenos (1143–1180), Nemanya ended his life as the unifier of the Serbian lands and the founder of the longest lasting and most powerful Serbian dynasty. All these achievements were made possible principally by the weakness of the Byzantine Empire after the death of Manuel I, in 1180, but it is clear that Serbia in Nemanya's time was very much a country between East and West, exposed to many Western influences, and, at the same time, strongly attracted by the East, Byzantium.[1]

The earth-shaking events of the Fourth Crusade, in 1204, drastically changed the situation in the Levant and affected much of southeastern Europe. The removal of Byzantium from Constantinople, the creation of a weak Latin Empire in its place, and the exclusively maritime interests of the only real victor of the Crusade, Venice, allowed the Balkan states to move in new directions and to develop new options. Bulgaria under Kaloian (1197–1207) and especially under John Asen II (1218–1241) profited the most initially,[2] but Serbia did not miss the opportunity either. Indeed, until 1204 Serbia was, basically, fighting against Byzantium to obtain independence. After 1204, Byzantium ceased to be an obstacle to Serbian ambitions and the Serbs—at least for a while—had to cope with other enemies.

Nevertheless, the East-West ambiguity in the Serbian position persisted. When its next leader, Stevan Nemanya's second son, Steven (who was married to the grand-daughter of the famous Venetian Doge and leader of the Fourth Crusade,

Enrico Dandolo), became a king and Serbia was elevated to the rank of kingdom, in 1217, the royal crown came from the West, from the Roman pope. Two years later, in 1219, Serbia achieved another landmark success—ecclesiastical independence. This development, however, originated in the East: the Serbian church was granted independence by the Byzantine patriarchate in Nicaea. Consequently, the autocephalous Serbian church became firmly attached to the Eastern Orthodox world—a fateful decision for all of Serbian history. That was the doing of Stevan Nemanya's very able youngest son Rastko/Sava, the highly talented and shrewd monk-diplomat-educator, who became the first archbishop and later a saint of the Serbian church.[3] Thus, the brother of the Serbian king, who was wearing a crown sent from Rome, was heading an Eastern Orthodox church in that same country. Serbia's position between East and West was, obviously, still very much a reality.

The next big upheaval in southeastern Europe, the disappearance of the Latin Empire and the return of Byzantium in Constantinople, in 1261, found Serbia on the threshold of a new process of growth. Indeed, this was the time—mid-thirteenth century—when a new and extremely important activity, mining, began in Serbia. I shall return to that phenomenon in a little while. Let me say now that mining of silver, copper, iron, and lead became very quickly the mainstay of the Serbian might and expansion. This was already visible during the reigns of King Uroš I (1243–1276) and his brother, King Dragutin (1276–1282), and became especially clear during the rule of the first great expansionist Nemanyid king, Milutin (1282–1321).

Milutin's period was, no doubt, a turning point in Serbian history. By this time mining was providing vast amounts of income for the ruler's coffers. Simultaneously, another very significant element emerged on the political scene of southeastern Europe: the unstoppable decline of Byzantium after the death of the Emperor Michael VIII Paleologos, in 1282. The combination of these two developments, Serbian mining and Byzantine decay, exercised a decisive influence on the orientation of Milutin's expansionist policies toward the southeast, toward the rich and poorly defended Byzantine lands in Macedonia and northern Greece.[4] Serbia was becoming an eastward-looking state, although links with the West always remained strong, especially in the economic sphere.

The eastward turn in Serbian politics was even reflected in the marriages of two thirteenth-century kings. Uroš I was married to the French Neapolitan Angevin Princess Helen, who brought a great deal of Western cultural influences to Serbia during her exceptionally long life. She died in 1314, having remained very influential during the rule of her two sons, Dragutin and Milutin, and even governing part of Serbian lands for over thirty years.[5] Milutin, for his part, was married at least four times, the most important marriage being the last one, in 1299, with the Byzantine Princess Simonis, daughter of the Emperor Andronicus II Paleologos (1282–1328). Never mind that the Serbian king at the time was at least forty-four years of age, and Simonis was only five.[6] As a matter of fact, Theodore Metochytes, the Byzantine envoy who traveled to Serbia several times to arrange the Byzantino-Serbian peace treaty and this marriage, wrote that Emperor Andronicus "was very scared because of her [i.e., Simonis] and worried very much lest she suffer some unexpected evil from this hostile old man [i.e., Milutin]."[7] And Georgios Pachymeres tells us that Andronicus felt that his little daughter "had been snatched from his arms by a barbarian, totally deprived of feeling of love and without anything honorable in his government."[8] The marriage, which the victorious Serbian king imposed on the weak Byzantine emperor, was of great consequence for Serbia, because Simonis and her retinue brought to the Serbian royal court and to the Serbian state a strong Byzantine influence, thus giving Serbia an added ideological push toward the East.

The culminating point of the Serbian medieval state and of Serbo-Byzantine relations came, of course, during the period of the mightiest Serbian ruler of all time, King and then Emperor Stefan Dušan (1331–1355, emperor from 1345). Dušan took advantage of the Byzantine internal disarray, especially of the long and exhausting civil war between John V Paleologos and John VI Cantacuzenus, which lasted from 1341 to 1347, to greatly expand the Serbian state toward the south and southeast. He thus created a Serbo-Greek state and when he proclaimed himself emperor, he took, quite appropriately, the symbolic title of "Emperor and Autocrat of Serbs and Greeks."[9] Dušan's ultimate goal was to conquer Constantinople and thus to become a "genuine" Roman, that is, Byzantine emperor. His empire contained large chunks of conquered Greek lands—as far east as Serres and as far south as the Gulf of Corinthos—and he took over the Byzantine imperial ideology. Dušan's court was full of Byzantine titles and ceremonies and the Serbian church was elevated for the first time to patriarchal rank, against the wishes of the patriarchate of Constantinople (the chasm was bridged only thirty years later). The administrative and legal structure of the Serbian Empire was largely based on Byzantine precedent. This was best reflected in the famous code of law, "Dušan's Code," issued in 1349 and revised in 1354, which is thoroughly permeated by Byzantine legal concepts.[10]

Dušan was also the first Serbian ruler to confront the Ottoman Turks and to become aware of the new, ominous menace they represented. He wanted to organize a broad anti-Ottoman coalition and to that effect he established contacts with the pope and wanted to be appointed by the pope "Commander-in-Chief of Christianity" against the "Infidels," while he himself would recognize the pope as "Father of Christianity." It should be mentioned that Dušan, while taking over the Byzantine imperial tradition and while always being a dedicated Eastern Orthodox Christian, was interested in collaboration with the papacy even before the appearance of the Ottoman threat. Certainly, the break between the Serbian church and Constantinople after the proclamation of the Serbian patriarchate contributed to Dušan's interest in contacts with Rome. In addition, one should not forget that Dušan had a sizable Roman Catholic population in the western, coastal areas of his state; that there was a large number of Roman Catholics, mainly from Dubrovnik, in the main mining and commercial centers of Serbia; and that some of Dušan's closest and most able collaborators were Roman Catholics from Dubrovnik and Kotor. Indeed, some of these men occupied very high positions in the Serbian government and were among the leading figures in negotiations in which Dušan engaged with the papacy to achieve his above-mentioned anti-Ottoman goals.[11] However, through it all, he continued to keep an eye on the possibility of conquering Constantinople and of establishing his authority in the Byzantine capital.

Clearly then, Serbia once again was maneuvering between East and West, but while negotiating with Rome, Dušan suddenly died, on December 20, 1355. One cannot help wondering what the fate of southeastern Europe would have been had he lived longer, conquered Constantinople, and realized his coalition with the papacy and the West. Would the Ottomans—confronted on the Bosphorus by a mighty Serbian Empire, stretching from the Danube in the north to Central Greece in the south, and from the Adriatic Sea in the West to the Black Sea in the east, and supported by Western Europe—have turned elsewhere, thus leaving southeastern Europe free of their invasion and plurisecular presence? Would the fate of Serbia, its links with the West, and its possible integration into Central and Western European cultural and civilizational trends, have been different and had different long-term consequences had Dušan's plan of collaboration with the papacy been implemented? Of course, those are questions without answers.

Dušan's premature death (he was about forty-eight when he died) marked the beginning of the end of Nemanyid Serbia. His weak young son Uros (1355–1371) was incapable of holding together his vast lands and of controlling the unruly regional lords. Even the joining to the imperial throne, in 1366, of one of the most able and powerful regional lords, Vukašin Mrnjavčević, with the title of king, did not do much to strengthen the central power.[12] There is in this, incidentally, a significant contrast between Serbia and Byzantium: it is clear, in fact, that the former strength of the Serbian state had resided solely and entirely in the forceful personality and exceptional prestige of the ruler (Dušan and before him Milutin), not on any established institutions. Contrary to that, in Byzantium, even as weak an emperor as John V Paleologos was able to survive on the throne for fifty years (1341–1391), amid the most turbulent events and most dramatic upheavals, thanks to the stability and enduring luster of the imperial institution.

It may be appropriate to note at this point that, in contrast to Helen of Anjou, wife of Uroš I, who was present and active in Serbia when that country was growing and developing, another woman named Helen was prominent in Serbian history at a time when that state was decaying. The second Helen distinguished herself in Serbian-conquered areas closest to the Byzantine heartland. The woman was Empress Helen, originally a Bulgarian princess, wife of the Emperor Stefan Dušan and mother of the young Emperor Uroš. According to John Cantacuzenus, Helen had played a decisive role in securing Serbian support for him back in 1342, when he had come to Dušan's court to seek help in his struggle against John V Paleologos. It was an eloquent plea made by Helen to Dušan and his main advisers that convinced the Serbian ruler to throw his support behind the Byzantine pretender. After Dušan's death, Cantacuzenus tells us, "Helen [Uroš's mother], distrustful equally of her son and of her husband's brother Symeon, having put under her control many cities and surrounded herself with a large army, held power herself, not attacking anyone nor waging war."[13] Indeed, we know that Helen, although she became a nun after her husband's death, ruled effectively in Serres from 1355 to 1365, probably recognizing the sovereignty of her son, whom she survived (she died, apparently, in 1376).[14] Thus, in a most difficult and turbulent time, when Serbia was falling apart, Byzantium was on the verge of collapse and the Ottoman tide was threatening to engulf everybody and everything in the area, Helen governed her region with ability and skill, which allowed her territory to survive for ten years under her rule—something that, under the circumstances, must be seen as a considerable success.

The rapid disintegration of Nemanyid Serbia did not help Byzantium, because by now both countries were falling victims to the overwhelming Ottoman might. The Serbian defeat at Maritsa, in 1371, at the hands of the Ottomans marked the beginning of the Ottoman expansion that, from that point on, never stopped until it reached Vienna, in the sixteenth century. In that same year, 1371, the Nemanyid dynasty died out with the demise of the young and childless Emperor Uroš.[15] Serbia, however, did survive. It suffered yet another defeat by the Ottomans at Kosovo, in 1389, and by now its contacts with Byzantium were increasingly replaced by dependence on the Turks, whose vassals both states became.

The last significant Byzantino-Serbian contact—one that took place considerably after the Nemanyid period—occured in 1402, after the battle at Angora, when the Serbian leader, Prince Stefan Lazarević, who had participated in the battle on the Ottoman side and had escaped after the Ottoman defeat, visited Constantinople and was given by the Byzantines the title of "Despot."[16] The Serbian despotate survived longer than the Byzantine Empire itself, which disappeared in 1453, with the Ottoman conquest of Constantinople. However, during the first half of the fifteenth century the links between Serbia and Byzantium became much more tenuous, while Serbia drew increasingly closer to Hungary, which was emerging as the mainstay of the anti-Ottoman struggle at the time. In the end Serbia fell to the Ottomans in 1459; its survival even to that date was due primarily to the wealth provided by its mines.

Mining had started in Serbia in the mid-thirteenth century and from the very beginning merchants from Dubrovnik—which had a treaty with Serbia ever since the times of Stevan Nemanya—seized the opportunity and became the chief intermediaries in the constantly growing export of Serbian minerals, especially silver, from the Balkan hinterland (Serbia and, from the first half of the fourteenth century, also Bosnia) to the West (Venice, Italy, and beyond). In the process the merchants of Dubrovnik immensely enriched themselves and their city, and they also contributed in a decisive way to the economic progress of Serbia and Bosnia and to the enrichment of their rulers and nobility.

There is much information on this topic in Byzantine and Serbian narrative and other sources, and especially in the extraordinarily rich and well-preserved Historical Archives in Dubrovnik.[17] Still, perhaps the most vivid and convincing illustration of the tremendous impact that wealth, produced by mining, had on Serbia at a very early date, comes from two reports on Byzantine embassies that visited Serbia in the second half of the thirteenth century. The first report is found in Georgios Pachymeres, who described the mission of the Byzantine ambassador John Vekos (later unionist patriarch John XI, 1275–1282), who in 1269 was sent to the court of the Serbian King Uroš I to negotiate an alliance and the marriage between a Byzantine princess and Milutin, the later king, younger son of Uroš I. When Vekos and his retinue arrived in the Serbian royal court, "they did not see anything worthy of and corresponding to royal power." King Uroš, "looking at their suite and servants, and especially at the eunuchs, wondered what could they be. When he heard from them [sc. the Byzantines] that that is the imperial rule and that such a retinue belongs to a princess, he [sc. Uros] said disapprovingly: 'Well, what is that? That is not the way we behave,' and having said that, he showed a young woman who was spinning the wheel and said, pointing with his arm: 'This is the way we treat the brides.' Everything there was very simple and poor, as if they lived off wild animals and stealing."[18]

This is not, certainly, a very flattering description of the Serbian court in 1269. However, thirty years later, in 1298, Serbia was visited by another Byzantine ambassador, Theodore Metochytes, who negotiated a peace treaty between the victorious King Milutin and the weakened Byzantine Empire, including the already-mentioned marriage between the Serbian ruler and the little Princess Simonis. Metochytes' description of the Serbian court is completely different from the one found in Pachymeres. When he arrived, in the evening, to the city where the court resided, Metochytes was lodged in a previously prepared house and sent "an abundance of all kinds of food, not hastily provided, but obviously earlier prepared from venison. Also, there was enough food for horses, and all of that was good." The next morning he was taken to see the king, accompanied by young noblemen "formally dressed, sent to show consideration to me, as is the habit. The whole ceremony . . . was very elegant, with much respect and pomp. . . . The king himself was dressed up and covered his body with festive clothes, overloading himself with precious stones, pearls and especially gold, as much as he was able to. The whole palace was resplendent with silk and gold-embroidered fabrics. The chosen ones, surrounding him [sc. Milutin] were outfitted and dressed up very unusually and more elegantly than was the case earlier, and all of this spectacle was modelled after the imperial and Roman nobility as much as possible."

After the audience with Milutin, Metochytes returned to his quarters to rest, because he had had a very exhausting trip through Byzantine and Serbian lands in winter-time. At his residence he was served by excellent servants, assigned to him and to his retinue by the royal court. "From this moment, every day from there [sc. the court] everything came here in abundance, even more and better than was necessary, and in such a quantity, that it could have sufficed perhaps not just for us, but had we been twice as many. Apart from venison, we got many different birds and other eatable animals, such as wild boars and deer, and in addition to that, usually every day we were sent from the archon's [sc. king's] table numerous tastily prepared foods and pastries on golden and silver dishes and plates, not because we needed this, but to honor us. . . . The king also sent us fresh and dried fruit and their best cakes, as well as portions of prepared fish, recently fished in nearby or more remote rivers, fresh or salted, including those large and fat Danubian [fish] which we [sc. in Constantinople] rarely get from there and that sometimes are sought, but cannot be found everywhere."[19]

The dissimilarities between the description of the Serbian court in 1269 and the one from 1298 are so glaring, that they need no comment. It should be pointed out, however, that not all the Byzantines held as favorable an opinion of Serbia as did Metochytes. Indeed, Nicephoros Grigoras, who visited Serbia somewhat later, in 1327, as part of a Byzantine embassy to the Serbian King Stevan Dečanski (1321-1331), stated his impressions this way: "Virtues look stronger when compared with bad things. So we, too [sc. those who visited Serbia] understood more fully how lucky we are, after we mixed with those barbarians and their horrible habits. Used to enjoy the imperial magnificence and to look upon our emperor as God's image on earth—[the emperor] who never stops and never tires going from one virtue to another—we had the impression, after our brief stay there [sc. in Serbia] as if we had come across insects adorned with necklaces and bracelets."[20] As is obvious, even this less than favorable description of the Serbian court could not avoid mentioning the adornments that people there wore. This makes it necessary to stress once more that it was the mineral wealth that made all the difference. Indeed, with the great expansion of Serbian mining in the fourteenth century and with the opening of new mines in various areas, Serbia's economic potential and military might grew substantially. Of particular importance was the fact that several Serbian mines produced large quantities of silver. Novo Brdo, in the Kosovo area, the richest of them all, produced silver mixed with gold and, in the first half of the fifteenth century, became the most important silver mine of Europe.[21]

In this connection, it is worthwhile noting, once again, the ambiguity of the

Serbian position between the East and West. Silver and other minerals generated wealth for Serbia by being exported, primarily through Dubrovnik, to the West. However, the income thus obtained was invested by the Serbian rulers—apart from military ventures—into religious and cultural enterprises entirely influenced by the East, Byzantium. Here I do not mean just the Byzantine-influenced refinement and luxury, prevalent in the courts of the Serbian rulers and nobility, but something much more important and valuable—the building of numerous monumental and magnificently decorated churches in monasteries.[22]

Serbian rulers had a long and illustrious tradition of building pious endowments, beginning with Studenitsa, built by Stevan Nemanya, a beautiful church which bears clear marks of Western, Italian, architectural influences, and with the famous Chilandar monastery on Mount Athos. Thirteenth-century churches and monasteries (e.g., Žiča, Mileševa, Sopoćani, etc.) show a growing Byzantine influence, especially in their majestic fresco paintings.[23] This was, of course, a consequence of the fact that the Serbian autocephalous church, after 1219, had become part of the Eastern Orthodox world. Nevertheless, throughout the thirteenth century Western influences in art and culture did not disappear from Serbia, championed particularly by Queen Helen of Anjou, wife of King Uroš I.

As time went on and as the Serbian expansion, especially from the time of King Milutin on, became decidedly oriented toward Byzantine lands, as the Serbian state included ever-more Byzantine territories, Byzantine influences, quite logically, became by far predominant in Serbian art and architecture. Gračanica is probably the best example of such trends, although, again, vestiges of Western cultural presence still persisted (e.g., in Decani).[24] The old dichotomy in the Serbian position between East and West persisted even at the time of that country's greatest ascent. A similar situation continued in the late fourteenth and in the fifteenth century, with the exquisite, elegant churches of the Morava school (e.g., Ravanica, Manasija, Kalenic, etc.), whose geographic location reflects the movement of the Serbian political, religious, and cultural centers northward under Ottoman pressure.[25] That period, however, is beyond the chronological framework of this paper.

It seems plausible to say, in conclusion, that Serbo-Byzantine relations during the period of the Nemanyid dynasty in Serbia show a peculiar, one might even say paradoxical characteristic: as political relations worsened, as mutual attitudes became more hostile, as Serbia more aggressively swallowed Byzantine lands, Byzantine ideological, administrative, legal, social, cultural, and artistic influences in Serbia became stronger and more pervasive. At the culminating point of the Nemanyid dynasty, in the days of the Emperor Stefan Dusan, the powerful Serbian Empire was so thoroughly permeated by the influences of the weak Byzantine Empire, that Dušan ruled, indeed, a Serbo-Greek state. The rapid collapse of Serbia after Dušan, the persistent Byzantine weakness and, above all, the inexorable expansion of the Ottomans changed all of that and quickly brought about the disappearance of both Balkan medieval empires.

NOTES

1. *Istorija srpskog naroda* (hereafter *ISN*), vol. I, ed. S. Cirković, Belgrade: Srpska književna zadruga, 1981, 209–211, 251–262 (J. Kalić). See also G. Ostrogorsky, *History of the Byzantine State*, Oxford: Basil Blackwell, 1968: 388, 398–399, 405–406. J. V. A. Fine, Jr., *The Late Medieval Balkans*, Ann Arbor: University of Michigan Press, 1987: 2–10, 23–28, 38–41.

2. Ostrogorsky, op. cit., 411, 427, 429, 435–438. Fine, op. cit., 29–32, 54–56, 80–87, 106, 124–133, 154–156. See also S. G. Evans, *A Short History of Bulgaria*, London: Laurence & Wishart, 1960: 61–67.

3. *ISN*, I, 297–301 (B. Ferjančić), 315–317 (D. Bogdanović). Also *Sava Nemanjic-Sveti Sava. Istorija i predanje*, ed.V. Djurić, Belgrade: Srpska akademija nauka i umetnosti (hereafter SANU), 1979.

4. *ISN*, I, 438–448 (Lj. Maksimović), 449–475 (S. Cirković). Ostrogorsky, op. cit., 464, 481, 489–490. L. Mavromatis, *La fondation de l'Empire Serbe: le Kralj Milutin*, Thessaloniki: Kentron Byzantinon Ereunon, 1978.

5. K. Jireček, *Istorija Srba*, vol. I, Belgrade: Naučna knjiga, 1952: 181–182, 187, 199. *ISN*, I, 347–348, 356 (S. Cirković), 402, 404–405, 421 (V. Djurić), 439, 447 (Lj. Maksimović), 449, 465 (S. Cirković).

6. Jireček, op. cit., I, 194. Ostrogorsky, op. cit., 489–490. Mavromatis, op. cit. 39–53. *ISN*, I, 446–447 (Lj. Maksimović). *Vizantijski izvori za istoriju naroda Jugoslavije* (hereafter *Izvori*), vol. VI, ed. F. Barišić and B. Ferjančić, Belgrade: Vizantoloski institut SANU, 1986, 171 (S. Cirković and B.Ferjančić).

7. *Izvori*, VI, 600 (N. Radosević).

8. Ibid., 58–59 (Lj. Maksimović).

9. Ostrogorsky, op. cit., 523–524. *ISN, I*, 523 (B. Ferjančić), 524–540 (M.Blagojević). See also G. C. Soulis, *The Serbs and Byzantium during the Reign of Tsar Stephen Dušan (1331–1355) and His Successors*, Washington, D.C.: Dumbarton Oaks, 1984. S. Cirković, *Srbija uoči carstva, Dečani i vizantijska umetnost sredinom XVI veka*, Belgrade: SANU, 1989: 3–13.

10. *Zakonik cara Stefana Dušana 1349 i 1354*, ed. N.Radojčić, Belgrade: SANU, 1960 (English translation: M. Burr, *Slavic and East European Review*, vol. 28, 1950, 198–217, 516–539).

11. Jireček, op. cit., I, 233–236. *ISN*, I, 553–556 (S. Cirković-R. Mihaljčić).

12. G. Ostrogorsky, "Serska oblast posle Dušanove smrti," in G. Ostrogorsky, *Vizantija i Sloveni*, Belgrade: Prosveta, 1970: 440–448. *ISN*, I, 584–591 (R. Mihaljčić). R. Mihaljčić, *Kraj srpskog carstva*, Belgrade: Beogradski izdavačko-grafički zavod, 1989: 94–114.

13. *Izvori*, VI, 394–397, 558–559 (S. Ćirković-B. Ferjančić).

14. Jireček, op. cit., I, 253, 314. Ostrogorsky: "Serska oblast, 435–439," *ISN*, I, 517 (B. Ferjančić), 569–571, 577 (R. Mihaljčić). Mihaljčić, *Kraj*, 207.

15. *ISN*, I, 601–602 (R. Mihaljčić). Fine, op. cit., 380. Mihaljčic, *Kraj*, 187–188.

16. Ostrogorsky, *History*, 557. M. A. Purković, *Knez i despot Stefan Lazarević*, Belgrade: Sv. arhierejski Sabor Srpske pravoslavne crkve, 1978: 63–64.

17. See, among others: M.Dinić, *Za istoriju*

rudarstva u srednjevekov-noi Srbiji i Bosni, 2 vols., Belgrade: SANU, 1955, 1962. *Zakon o rudnicima despota Stefana Lazarevića*, ed. N. Radojčic, Belgrade, 1962. S. Ćirković, "Dubrovcani kao preduzetnici u rudarstvu Srbije i Bosne," *Acta historico-oeconomica Iugoslaviae*, vol. 6, Zagreb, 1979, 1–20. S.Ćirković, "The Production of Gold, Silver and Copper in the Central Parts of the Balkans from the 13th to the 16th Century," *Precious Metals in the Age of Expansion*, ed. H. Kellenbenz, Stuttgart: Klen-Cotta, 1981: 41–69. S. Ćirković-D. Kovačević Kojić, "L'économie naturelle et la production marchande aux XIIIe–XVe siècles dans les régions actuelles de la Yougoslavie," *Balcanica*, vol. 13–14, Belgrade: SANU, 1982–1983: 45–56. D. Kovačević-Kojić, "O rudarskoj proizvodnji u srednjovjekovnoj Bosni," *Godišnjak Društva istoričara Bosne i Hercegovine*, vol.34, Sarajevo, 1983, 113–122.

18. *Izvori*, VI, 26 (Lj. Maksimović).

19. Ibid., 110–114 (I. Djurić).

20. Ibid., 626 (N. Radosević).

21. Ćirković, *The Production*, 52.

22. B. Krekić, "La Serbie entre Byzance et l'Occident au XIVe siècle," *The Proceedings of the 13th International Congress of Byzantine Studies*, Oxford: Oxford University Press, 1967: 62–65.

23. *L'art byzantin du XIIIe siècle*, ed. V. Djurić, Belgrade: Faculté de Philosophie, Departement de l'histoire de l'art, 1967. D. Bogdanovic, V. Djurić, and D. Medakovic, *Chilandar*, Belgrade: Jugoslovenska knjiga, 1978. *ISN*, I, 273–296, 389–433 (V. Djurić). S. Ćirković,V. Korać, and G. Babic, *Studenica Monastery*, Belgrade: Jugoslovenska revija, 1986. *Mileševa u istoriji srpskog naroda*, Belgrade: SANU, 1987. *Studenica i vizantijska umetnost oko 1200. qodine*, ed. V. Korać, Belgrade: SANU, 1988.

24. *L'art byzantin au début du XIVe siècle*, ed. S. Petković, Belgrade: Faculte de Phil., Départ. de l'hist. de l'art, 1978 (on Gračanica see esp. pp. 127–212). S. Ćurčić, *Gračanica, Milutin's Church and Its Place in Late Byzantine Architecture*, College Park: Pennsylvania State University Press, 1979. *ISN*, I, 476–495, 641–663 (G. Babic-Djordjević). *Zaduzbine Kosova*, ed. A. Jevtić, Prizren-Belgrade: Eparhija raškoprizrenska, Bogoslovski fakultet u Beogradu, 1987: 14–180. *Dečani i vizantijska umetnost sredinom XIV veka*, Belgrade: SANU 1989.

25. *L'école de la Morava et son temps*, ed. V. Djurić, Belgrade: Faculte de Phil., Depart. de l'hist. de l'art, 1972. *Manastir Ravanica Spomenica o šestoj stogodišnjici*, Belgrade, 1981. *ISN*, vol. II, ed. J. Kalić, Belgrade: Srp. knjiž. zadruga, 1982: 144–191 (G. Babić-Djordjević–V. Djurić), 314–329 (S. Ćirković).

4
The Iconology of Royal Ritual in Sixteenth-Century Muscovy

Michael S. Flier
Harvard University

We were told that in all the Muscovite Land only two holidays a year were celebrated with particular solemnity, namely, Epiphany and Palm Sunday....
—Paul of Aleppo, 1655[1]

Introduction

Archdeacon Paul of Aleppo was only one of a number of foreigners who noted the exceptional celebrations of Epiphany and Palm Sunday in Muscovy of the sixteenth and seventeenth centuries.[2] In the city of Moscow itself the heads of church and state participated in religious rituals that figuratively replicated two historical events in the life of Christ: his baptism by John the Forerunner (John the Baptist) in the River Jordan and his triumphant entry into Jerusalem a week before his resurrection. The Orthodox Church celebrates the Baptism on Epiphany (Theophany) Day, January 6, and the Entry into Jerusalem on Palm Sunday, the Sunday before Easter. It is remarkable that these two great feasts alone were accorded special ritual status, whereas others like Christmas, Presentation, and Transfiguration were not. Equally noteworthy is that neither of these Muscovite royal rituals was Byzantine in origin.[3]

The accumulated information about the Epiphany and Palm Sunday rituals in Moscow shows enough similarity in chronology, imagery, and symbolism to suggest a common cultural function. It is the purpose of the present study to indicate what this might be. In the course of the discussion I will speak against the current "submission hypothesis," which sees both rituals as expressions of the submission of the tsar to the authority of the church, specifically the metropolitan/patriarch. Instead I suggest that the royal Epiphany and Palm Sunday rituals in Moscow be viewed as artifacts of a cultural text that responded to the eschatology of Moscow/New Jerusalem. In this capacity the rituals actually enhanced the person of the tsar, his place in Russian history, and his potential role in the world beyond time. We begin with details about the rituals themselves before turning to their development and significance.

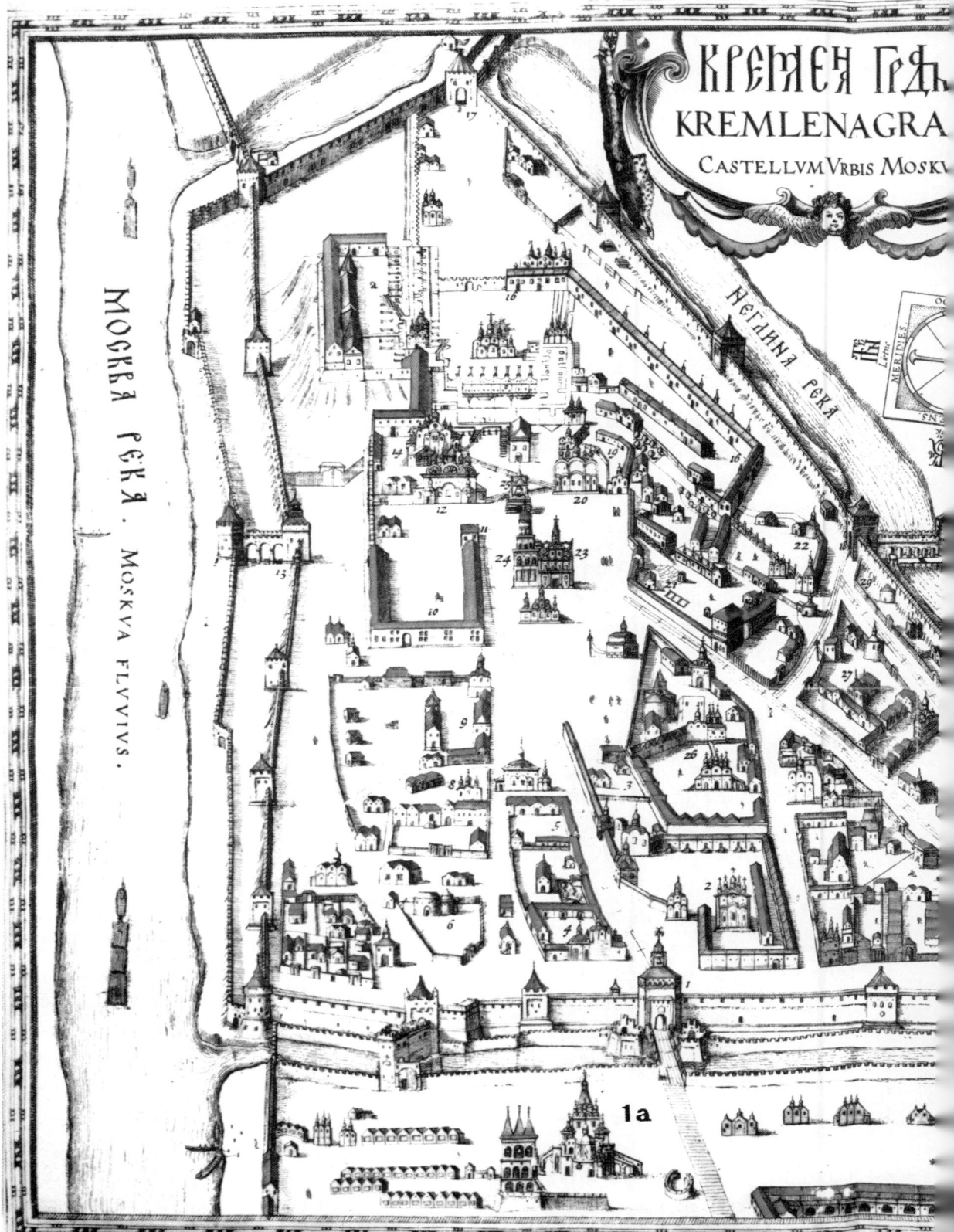

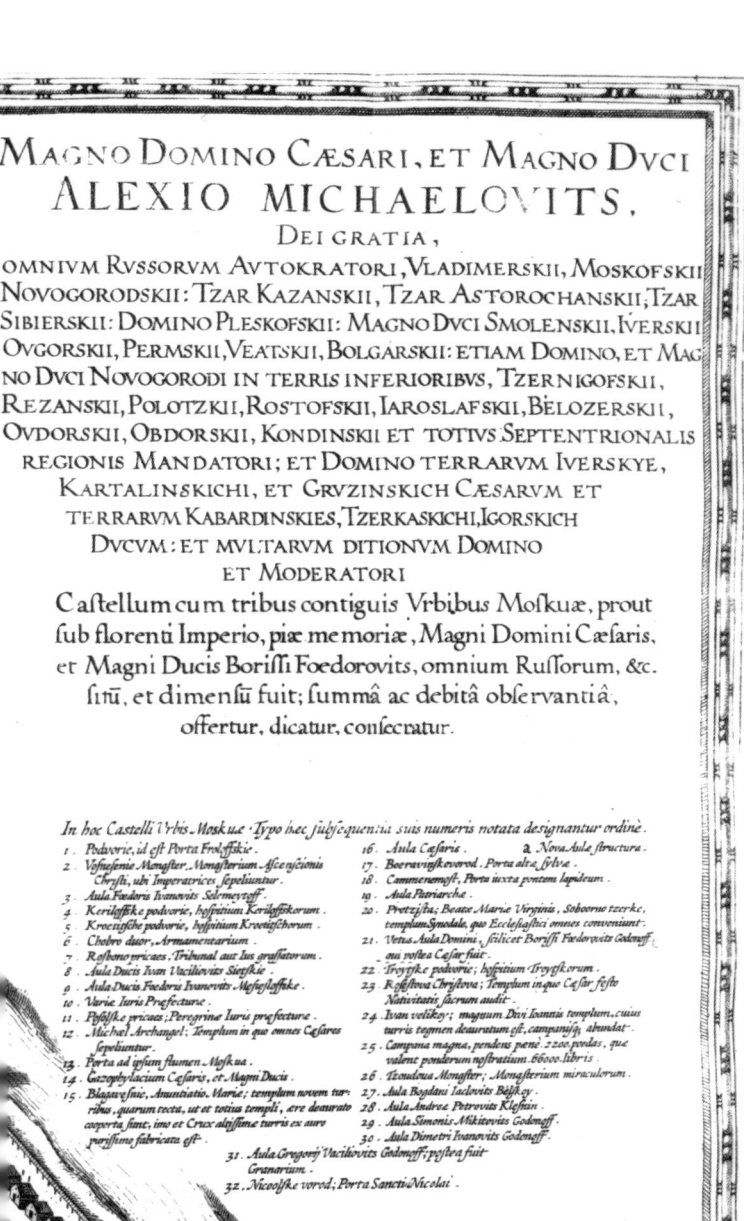

Figure 1 Plan of the Moscow Kremlin [Kremlenagrad]. Beg. 1600s. Supplement to M.V. Posokhin et al., eds., *Pamiatniki arkhitektury Moskvy. Kreml'. Kitai-gorod. Tsentral'nye ploshchadi.* (Moscow, 1982). Reproduced with permission.
1. Savior (Frolov) Gates.
1a. Cathedral of the Intercession on the Moat (St. Basil's Cathedral), Red Square, and Lobnoe Mesto.
12. Cathedral of the Archangel Michael. 14. Cathedral of the Annunciation.
20. Cathedral of the Dormition.

The Palm Sunday Ritual

The earliest description of the Palm Sunday Ritual in Moscow is recorded by an anonymous member of Anthony Jenkinson's English entourage in the spring of 1558:[4]

On Palme sunday they have a very solemne procession in this maner folowing.

First, they have a tree of a good bignesse which is made fast upon two sleds, as though it were growing there, and it is hanged with apples, raisins, figs and dates, and with many other fruits abundantly. In the midst of the same tree stand 5. boyes in white vestures, which sing in the tree before the procession. . . .

The account describes a long procession of young acolytes bearing traditional ecclesiastical paraphernalia—tapers, banners, icons—and they in turn are followed by more than a hundred richly vested priests and then by half of the members of the Muscovite nobility. The focal point of the procession is a reenactment of Christ's triumphant entry into Jerusalem on Palm Sunday:

First, there is a horse covered with white linnen cloth down to the ground, his eares being made long with the same cloth like to an asses eares. Upon this horse the Metropolitane sitteth sidelong like a woman: in his lappe lieth a faire booke [the Gospels], with a crucifix of Goldsmiths worke upon the cover, which he holdeth fast with his left hand, and in his right hand he hath a crosse of gold, with which crosse he ceaseth not to blesse the people as he rideth.

There are approximately 30 sons of priests who spread their garments in the path of the approaching Christ. As soon as the horse passes over the garments, the youths pick them up and run ahead to spread them out again:

One of the Emperours noble men leadeth the horse by the head, but the Emperour himselfe goyng on foote, leadeth the horse by the ende of the reine of his bridle with one of his hands, and in the other of his handes he had a braunch of a Palme tree: after this followed the rest of the Emperours Noble men and Gentlemen, with a great number of other people.

Beginning at the Cathedral of the Dormition (fig. 1, no. 20) the procession made the rounds of the major Kremlin churches (fig. 1, nos. 12, 14) before returning to the Dormition for dismissal. The branches of the tree were distributed by the metropolitan to the assembled throng along with gifts to ranking members of the court. The metropolitan gave the tsar 200 rubles, apparently a payment for services rendered.

Two specialized studies have provided evidence that the central component of the Palm Sunday Ritual, the Procession on the Ass, first appeared in Russia at the end of the fifteenth century in two distinct contexts: the installation ceremony for the metropolitan in Moscow (1495), and the Palm Sunday Ritual in Novgorod.[5] The Palm Sunday Ritual was apparently introduced in Moscow as a royal ceremony in expanded form (decorated tree, children, boyars, merchants) sometime between 1547, when Ivan IV was crowned as tsar, and 1558, when the Jenkinson entourage observed its performance. Knowledge of the ritual was probably due to Macarius,

Figure 2 The Palm Sunday Ritual in Moscow, April 10, 1636. Engraving from Adam Olearius, *Vermehrte Newe Beschreibung Der Muscowitischen und Persischen Reise* (Schleswig, 1656), p. 132a.

who left his post as archbishop of Novgorod to become metropolitan of Moscow in 1542. No earlier than 1560, the ceremony was extended beyond the walls of the Kremlin to the newly completed Church of the Intercession on Red Square (St. Basil's Cathedral, fig. 1, no. 1a).[6] Following a brief service in the Chapel of the Entry into Jerusalem, the procession made its way back to the Dormition inside the Kremlin walls (cf. seventeenth-century engravings of the Palm Sunday Ritual, figs. 2, 3).

The source for the Novgorod Palm Sunday Ritual with the Procession on the Ass and its later Moscow variation have interested scholars for some time. Ostrogorsky[7] assumed that the reenactment of the Entry may have been influenced by a similar ritual in Jerusalem itself, but the ritual gesture of the tsar pulling the reins of the ass, the equerry service (*Stratordienst*), could not. Faithfulness to historical circumstances would not have permitted an equerry in the Jerusalem ritual, since none is mentioned in the Gospel accounts of the Entry. Ostrogorsky proposed a Western source for the equerry service, the *Donation of Constantine*, the eighth-century forgery in which Emperor Constantine grants to Pope Sylvester primacy over the Christian church in Rome and its environs. A later interpolation in the *Donation* notes that Constantine crowned Sylvester with a white cowl, served as equerry for the pontiff by holding the horse's bridle as a sign of deference to the first pope, St. Peter, and ordered that all Peter's successors and they alone would wear the white cowl. Specifically

Abrieß der Muscowitischen Procession am Palm Sontag

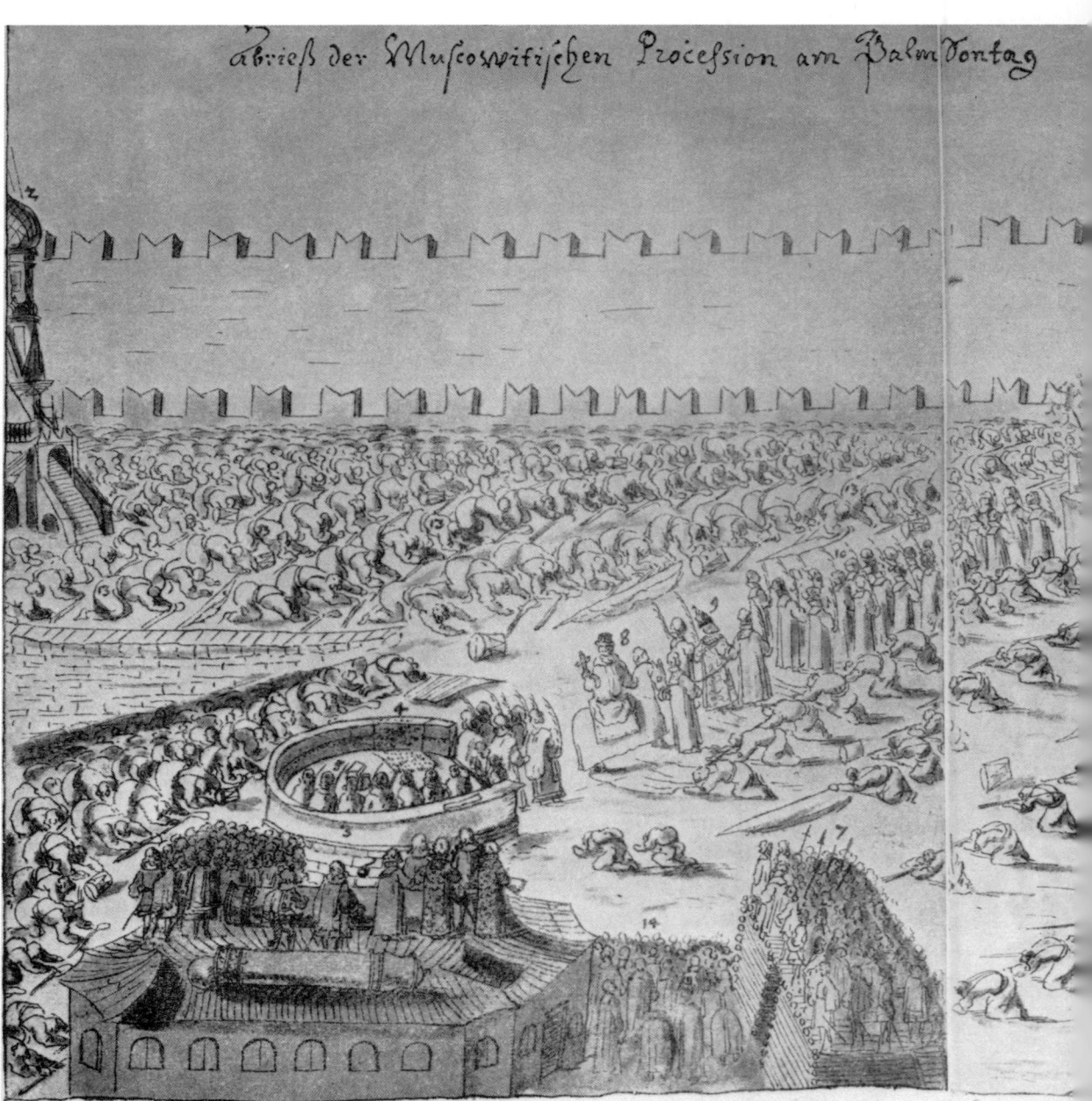

Anno 1662 den 2 April/23 Marti ward in Moscau eine solenne Procession gehalten in welcher der Zaar außm trum geleitet ward, nach dem er den Segen vom Metropoliten empfangen den Reichs Cantzler an der Röm. ihre gesundtheit sich zuerkundigen geschicket, Hat Fhr: Danielowitz Miloslausky alß Schwie-zer bater dem silbern Schießbecken zu halten angenommen, der Zaar immittler Zeit so lange mit entblöß-tem Haupte nach vollendeten Ceremonien ein pferdt mit weißer leinwandt bedecket worauff der Metro-polit gesessen den weg mit allerhandt fürb lahten untergespreitet.

Num. 1 Die Schloßpforte. num. 2. Die Kirche Jerusalem 3. Das Amphitheatrum 4. des Zaaren standt 5. Der Metro-Gesandten gestanden. 7. ein von Holtzern balcken erbawter und mit brettern belegter Schawot war der Schwedischen gehende Boiaren trügen palmen in händen 11 Ein mit rohtlahten umzogener Schlitten darauff ein Dür-rer baum mit 6 mit rohtlahten bedeckten pferden gezogen. 12 Die vorhergehende Clerisey mit bildern und Creützen vor welcher Zwo- vollbrachten Ceremonien allererst auff alß die procession albereit vor über und in der Schloßpforten gewesen. 14

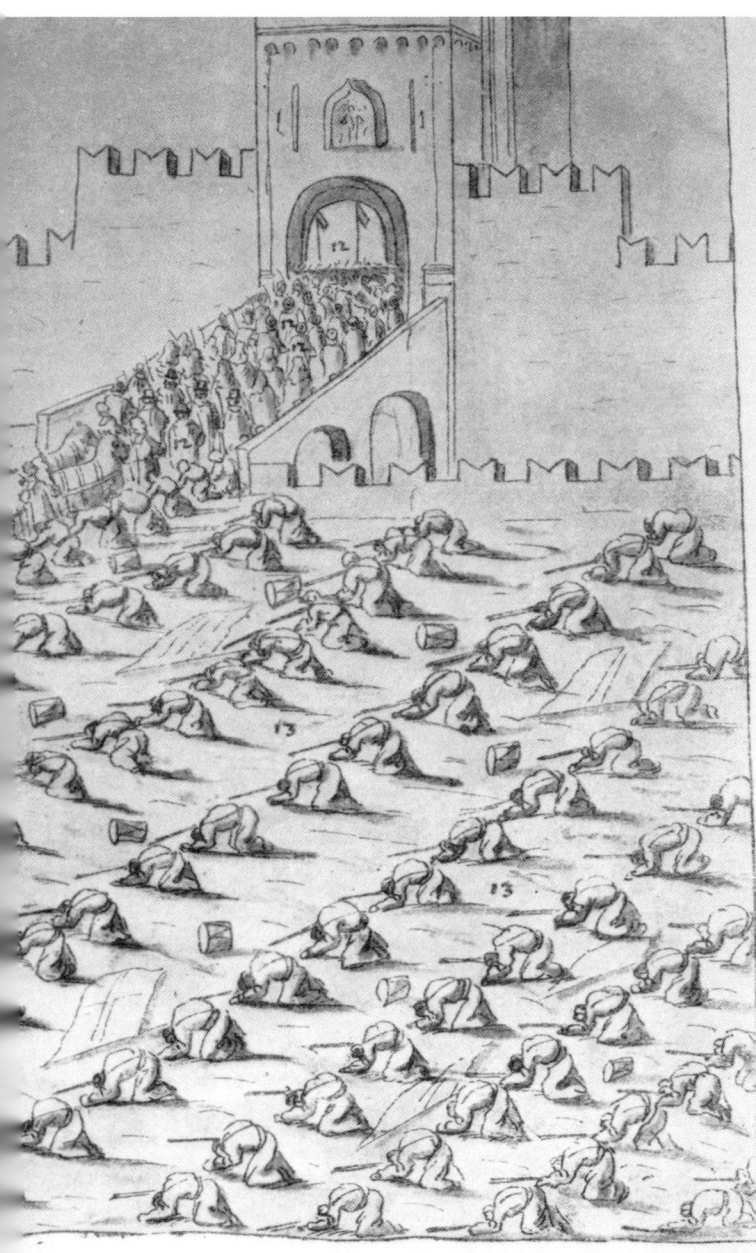

Figure 3 The Palm Sunday Ritual in Moscow, March 23, 1662. Engraving from F. Adelung, *Al'bom Meierberga. Vidy i bytovye kartiny Rossii XVII veka* (St. Petersburg, 1903), pl. 73.

Figure 4 *Entrance of Pope Sylvester into Rome* [Emperor Constantine leading the pope's horse]. Fresco. Oratory of St. Sylvester in the Church of the SS. Quattro Coronati, Rome. 1246. Reproduced with permission from Guglielmo Matthiae, *Pittura romana del Medioevo*, 2d ed., 2 vols. (Rome, 1988), v. 2: *Secoli XI–XIV*, pl. 132.

the passage that reads . . . et tenentes frenum equi ipsius pro reverentia beati Petri stratoris officium illi exhibuimus . . . [8] has been used since the eighth century in Western Europe to justify the symbolic respect and submission of secular to ecclesiastical authority shown through the performance of the equerry service (see fig. 4). In the earliest documented case, Pepin the Short, king of the Franks, held the reins of the horse mounted by Pope Stephen II at Ponthion in January 754.[9]

In two recent studies[10] I have maintained that the threat to secularize church property was insufficient grounds for the introduction of such a major change in ritual with its putative symbol of secular submission, the equerry service. One need only recall that the Procession on the Ass is included not only in the Novgorod Palm Sunday Ritual, but in the installation ceremony for the metropolitan in Moscow, in which the struggle between church and state is not an issue.[11]

In both cases the chief prelate is likened to Christ during his triumphant entry into Jerusalem, when he is hailed as humble victor over death (the raising of Lazarus) and leader of the flock. The emergence of this profoundly eschatological image of the Savior in the ritual was surely not limited to the church's defense of property, but undoubtedly intended to counter the heresies of the Judaizers in the face of the impending Apocalypse. According to Orthodox belief human history would last seven millennia, one cosmic week. At the onset of the Eighth Millennium, Christ would appear at the Second Coming and sit at the Last Judgment. After the General Resurrection the righteous would be permitted to share life eternal in the New Jerusalem, while the rest would be cast into the flames of Hell. The Eighth Millennium was expected to commence in 1492.

The focus of the Palm Sunday liturgy and the meaning of Christ's Entry are eschatological, concerned with the promise of the General Resurrection, of life anew at the Apocalypse, the End of Time. Against the background of such a cataclysm the Procession on the Ass had a special poignancy, emphasizing the correlation between Christ the Shepherd and the chief prelates of the church and promulgating their function as leaders when the end came. Transported to Moscow during the reign of Tsar Ivan IV, the Palm Sunday Ritual continued to be viewed in eschatological terms and was not simply a mark of secular submission. We will return to this issue after a brief review of the Epiphany Ritual in Russia.

The Epiphany Ritual

There are two rather complete descriptions of the Epiphany Ritual from the Jenkinson entourage during the 1557–1558 journey. The first is by Jenkinson himself:

The 4. [sic] of Januarie, which was Twelftide with them, the Emperour, with his brother, and all his Nobles, all most richly apparelled with gold, pearles, pretious stones, & costly furres, with a crowne upon his head, of the Tartarian fashion, went to the Church in procession, with the Metropolitan, and divers bishops, and priests. . . . [T]hen came he out of the Church, and went with the procession upon the river, being all frozen, and there standing bare headed, with all his Nobles, there was a hole made in the ice, and the Metropolitan hallowed the water with great solemnitie, and service, and did cast of the said water upon the Emperours sonne, and the Nobilitie. That done, the people with great thronging filled pots of the said water, to carry home to their houses, and divers children were throwen in, and sicke people, and plucked out quickly againe, and divers Tartars christened: all which the Emperour beheld. Also there were brought the Emperours best horses, to drinke at the said hallowed water. All this being ended, he returned to his pallace againe. . . .[12]

The second, anonymous, description provides more details about the ritual itself:

Every yeere upon the twelfe day they use to blesse or sanctifie the river Moska, which runneth through the citie of Moskovia, after this maner.

First, they make a square hole in the ice about 3. fathoms large every way, which is trimmed about the sides and edges with white boords. Then about 9. of the clocke they come out of the church with procession towards the river in this wise.

First and foremost there goe certaine yong men with Waxe tapers burning, and one carying a great lanterne: then follow certaine banners, then the crosse, then the images of our Ladie, of S. Nicholas, and of other Saints, which images men carrie upon their shoulders: after the images follow certaine priests to the number of 100. or more: after them the

Metropolitan who is led betweene two priests, and after the Metropolitan came the Emperour with his crowne upon his head, and after his majestie all his noble men orderly. Thus they folowed the procession unto the water, & when they came unto the hole that was made, the priests set themselves in order round about it. And at one side of the same poole there was a scaffold of boords made, upon which stood a faire chaire in which the Metropolitan was set, but the Emperours majestie stood upon the ice.

After this the priests began to sing, to blesse and to sense, and did their service, and so by that time that they had done, the water was holy, which being sanctified, the Metropolitane tooke a little thereof in his handes, and cast it on the Emperour, likewise upon certaine of the Dukes, and then they returned againe to the church with the priests that sate about the water: but y preasse that there was about the water when the Emperour was gone, was wonderful to behold, for there came about 5000. pots to be filled of that water: for that Muscovite which hath no part of that water, thinks himselfe unhappy.[13]

The event was called Procession to the Jordan (Khozhdenie na Iordan'), with the specially marked form of Jordan (*Iordan* with palatalized *n*') used to indicate that part of the Moscow River exposed by the large hole in the ice.

The sources are silent about the precise beginnings of the Epiphany Ritual in Russia. Paul Bushkovitch has been able to narrow down the likely time of its introduction to the period between 1477 and 1525.[14] Ambrogio Contarini makes no mention of it in the otherwise detailed account of his stay in Moscow in 1476–1477 (including court ceremonies in December and January). Paolo Giovio provides a brief description of it in his book on Dmitrii Gerasimov's embassy to Pope Clement VII in 1525–1526. Maksim Grek responds to an anonymous inquiry, apparently concerning a Russian Epiphany ritual by a river; he provides a brief eyewitness account of Greek practice on Mouth Athos regarding the sanctification of the waters at the beginning of each month at each parish church, except for January, when an icon procession makes its way to a nearby river or stream on Epiphany morning. Maksim's reply, probably to a church prelate, is dated 1518–1525, the most plausible time period when such a ritual was established in Moscow. There is no concrete evidence of the tsar's participation in the Epiphany Ritual in Moscow before 1558, but it is likely that he and the rest of the nobility participated in the Blessing of the Waters in some capacity before that time.

Bushkovitch finds the primary justification for the Russian Epiphany Ritual in the church's desire to combat folk rituals associated with the period between Christmas and Epiphany, the so-called *sviatki*.[15] Christmas Eve and Epiphany Eve were characterized by dancing, debauchery, and defilement. Revelers played satanic games, blasphemed, wore wicked costumes and masks, and concluded their devilish practices by washing themselves in the river before returning to their homes to collapse from exhaustion.[16] The church could battle against such behavior not only by establishing a rival celebration, but by endowing specific aspects of folk behavior with Christian significance. At the nearby river, a ritual cleansing in the folk tradition was easily reinterpreted as spiritual purification in

Christian tradition. Bushkovitch correctly links the watering of horses in the sanctified water following the Epiphany Ritual with the folk belief that evil spirits were released from Hell in the week preceding Epiphany.

As outlined by Bushkovitch, the major points of change in the Epiphany Ritual occurred in the seventeenth century and involved the relative positions of the tsar and patriarch. In the 1620s the patriarch stood on the ice and the tsar sat on his throne; by the 1670s the patriarch and the tsar stood by their respective thrones, although the prelate's throne was somewhat higher.[17]

Church Ceremony as Royal Ritual

Both the Palm Sunday and Epiphany Rituals appear in part to have been responses to perceived threats to the established church, whether in the form of heretical teachings from within or folk beliefs and superstitions from without. Both rituals are dogmatic, underscoring Christ's function as messiah and savior and the reality of the Trinity at his baptism. Additionally they are integrative, consolidating the flock and making ready a people worthy of salvation. It is against this larger issue that their elevation to annual *royal* rituals, featuring the tsar and the metropolitan, must be considered.

The Palm Sunday Ritual apparently arose in Novgorod; the Epiphany Ritual has no traceable locus. The former was restricted to Novgorod and Moscow in the sixteenth centuries but spread to other diocesan centers in the seventeenth century before being confined to Moscow in 1668. The latter seems to have had a nonlocalized, universal character from the very beginning, if one can judge from early reports and the continuation of such rituals in small villages well into the nineteenth century.[18] From the available evidence both ceremonies were elaborated as royal rituals in Moscow during the reign of Ivan the Terrible, probably in the early 1550s following his coronation (1547) and defeat of Kazan' (1552). It was these events on which he could stake his claim as the undisputed emperor of his realm and the hero of a great Christian victory over the infidel Kazan' Tatars, the Muslim "Sons of Hagar."

The establishment of the Epiphany and Palm Sunday ceremonies as royal rituals suggests a common motivation, a correlative function, for both. In interpreting that motivation, that function, and its significance for Ivan's reign, it is useful to consider each ritual in light of the four levels of reference I distinguished in my previous studies: performatory, iconographic, historical, and eschatological. After reviewing the results of that analysis of the Palm Sunday Ritual, I will show its applicability to the Epiphany Ritual.

The level of immediate performance provides evidence for the submission hypothesis, a reading in which the tsar's role in the Ritual is viewed as symbolic of the submission of secular authority to that of the church[19] or to the metropolitan himself.[20] Indeed, the Ritual appears to reverse the usual hierarchal superiority accorded the head of state, who sits while others stand or is seated on a level higher than those seated in his presence.[21] In the Procession on the Ass the tsar walks, the metropolitan rides; the tsar is below on the ground, the metropolitan is above seated on the ass. This component of the Ritual certainly signals inequality interpretable as submission, as we see in the sixteenth-century Jenkinson account:

The Metropolitane is next unto God, our Ladie and S. Nicholas accepted: for the Emperours majestie judgeth and affirmeth him to bee of higher dignitie then himselfe: for that saith he is Gods spirituall officer, and I the Emperour am his temporall officer, and therefore his majestie submitteth himselfe unto him in many things concerning religious matters, as in leading the Metropolitans horse upon Palme sunday, and giving him leave to sit on a chaire upon the 12. day [Epiphany], when the river Mosko was in blessing, and his majestie standing on the ice.[22]

If inequality is indeed signaled at the immediate level of performance by the tsar, then it is *purposeful* inequality, designed to enhance the image of the tsar. He performs a topos of humility as a *podvig*, a pious deed. That the most powerful person in Muscovy would so humble himself before his court and selected foreigners must have impressed all in attendance. And as a model for ritual humility, the tsar could look back past Emperor Constantine to Christ, who humbled himself before John the Forerunner by undergoing baptism (Matt. 3:13–17) and who entered Jerusalem on the back of an ass (Matt. 21:4–5) instead of a horse.

The Palm Sunday Ritual provides a regulated context in which the tsar's topos of humility is to be performed. It is a mistake, however, to attribute to the symbols in one context the same value they have in others. The tsar's humility is *not* directed toward the metropolitan as head of the church but toward the metropolitan as the representation of Christ. This is an important distinction noted by the 1678 Synod: ". . . our most pious autocrats deign to be in it, in order to show the Orthodox people the image of their humility and submission before Christ the Lord. . . ."[23] Under no other circumstances does the tsar perform the equerry service for the metropolitan, even during the latter's installation ceremony, which contains the Procession on the Ass.[24]

The actuality of the Palm Sunday context undercuts Ostrogorsky's interpretation of the equerry service relative to Moscow. The Western examples of medieval kings and emperors performing the equerry service for the pope are primarily motivated by political intent, involving alliances with the papacy; in the Russian Palm Sunday Ritual the equerry service is incorporated into a *religious* ritual, as Ostrogorsky himself notes,[25] thus taking on a different significance, one best understood at the iconographic level.

Not all the elements in the Muscovite Palm Sunday Ritual are found in the Gospel accounts of the Entry into Jerusalem. Christ rides the ass into Jerusalem on his own; there is no equerry service. There are no children specifically mentioned as cutting down palm branches or spreading clothing in front of the

Figure 5 *Entry into Jerusalem*. Obverse of two-sided icon. Novgorod. Cathedral of Holy Sophia. End 15th–beg. 16th century.

procession. Trees are mentioned in passing as the source of branches, and fruit is nowhere to be found. In "Breaking the Code" I suggested that the inspiration for much of the Ritual was to be found rather in the liturgy of the feast and especially in the visualization of the event in Orthodox iconography.

Icons of the Entry for the festival tier (fig. 5) of the iconostasis typically depict Christ riding sidesaddle on the ass, with children cutting off branches from a fruit-bearing tree, preparing to hail him as the victor. The dominant role of children in the depiction is due to reliance on the apocryphal Gospel of Nicodemus. It is children, and not the undifferentiated crowd or multitude, as in the Gospel account, who are typically described spreading garments in the path of Christ, an ancient symbol of an anointed king.

The Palm Sunday Ritual in Moscow can be viewed as a dynamic manifestation of the Palm Sunday icon. As a living tableau, the participants become, according to the Byzantine doctrine of images, tangible representations of the intangible. The Ritual provides counterparts of all the roles in the icon—disciples, townspeople, boys in the tree, boys spreading garments in the path of the procession, and the fruit-laden tree itself. The disguised horse represents the ass, and the metropolitan, the Savior.[26] In fact, the only major element in the ritual without a counterpart in the icon or the historical event behind it is the tsar himself. But by juxtaposing himself to the representations of the holy personages, the living tsar is himself provided with an aura of holiness. His singular status is enhanced by virtue of a shift of genres, from static icon to dynamic ritual. He is the touchstone of the present that functions to unite the past event with future promise. In this context I have also suggested in "Breaking the Code" that Tsar Ivan IV embodies the image of the humble shepherd leading the way for Christ to enter Jerusalem, for the Orthodox faithful to achieve salvation. In doing so he elicits immediate historical and eschatological connections.

The introduction of the second version of the Palm Sunday Ritual illuminated the analogue of the Entry in contemporary history. The Procession on the Ass was extended out of the Kremlin onto Red Square to the Church of the Intercession on the Moat (fig. 6). This unique edifice, consisting of eight chapels around a central tent tower, was built by Ivan to commemorate the momentous victory of Moscow over the Kazan' Tatars in 1552. In the context of an annual church feast that celebrates a triumphant entry into the holy city of Jerusalem, Ivan's procession to the Jerusalem Chapel of a cathedral dedicated to his victory over the Kazan' infidels recalled that in real life, he too was a victor. He had entered a city of unbelievers—Kazan'—in triumph. And he returned to Moscow, the New Jerusalem, as a victor. According to the Nikon Chronicle, as he approached Moscow following the victory, he was greeted outside the city by the metropolitan, other church dignitaries and his court as one of the great heroes of Orthodoxy. Following a speech by Metropolitan Macarius, in which the tsar is compared to Constantine the Great, Alexander Nevskii, and Dmitrii Donskoi,

Figure 6 Barma and Postnik. *Cathedral of the Intercession on the Moat*. Northwest elevation. 1555–61. The Chapel of the Entry into Jerusalem is at the head of the gallery staircase in the foreground.

the entire entourage fell on their knees before him, shedding tears of joy and gratitude for his victory and safe return. Ivan then removed his military garb, donned his imperial garments, including the holy regalia of Monomakh, and walked *on foot* into Moscow to a tumultuous outpouring of popular exaltation and joy.[27] By leading the iconographic Christ in a procession from the Cathedral of the Dormition, where he was crowned by God as tsar, to the Jerusalem Chapel of the Intercession, which represented his triumph over Kazan', Ivan was able to commemorate his own conquest, his own Christian victory, his own claim to immortality. This tangible evidence of Ivan's heroic posture served to reinforce the iconographic dimension of the Ritual in which Ivan demonstrated both his humility before Christ and his strength as shepherd of the flock. Fortuitously the annual celebration of this achievement was made to coincide with one of the most important feasts of the church calendar.[28]

An eschatological interpretation of the Palm Sunday Ritual was favored by an Orthodox understanding of history and the iconography of the Entry itself. The Procession on the Ass was apparently introduced into Muscovite Rus' in the late fifteenth century, at a time when the Orthodox faithful were taken with thoughts of the Apocalypse, the Second Coming, and the Last Judgment. The Procession was included in the Palm Sunday Ritual in Novgorod and the Installation Ceremony for the metropolitan in Moscow. When the fateful year of 7000 (1492) came and went, however, concern with the End Times did not fade away. The church took the position that the End of the World would occur but the precise time was God's alone to know (Matt. 24:36, Mark 13:32).[29] If the Eastern Slavs were the last great people to accept Orthodox Christianity, nonetheless Muscovite Rus' had succeeded through purity of faith in being its final stronghold before the Second Coming of Christ and the End of Time. This representation of Moscow's eschatological significance was forcefully articulated by Monk Philotheus in various epistles, most notably in his prophetic letter to Ivan's father, Basil:

And now I beg you and implore you once more: Pay heed to what I have written above, for the Lord's sake. For all Christian kingdoms have come together in your kingdom. After this we expect the kingdom without end. . . . And if you rule [lit. put in order, arrange] your kingdom well, you will be a son of light and a resident of the heavenly [lit. higher] Jerusalem, as I have written to you above. So now I say: Be watchful and take heed, o pious tsar. For all Christian kingdoms have come together in yours alone, inasmuch as two Romes have fallen, and a third stands, and a fourth there shall not be [cf. Rev. 17:10]. Indeed your Christian kingdom will not be left to others, according to the great Theologian [Saint John the Divine, but actually from Daniel 2:44]. The word of the blessed David had been fulfilled for the Christian Church. This is my rest forever. Here I will dwell, for I have desired it [Psalms 132 (131):14].[30]

As I indicated in "Ivan the Terrible: Emperor as Mythmaker," apocalyptic imagery increases from the late fifteenth century on. In the so-called short version of Ivan IV's coronation ceremony, which is assumed to be the one actually used in 1547,[31] the dramatic moment when Metropolitan Macarius removes the life-giving cross from a golden plate and places it on Ivan is accompanied by a prayer for the tsar's just and lengthy reign. The invocation begins "O Lord, our God, King of Kings and Lord of Lords,"[32] a direct allusion to the Parousia of Christ as the Righteous Judge from Revelation 19:11–16.

The Apocalypse was a dominant theme as well in the decoration of the principal public locales of the tsar's daily life in the Kremlin. Events or themes from the Book of Revelation adorned the interiors of the palace church (Cathedral of the Annunciation), the cathedral church (Cathedral of the Dormition), and the throne room of the Golden Hall.[33]

Surely the concentration of apocalyptic imagery in a space as confined and emblematic as the Moscow Kremlin would create a context that insured that the introduction of the Palm Sunday Ritual by Ivan IV and Metropolitan Macarius would be read not only as a retrospective historical re-creation, but an anticipatory eschatological model for Moscow as the New Jerusalem. This duality is inherent in the original symbolism of the Entry itself.

The iconography of the Christian Entry into Jerusalem derives from Roman imperial imagery, specifically, the representation of the emperor's triumphant departure or arrival—*profectio* or *adventus*—into a city. Kantorowicz has shown quite convincingly that the Entry of Christ can be viewed in two ways—as a historical event, where the representation alludes to specific historical circumstances—or as an abstracted, eschatological event, where the representation alludes to the messianic significance of the Entry.[34] In the latter case, the imagery of the mounted Roman emperor led by a winged Victory is transformed into the King of the Jews led by an angel, the precursor mentioned in both the Old and New Testament:

Exodus 23:20. Behold, I send an Angel before thee, to keep thee in the way, and to bring thee into the place which I have prepared.

Mark 1:2-3. As it is written in the prophets, Behold, I send my messenger before thy face, which shall prepare the way before thee.

In Christian doctrine, this harbinger of the coming of the Lord is John the Baptist, the Orthodox John the Forerunner.

Although the historical *Adventus* represented by the Entry into Jerusalem on Palm Sunday can be distinguished from the eschatological *Adventus* represented by the Second Coming, Kantorowicz notes that occasionally one concept would supersede or even replace the other in medieval thinking. He cites the Muscovite Palm Sunday Ritual as the unique example in which the two images are blended.[35] The reenactment of the Entry presents the historical image; the tsar pulling the ass at the end of a long rein presents the eschatological image. Kantorowicz's astute observation can be fleshed out if the context of the Ritual's introduction into Moscow's court ceremonial is considered. By leading the way in the Procession on the Ass, Ivan as the humble shepherd of the flock at the historical level can be identified on the eschatological level as the harbinger of the Lord, John the Forerunner (John the Baptist), who happens to be his own patron saint. What is crucial here is that the eschatological image suspends the facts of history (John the Forerunner was killed before the historical Entry into Jerusalem occurred) to focus on the dynamic tension between the humble precursor and Christ at the Second Coming, between the messenger of promise and the Redeemer of the Righteous. For Moscow, which increasingly saw itself as the New Jerusalem, the apocalyptic connotations of the Ritual were an annual reminder that the Last Judgment might come at any time. The Ritual provided a model of a humble and powerful ruler prepared to lead the Orthodox faithful to salvation at the end of history as well as within it.

The four levels of reference indicated in the analysis of the Palm Sunday Ritual are applicable to the Epiphany Ritual as well. At the level of performance once again we see all the elements used to support the submission hypothesis, a reading in which the tsar's role in the Ritual is viewed as symbolic of the submission of secular authority to that of the church or to the metropolitan himself. It is the tsar who stands on the ice while the metropolitan sits. It is the tsar who must remove his crown while the metropolitan keeps his head covered. Nonetheless, within the purview of a holiday that celebrates Christ's baptism, in which he *humbles himself* before John the Forerunner (Matt. 3:13–17), the purposeful humility of the tsar in imitation of Christ is perfectly in order. Bushkovitch, however, follows a different line of reasoning here, reading a political message over the religious one:

> Like other Byzantine court rituals, it [the Epiphany Ritual] celebrated the greatness and glory of the emperor, the image of Christ on earth. . . . As a court ceremony, the Russian rite not only differed from the Byzantine ceremony in form, it presented an entirely different message. The Tsar was not elevated above the court and the church [the Byzantine emperor stood on a raised platform—M.S.F.], instead he followed the Metropolitan in procession, leading the boyars but not physically above them. By the decorated hole in the ice, the *Iordan'* he *stood*, and stood bareheaded according to Jenkinson, before the Metropolitan seated on an elevated throne. In the Russian language of ritual, as well as the European, the Tsar showed his respect for the Metropolitan, not the other way around. The Byzantines honored the Emperor, the Russians honored the church. The purpose of the Russian ceremony, well understood by the still Catholic English, was to bless the water of the Moscow river, and by that holy water to sanctify the Tsar, aristocracy, and eventually the people of the Russian state. The Byzantines, by contrast, used the ceremony to underline the Christlike image of the Emperor.[36]

Consideration of the levels of reference beyond performance reveals a different, less political interpretation of what remains a royal *religious* ritual. We see that the Russians were less concerned with isolating and glorifying the emperor in the present than in presenting him within an iconographic model that had more important ramifications for the future, beyond the confines of human history.

The iconographic pattern that links tsar and metropolitan as John the Forerunner and Christ in the ritual *ending* of Palm Sunday finds its reversed counterpart in the ritual *beginning* of Epiphany. In the Blessing of the Waters it is the metropolitan in the image of John the Forerunner who first casts holy water on the tsar in the image of a humble Christ, standing bareheaded on the ice of the symbolic River Jordan. As in the case with Palm Sunday, the icon of the Baptism (fig. 7) provided the inspiration for the elevated platform on which the metropolitan performs the Blessing of the Waters: Christ *stands* in the midst of the River Jordan, while John, standing *above him* on the rocky banks of the river, baptizes him, his right hand on the *bare head* of the Savior. Thus the ritual not only reenacts a holy event from the life of Christ but presents the highest echelons of church and state in a living icon of that event.

Bushkovitch makes much of the fact that the tsar stands while members of the clergy sit during the ceremony. This distinction is better understood as the result

Figure 7 *Baptism*. Obverse of two-sided icon. Novgorod. Cathedral of Holy Sophia. End 15th–beg. 16th century.

of the level of performance intersecting with the level of iconography. It is liturgical prescription and not imperial submission that governs the sitting and standing of the officiating clergy during a religious service. According to strict Russian Orthodox practice the reading during Vespers of the *paremii* (selections from the Holy Scriptures that prefigure or illuminate the events or holy persons celebrated) requires the clergy to stand during readings from the New Testament

Figure 8 *Baptism of Saint Vladimir*. Fresco on lower southeastern wall adjacent to throne. Golden Hall throne room. 1547–56. Reconstruction by K.K. Lopialo from O.I. Podobedova, *Moskovskaia shkola zhivopisi pri Ivane IV. Raboty v moskovskom kremle 40-kh–70-kh godov XVI v.* (Moscow: Nauka, 1972), 199.

and sit during readings from the Old.[37] The Vespers portion of the Epiphany service contains thirteen *paremii*, all from the Old Testament. The interpolated troparion of the feast specifically refers to the Creator who enlightens those sitting in darkness (*siediashchie vo tmie*). During the Blessing of the Waters itself, three *paremii* are read from the Book of Isaiah, requiring that the officiating clergy be seated.

The historical level of reference is illuminated by the juxtaposition of Epiphany and Palm Sunday as celebrations of events in the life of Christ. As signs of the beginning and ending, respectively, of Christ's public ministry, the Epiphany and Palm Sunday Rituals invited reference to parallels within history as well, specifically Russian history. I have discussed above the association of Christ's Entry into Jerusalem on Palm Sunday with Ivan IV's entry into Moscow following his defeat of Kazan', an "apocalyptic" event in an age concerned with the *end* of Russian history. The participation of Tsar Ivan IV in the annual Epiphany Ritual forged a link not only with Christ, but with Saint Vladimir, whose baptism in 988 signalled the rebirth of Rus' as a Christian land, the *beginning* of enlightened Russian history.

The arrangement of frescoes in the Kremlin's Golden Hall demonstrates the singular importance of this event to his reign. The wall paintings of the antechamber were devoted primarily to Old Testament battle scenes, whereas those of the throne room were dedicated to two great heroes of Kievan and Muscovite Rus', especially Saint Vladimir the Baptizer and Vladimir Monomakh. The historical fresco immediately adjacent to Ivan's throne is of particular importance, serving as background for his official presentation at court. This fresco depicts the baptism of Vladimir (fig. 8), in which ruler and ruled are symbolically reborn into the light of Christianity, the commencement of a new age for Rus'. When Ivan himself was anointed as the first officially crowned tsar, the coronation ceremony was held on January 16, 1547, the first Sunday following the apodosis or final afterfeast of Epiphany, January 14. The beginning of his reign as emperor would coincide with the celebration of the beginning of Christ's public ministry, with its obvious allusion to the baptism of Vladimir and all Rus'.

In addition to the similarities between the Epiphany and Palm Sunday Rituals at the referential levels of performance, iconography, and history, one finds a common eschatological basis in the Jewish and derivative Christian calendars. Of the three messianic/eschatological feasts in the Jewish liturgical year, two are developed directly in the Christian calendrical tradition. Passover and Shavuot, the Feast of Weeks (the early grain harvest), find parallels in Easter and Pentecost. The third festival, Sukkot, the Feast of Tabernacles (the harvest of the vine), has no direct parallel. Students of comparative liturgics have provided a convincing argument that the original symbolism of the Feast of Tabernacles as the beginning and ending of the sacerdotal calendar was connected with both the messianic vocation of the Savior and the theme of the water of life. Because of differences among calendars in the ordering of months, these themes were eventually redistributed in the celebration of Christ's Baptism (Epiphany) and the messianic Entry of the Savior into Jerusalem on Palm Sunday. The baptism of Christ marks the beginning of his public ministry, and the Entry into Jerusalem its end. Set between the frames of the birth and death of Christ Incarnate, these two pivotal feasts lead directly to the Resurrection and the promise of life eternal.

The liturgy of the Epiphany contains numerous eschatological allusions from the Old Testament (the Great Flood, Jonah and the whale, the crossing of the Red Sea, the three children in the fiery furnace) as well as from the New. Prominent are the frequent references to John baptizing with water, but Christ with the Holy Spirit and with fire. Canticle 6 of Matins in the Epiphany service, for example, reads:

Christ baptizes in the fire of the Last Day those who are disobedient and believe not that he is God: but through the Spirit and by the grace that comes through water He grants a new birth to all those who acknowledge His divinity, delivering them from their faults.[38]

The symbolic value of fire in reference to the End Times may explain why the phrase *i ognem* ("and with fire") was added to the Blessing of the Waters during the reign of Boris Godunov. Bushkovitch views this addition as the influence of folk interpretation on the Ritual[39] but in fact, it is more likely to be viewed as an explicit expression of the eschatological link in baptism between the Holy Spirit and fire found in the Gospels:

Matt. 3:11. I [John the Baptist] indeed baptize you with water unto repentance: but he that cometh after me is mightier than I, whose shoes I am not worthy to bear: he shall baptize you with the Holy spirit, and with fire (cf. Luke 3:16).

The Iconology of Royal Ritual

In this analysis of the sixteenth-century Muscovite royal rituals associated with Epiphany and Palm Sunday, I have attempted to uncover conventional patterns that permitted the identification of the tsar and the metropolitan with John the Forerunner and Christ at a crucial turning point in Russian history. I have suggested that the cultural system or paradigm that stimulated the development of these and related cultural artifacts was one informed by concern for the apocalypse. In Panovskian terms, the iconology of these court rituals was eschatological. Their functional complementarity is a manifestation of this common stimulus beyond their simple association with the ecclesiastical calendar.

The powerful historical-eschatological force of the Epiphany and Palm Sunday Rituals still maintained their hold on Muscovite Rus' when Paul of Aleppo acknowledged their singular importance in 1655. These two major royal rituals elaborated at the Muscovite court are to be understood as marks of royal mission rather than submission, direct expressions of Moscow's belief in her messianic purpose to bring the Orthodox faithful to salvation after the fall of Constantinople. The Byzantine models, which exalted the emperor in the here and now, were inappropriate for loftier eschatological concerns. It was not the deposed Byzantine emperor, but the Muscovite tsar, crowned as God's representative on earth, who would hold the reins of power and, in humble imitation of Christ's earthly ministry, lead Orthodox Christianity to its final destiny.

Notes

1. *Puteshestvie antiokhiiskogo Patriarkha Makariia v Rossiiu v polovine XVII veka, opisannoe ego synom, arkhidiakonom Pavlom Aleppskim*, trans. F. Murkos, 5 pts. (Moscow, 1896–1900), pt. 2: *Ot Dnestra do Moskvy* (Moscow, 1897), 195.

2. A survey of these accounts may be found in Konstantin Nikol'skii, *O sluzhbakh russkoi tserkvi, byvshikh v prezhnikh pechatnykh bogosluzhebnykh knigakh* (St. Petersburg, 1885), 45–97; and Paul Bushkovitch, "The Epiphany Ceremony of the Russian Court in the Sixteenth and Seventeenth Centuries," *The Russian Review* 49, no. 1 (1990), 1–17.

3. Nikol'skii, *O sluzhbakh*, 46–47; the traditional Blessing of the Waters on Epiphany day is, of course, Greek in origin (p. 288); V. Savva, *Moskovskie tsari i vizantiiskie vasilevsy. K voprosu o vliianii Vizantii na obrazovanie idei tsarskoi vlasti*

moskovskix gosudarei (Kharkov: Tipografiia i Litografiia M. Zil'berberga i Sv'ia, 1901), 104, 167–175; Bushkovitch, "Epiphany Ceremony," 4–7.

4. The commentary of Anthony Jenkinson and his entourage (1557–58 [publ. 1589]) in Richard Hakluyt, *The Principall Navigations Voiages and Discoveries of the English Nation*, facsim. ed., intro. David Beers Quinn and Raleigh Ashlin Skelton (Cambridge: Cambridge University Press, 1965), 341–342. It is this description that serves as the primary source for Karamzin: N.M. Karamzin, *Istoriia gosudarstva rossiiskogo*, 5th ed., 12 vols. in 3 bks. (St. Petersburg: Tipografiia Eduarda Pratsa, 1842–43/1988), bk. 3, vol. 9, ch. 7, cols. 275–276 and n. 834.

5. Nikol'skii, *O sluzhbakh*, 45–97; Miroslav Labunka, "The Legend of the Novgorodian White Cowl: The Study of Its 'Prologue' and 'Epilogue,'" unpublished doctoral dissertation (Columbia University, 1978).

6. The chapels surrounding the tent tower were officially consecrated on October 1, 1559/1560: *Polnoe sobranie russkikh letopisei*, 38 vols. to date (St. Petersburg [Petrograd, Leningrad]-Moscow: Various publishers, 1846–1989 [hereafter PSRL]), v. 13, 320 (s.a. 7068/1560). The first Palm Sunday after the consecration would have come in the spring of 1560. The entire church was completed and consecrated in 1561: *PSRL*, v. 13, 334 (s.a. 7069/1561).

7. Georg Ostrogorsky, "Zum Stratordienst des Herrschers in der byzantinisch slavischen Welt." *Seminarium Kondakovianum*, vol. 7 (1935), 196–199.

8. "... and holding the bridle of his [Pope Sylvester's] horse, in deference to the blessed Peter we [Constantine], rendered to him the service of equerry... "

9. Ostrogorsky, "Zum Stratordienst," 187.

10. Michael S. Flier, "Breaking the Code: The Image of the Tsar in the Muscovite Palm Sunday Ritual," in *Medieval Russian Culture II*, ed. Michael S. Flier and Daniel Rowland (in preparation), and "Emperor as Mythmaker: Ivan the Terrible and the Palm Sunday Ritual," in *Rossica*, ed. Claudio Ingerflom, T. Kondrat'eva, R. Wortman, and B. Uspensky (New York: Sharpe, and Moscow: Progress, in press).

11. It is not the tsar, but a high-ranking boyar who serves as equerry for the newly confirmed head of the church.

12. Hakluyt, *The Principall Navigations*, 336–337. Jenkinson's reference to the "Emperours sonne" as the recipient of the sprinkling of holy water, and not the emperor himself, is puzzling. There is no mention of a son earlier in the same text: "the Emperour, with his brother, and all his Nobles" and "he [the Emperour] ... went ... and standing bare headed, with all his Nobles." In the anonymous text (see below) written by a member of the Jenkinson party, holy water is cast directly upon the emperor himself. Pragmatically it makes little sense that Ivan's young son Ivan (b. March 28, 1554), less than four years old in January, 1558, would have been exposed to the harsh January weather in this manner; the tsar's other son, Fyodor, was even younger (b. May 11, 1557). It is more likely that the text here is corrupt and what was meant was "the Metropolitan ... did cast of the said water upon the Emperours [per] sonne, and the Nobilitie."

13. Ibid., 341.

14. Bushkovitch, "Epiphany Ceremony," 10–11.

15. Ibid., 12–14.

16. The occurrence of identical rituals on June 24, the Nativity of John the Forerunner, points to an ancient source, the biannual celebration of the summer and winter solstices, the extreme points of the solar cycle.

17. Bushkovitch, "Epiphany Ceremony," 9–10.

18. Bushkovitch, "Epiphany Ceremony," 8, 13, 16.

19. Ostrogorsky, "Zum Stratordienst," 201; Labunka, "Legend," 245; Robert O. Crummey, "Court Spectacles in Seventeenth-Century Russia: Illusions and Reality," in

Essays in Honor of A. A. Zimin (Columbus: Slavica Publishers, Inc., 1985), 134.

20. Bushkovitch, "Epiphany Ceremony," 3.

21. Crummey, "Court Spectacles," 136–138.

22. Hakluyt, *Principall Navigations*, 343–344.

23. *Akty sobrannye v bibliotekakh i arkhivakh Rossiiskoi Imperii Arkheograficheskoiu ekspeditsieiu Imperatorskoi Akademii nauk*, 4 vols. (St. Petersburg, 1836), v. 4: *1645–1700*, no. 223, p. 309.

24. Cf. *PSRL*, v. 26 (1959), 326 (s.a. 7003/1495); *Akty sobrannye*, v. 1: *1294–1598*, no. 184 (Feb. 6, 1539), 160–161; no. 264 (Feb. 20, 1564), 299–300.

25. Ostrogorsky, "Zum Stratordienst," 202–203.

26. In a letter to Aleksei Mikhailovich dated March 30, 1659, the estranged Patriarch Nikon wrote to complain about Metropolitan Pitirim taking his place in the Muscovite Palm Sunday Ritual, saying that it was terrifying for him as patriarch to represent (*izobrazhat'*) the person of Christ, i.e., to take on the image of God, to be a living icon. See V.M. Zhivov and B.A. Uspenskii, "Tsar' i Bog. Semioticheskie aspekty sakralizatsii monarkha v Rossii," in *Iazyki kul'tury i problemy perevodimosti*, ed. B. A. Uspenskii (Moscow, 1987), 110.

27. *PSRL*, v. 13 (1965), 225–227 (s.a. 7061/1553).

28. Cf. M.A. Il'in, "O naimenovanii pridelov sobora Vasiliia Blazhennogo," in *Novoe v arxeologii. Sbornik statei posviashchennyj 70-letiiu Artemiia Vladimirovicha Artsikovskogo* (Moscow: Moscow State University, 1972), 292.

29. N. A. Kazakova and Ia. S. Lur'e, *Antifeodal'nye ereticheskie dvizheniia na Rusi XIV-nachala XVI veka* (Moscow-Leningrad: ANSSSR, 1955), 399–406; M.V. Alpatov, *Pamiatnik drevnerusskoi zhivopisi kontsa XV veka. Ikona "Apokalipsis" Uspenskogo sobora Moskovskogo kremlia* (Moscow: Iskusstvo, 1964), 33.

30. V. Malinin, *Starets Eleazarova monastyria Filofei i ego poslaniia. Istoriko-literaturnoe issledovanie* (Kiev: Tipografiia Kievo-Pecherskoi Uspenskoi Lavry, 1901), App. IX, 54–55.

31. Savva, *Moskovskie tsari*, 146.

32. *PSRL*, v. 13, 150 (s.a. 7055/1547).

33. I. Ia. Kachalova, N. A. Maiasova, and L. A. Shchennikova, *Blagoveshchenskii sobor Moskovskogo kremlia. K 500-letiiu unikal'nogo pamiatnika russkoi kul'tury* (Moscow: Iskusstvo, 1990), 21, 30ff.; Alpatov, *Pamiatnik*; O.I. Podobedova, *Moskovskaia shkola zhivopisi pri Ivane IV. Raboty v Moskovskom kremle 40-kh–70-kh godov XVI v.* (Moscow: Nauka, 1972), 22–68.

34. Ernst H. Kantorowicz, "The 'King's Advent' and the Enigmatic Panels in the Doors of Santa Sabina," *Art Bulletin* 26, no. 4 (1944), 221ff.

35. Ibid., 229.

36. Bushkovitch, "Epiphany Ceremony," 5, 8.

37. N.D. Uspensky, *Evening Worship in the Orthodox Church*, trans. and ed. Paul Lazor (Crestwood, N.Y.: St. Vladimir's Seminary Press, 1985), 100. Uspensky cites a seventeenth-century *ordos* with the directive: "At the vespers of a feast, according to custom they place a bench at the right choir so that the abbot and the priests may sit during the *paroimiai*."

38. Translation from the Greek by Mother Mary and Archimandrite Kallistos Ware, *The Festal Menaion*, intro. Georges Florovsky (London: Faber & Faber, 1969), 373–374.

39. Bushkovitch, "Epiphany Ceremony," 14.

5
The Least Affected Social Group in the Ottoman Balkans: the Peasantry

Peter F. Sugar
University of Michigan

Let me begin by reminding you of two well-known and obvious facts. First, whenever we speak of the Balkans we generalize because even at any given moment, let alone at different historical periods, various regions south of the Danube-Save line differed greatly from each other. Second, in spite of their long overlordship in the lands of their large empire, the Ottomans were never able to absorb their subjects into an Ottoman society and culture although they influenced the life of every ethnic/national and social group over which they ruled.

The facts on which this presentation is based are also well known to students of Ottoman and Balkan history; what might be somewhat original is my interpretation of these facts. The title of my presentation is based on my belief that in the mixture of Byzantine, Turkic, and Islamic elements that produced the Ottoman system the Byzantine was the strongest. In this I return to the interpretation of Iorga and disagree with some more recent students of the Ottoman state. Furthermore, I believe that it was the peasantry that remained more closely and for a longer period of time in the frame of mind it acquired during the Byzantine centuries than any other social or professional class or group and that, by the time the Ottoman system began to fall apart, this somewhat Ottomanized Byzantine heritage was so strong that it survived the drastic changes in the countryside, the shift from the *timar* system to that of *çiftliks*, and allowed those who were the first harbingers of something new and western, the early nationalists, to turn to the peasantry for support. More than twenty-five years ago, Wayne S. Vucinich made the unequivocal statement: "National rebirth came from the village and not from the city."[1]

The Balkan peasantry was most directly affected by two Ottoman institutions, one mainly political/administrative, the other economic. The administrative one was described perfectly by Dimitri Obolensky when he wrote about a different state. He stated that "the basic units of the Byzantine provincial administration were the themes. These were districts in which soldiers were settled on small farms which they held on condition of hereditary military service, and whose governors (usually called 'strategi,' generals) exercised, under direct control of the emperor, the supreme military and civil command. Each theme was thus . . . a miniature state with its own army, police and civil administration."[2] All one has to do to make this sentence fit the Ottoman Empire perfectly is to change themes into *eyalets* and strategi into *valis*. We can take this similarity of the Byzantine and Ottoman administrative system a step further. Speros Vryonis informed us that the strategoi could do everything in their themes "save for the assessment and collection of taxes, which were effected by agents directly under Constantinople . . . ."[3] The taxing agent in the Ottoman Empire was the *defterdar* of every given *eyalet* who operated independently of the *vali*. The Vryonis volume deals with Anatolia not the Balkans. This fact reminds us of another well-known, but often neglected, historical truth. The Byzantine-Turkish coexistence, as far as institutions were concerned, antedated the appearance of the Ottomans by several centuries. Osman and his successors had ready made models in the various Seljuq and Karaman principalities of Anatolia.[4]

The economic institution most important for the Balkan peasantry was the *timar* system. This too was known already in Seljuq Anatolia and was, to a considerable extent, built on a Byzantine model. Obolensky gives us another sentence clearly showing this relationship: the "pronoia . . . was held for a limited time, usually until the recipient's death, and was, until the second half of the thirteenth century, unalienable."[5] Here we have a principle described which, with small modifications, became the *timar* system. By the fourteenth century not only the Byzantine pronoia, but also its Balkan versions in the Second Bulgarian Empire (1204–1241) and in the realm of Stepan Dušan (1331–1355) became alienable as was the Ottoman *timar*. The one important difference was that pronoias were given to lords, while timars were assigned not only to them but also to the soldiers on small farms mentioned in the first quotation from Obolensky.

Before going any further, let me attempt to answer a question that will certainly be asked: What about the cities; these too were parts of *eyalets* subject to the *valis's* jurisdiction? Two important differences made the cities much more susceptible to Ottomanization than the rural areas. Turks did not settle in the countryside except in what is today European Turkey and some adjacent areas in today's Bulgaria. The *timarll* was a lone Ottoman among numerous native neighbors. Cities not only acquired Ottoman garrisons and served retired Ottoman dignitaries (Ayans), but their major economic functions, grouped into handicraft and merchant guilds, were absorbed into their Ottoman equivalents. I cannot go into detail about this process that, once again, was facilitated by long contact between Greek and Turkish societies. Gibb and Bowen made it clear that "there seems to have been a strong resemblance, as in so many Byzantine and Moslem institutions, between the guild systems of the two communities."[6] The city became truly Ottoman, Turkified, and it was not until the decline of the

Ottoman system, in the 18th century mainly, that the re-Christianization of the cities began.7

By that time even the physical aspects of the cities had changed. Major churches acquired minarets and became mosques. The various quarters, organized along professional and religious lines, gave the cities the checkerboard-like organization the remains of which are reflected to the present day in street and district names of numerous Balkan cities.8 When the cities reacquired their non-Moslem majorities, the new inhabitants fit into this pattern for several decades without changing it.

While at the beginning of modern Balkan history the countryside supplied the followers of the early nationalists, the cities turned into the foci of the various *ayans* (the second meaning of the expression is local lord) who tried to carve out states of their own in the Balkans well into the early nineteenth century.9

The countryside, on the other hand, retained its old physiognomy. The visible signs of the change in supreme masters were minimal at best. More often than not, any given region's *timarll* was the sole Moslem/Turk whose presence changed the countryside little if at all and who, given his military duties, was away for about half of every year. The more important question to ask is: How much did the life of the rural population change when Byzantine rule was replaced by the Ottoman?

To answer it, one has to look at three aspects of the peasantry's life, the ones that were the most meaningful for it: work and related obligations, family and religion.

While the replacement of the Christian landlords by the *timarlls* probably meant very little at first to the average peasant—simply a change of masters—he rapidly discovered that while the new system did not differ from the old it was more secure and less arbitrary. He certainly never knew that under Ottoman rule, like everybody else, he too had a *hadd*—something like a bill of rights—that the authorities protected. What he knew was that his obligations were fixed and did not fluctuate according to the master's whim. His *çift* was unalienable and covered enough ground, between 60 to 150 *dönüm*, depending on the quality of the soil, to support him and his family.10 He could not acquire more, but this was something he could only rarely do in Byzantine times and, therefore, he did not miss this right. If he saw some serious change, it came in the payments he had to make to lord and state. While these were usually unchanged in almost all respects because the Ottoman habit was to confirm local laws and customs in the *kanunnames* they issued for each conquered region, his new lord, the *timarll/sipahi* was entitled to a cash payment, the *çift resmi* of twenty-two akçes per year, "the equivalent of the hay, fodder, wood and services which the peasant had owed to the fief-holder in Byzantine days."11 Unlike the guild master in the town, the peasant could produce more than the amount on which he was taxed by lord and state and keep the difference. Yet, this extra income did not mean much given the fact that he could not buy land beyond the one the *çift* assured him. This piece of land could be passed on to his children, but could not be divided among them, as smaller units would not support a family and make it produce the required taxes. This fact directs our attention to the second of the three aspects that dominated the peasantry's existence.

Some of you might have noticed that I have not used the expression village in my presentation. The Balkans simply had no villages prior to the transformation of the *timar* system into the *çiftlik* economy. Around the peasants' houses were their fields and those belonging to their lords' estates, *kiliç* in Ottoman days, which they also worked. The countryside resembled somewhat, although in a much smaller edition, the old farm country in our United States. At least in the early Ottoman centuries, when wars ravaged the Balkans repeatedly, just as they did in Byzantine days, there was enough empty land for the establishment of new *çifts* when the family grew too large to live off the yield of the original homestead. This too was nothing new and simply continued the pattern established in Byzantine days.

I am certain that most of you expect me to speak of the *Zadruga* or its equivalent in languages other than Serbian in this connection. A recent study convinced me that the *Zadruga* did not exist in the Balkans prior to the late 18th century.[12] What existed was a vague understanding of the extended family out of which the *Zadruga* grew in the years in which the *çiftlik* dominated the countryside. What occurred is easily understood.

Given the unalienable and indivisible family holding, younger sons had to move. Given the availability of land, they did not have to move far and remained in contact with their father and older brother. While the *timarll* was pleased by acquiring an additional taxable on land belonging to his holding but previously fallow, it was simpler for him to deal with the new tenant through the old who, given the family structure, had the new one's respect. This was the beginning from which in more difficult and dangerous times the *Zadruga* developed. This is a very important point to remember. It was an organic development that, probably, would have occurred in the Byzantine countryside too if the life in the Balkans would have been as stable in the late Byzantine centuries as it was in the early Ottoman ones. Given the quasi-feudal structure, the availability of land and the natural tendency of relatives to support each other this was an almost unavoidable development. Unavoidable it might have been, but it gave the rural people a great advantage over the urban dwellers in the long run. The importance of the *Zadruga* in the last Ottoman centuries in the Balkans is well known. The villages had them; the cities did not.

The younger sons of a peasant could move out yet stay in physical proximity with their paternal home. The younger sons of guildsmen could not act in the same manner. Given the fixed number of workshops of each profession in each town with its journeymen and apprentices also fixed, younger sons had to move into other cities unless they were lucky enough to marry the daughter of a guildmaster who had no sons. In this latter case they became members of their father-in-law's family. The extended family and subsequently the *Zadruga* could not develop in the cities.

The third basic factor in the life of the inhabitants of the Balkans under Ottoman rule was their religion. This is a topic about which much has been written and which is controversial to the present day. The usual topics deal with conversions from Christianity to Islam, the role of the Bogomils and other heretics, the Orthodox and other millets, the position of Jews in the Ottoman Empire, the Slavonic versus the Greek rites, and the role of the Phanariotes, to mention only a few topics. I will not even touch on these. I am limiting myself to the religious beliefs and practices of the great majority of Orthodox Balkan Christians who understood very little of theology, were more often than not illiterate, but for whom religion, as they understood it, was a very important part of existence. In short, I am interested in the context of this short presentation in folk religion.

Folk religion, whatever denominations are investigated, is a mixture of any given religion's basic tenets and teachings, often not clearly understood, and of local beliefs and superstitions often going back to long-forgotten pagan beliefs. A pagan stone altar could easily become a holy place of primitive Christianity in a new guise; for example, as the spot where a saint appeared or a miracle occurred. This Christian saint can and was equated more than once in the Ottoman-ruled Balkans with a Moslem holy man in whose powers a given *derviş* order or the *akhi* of a given guild believed. What is essential is that the believer feels secure in this and possibly the next life because, as far as he is concerned, he not only does the right thing, but uses the proper charms and incantations often not even fully understood in his daily life. If you want a contemporary American example, think of the field-goal kicker who crosses himself before he kicks.

Once again, the population of rural areas was better protected in its beliefs than were those living in cities and towns. First of all, the peasantry did not see churches transformed into mosques. The urban dweller not only lost some of his favored places of worship but also had to accept *şeyhs* and *kethüdas* with their Moslem patron saint and insignias as the leaders of the guild in which he worked. While folk religion made this relatively easy for most guild members, the change was obvious and drastic. If it did nothing else, it prevented non-Moslems from reaching the most important leading positions in their guilds.

It was also in the cities that learned theologians and bishops resided who, quite correctly, opposed folk-religious practices and beliefs. Finally, it was in the cities and towns that religious issues produced ethnic controversy. Steven Runciman wrote: "the Church was run more and more in the interest of the

Greek people and not of Orthodoxy as a whole."[13] Runciman blames the Phanariots and their influence over the patriarchate for this development. He was certainly correct in blaming this group, but the trend which they turned into a torrent was there from the moment Mehmed II placed Gennadius in charge of the Orthodox patriarchate and millet. The most visible result of this policy was the Graecification of the hierarchy and the disappearance of Church Slavonic from the liturgy in churches which they controlled. Once again, this occurred mainly in cities and towns where not only the better-educated clergy resided, but where one also found the better educated laymen who understood what was going on.

The peasantry could avoid not only Moslem administrators and judges, but even the Christian law courts and authorities, as long as its members settled their problems and disputes among themselves according to local custom and habit. Furthermore, they had their own clergy. "The monastic Christian clergy . . . supplied the bishops and patriarchs . . . while the secular clerics, who served in the parishes and often shared a common lot" with their parishioners were usually of local origin.[14] "The peasants respected the parish priest because he was one of them," usually a scion of the dominant local extended family. "The village priest lived and died in the social circle in which he grew up. To eke out a living [he] . . . tilled his own fields."[15] That he was often illiterate without theological training and had learned his profession by being apprenticed to his predecessor made little difference to those who made up his flock. What was important to them was that they spoke the same language, that of the local folk religion, and trusted and understood each other. Life went on and souls were saved in an old, time-honored manner that neither the Ottoman authorities nor the *millet başi*–patriarch could change and influence.

As indicated at the beginning of this presentation, it is my contention that the Ottoman system was more heavily indebted to Byzantine models than to any other as far as its administrative organization was concerned and that as a result the Ottoman Balkans were less a departure from the Byzantine Balkans than is generally assumed. I also suggested that the least affected social group living in the Balkans was the peasantry.

If I am correct, and at least I believe that I am, this pattern does not fit into Balkan, Byzantine, or Ottoman history and appears to be unique in the long-range history of this area and states. Whenever invasions, settlements, or conquests occurred, at least partial absorption also resulted. The second point I made at the very beginning of my presentation stressed that in this respect the Ottomans were an exception. Exceptions are never or very seldom accidents in history. Let me end by trying to show why the Ottoman case was different from the other drastic changes that occurred in what was first the realm of the Byzantines and later of the Ottomans.

Irrespective of the date which one accepts as the beginning of the Eastern Roman or Byzantine Empire—either from 330 when Constantine dedicated his new capital to himself or from the rule of Valentian I (364–375), the first emperor who claimed to rule only the East—the Byzantine Empire was a well-established, powerful state by the time the first Slavs appeared in the Balkans roughly some 200 years later. This in-migration of "barbarians" ended with the arrival of the Vlachs probably in the 10th century. What we have here is a rather slow demographic change, about 400 years, giving the emperors opportunity and time to deal with the newcomers. Furthermore, these migrants admired the state into which they moved either peacefully or by force, and whenever they were strong enough to make decisions of their own they imitated it. The result is well known. Byzantium did not absorb the newcomers who retained their languages and leading social elements but converted them successfully not only in a religious sense but also in serving as a model for the states which Serbs, Bulgars, and some others were able to form on occasion. The realm of Byzantium was only seldom united under one ruler, but it was always Byzantine in its organization, administration, religion, and customs even when it was divided politically. Time and a superior civilization turned the non-Greeks of the Balkans into Byzantines speaking other tongues.

Roughly the same time period, about 400 years elapsed, as the already-mentioned Vryonis volume has clearly shown, between the first Turkish/Moslem attacks on Byzantium in Asia Minor and—to use his expression—the Islamization of that region. In the end of this process, Anatolia was mainly Moslem and Turkish with the Greeks, Armenians, and other people as a distinct minority. To what extent and why was the result of these later 400 years of Byzantine and invader conflict different from the earlier one? At first sight, the difference appears to be drastic. Eastern Rome had to vacate Asia Minor, and Christianity was replaced, to a considerable extent, by Islam. It looks like a true conquest, like the absorption of the Greek and Byzantine world into the Turkish and later Ottoman. Yet, what we have is mutual absorption. While politically and religiously the various Turkish states and their religion were victorious, these states—just like the Serb and Bulgarian ones in the Balkans—have learned statecraft, diplomacy, and administrative practices from the Byzantines whose methods and offices they used when running their establishments. This curious case of mutual absorption was the result of 400 years of coexistence in a somewhat limited geographic region of two mature cultures and civilizations. This is why the Byzantine experiences in the Balkans and Anatolia differed. In the Balkans Byzantium had a civilizing mission; in Anatolia it faced a competitor in the high civilization of the Arabs and Persians that the Turks brought with them when they moved in.

The inability of the Ottomans to absorb the people in the Balkans becomes almost obvious if one compares the first two developments with the one to which this essay was devoted. First, the rapidity of change has to be considered. The first permanent Ottoman/Turkish settlement in the Balkans dates from 1354, and only 100 years later the entire region south of the Danube-Save line was in Ottoman hands, including Constantinople. The slow melting together of original and new populations, which occurred in Anatolia, could not and did not occur in the Balkans. The early Ottomans, except those few who transformed the cities, were soldiers constantly on the move. Furthermore, they were not numerous enough to settle a new region. The manpower shortage of the Ottomans is an important and often-neglected fact. But, it was not only the speed of conquest by an army not followed by settlers that made the difference. The Ottomans were totally familiar with, if not the result of, the Anatolian symbiosis and were perfectly satisfied to leave unchanged what they found in the Balkans that resembled, in many respects, the situation to which they were used. They did not even try to introduce change when not pushed to it by their business and religious upper elites who, quite naturally, centered in the cities. What happened here was not the encounter between Roman and barbarian or the slow symbiosis of Christian and Moslem cultures. For the Ottomans the Balkans looked familiar and did not require change. Therefore, as long as the population of the Balkans was peaceful and paid taxes, it could be left alone. Thus, in a sense, the Byzantine world in the countryside did not change with the Ottoman conquest. The small adjustments that the change of overlords required were easily made and brought no fundamental change. When the Ottoman system became corrupt, unable to adjust, and finally broke down, something which in the rural areas was most drastically illustrated by the *çiftlik*-centered economy and life replacing the *timar*-based existence, only then did the Byzantine heritage begin to disappear. This process was brought to an end by the appearance of modern, Western influences, first and foremost nationalism. This reading of the Byzantine-barbarian versus Byzantine-Turkish and finally the Byzantine versus Ottoman encounters is the novel interpretation to which I alluded earlier and that, I assume, will produce the most questions and criticisms.

Notes

1. Wayne S. Vucinich, "The Nature of Balkan Society under Ottoman Rule," *Slavic Review*, XXI/4 (December, 1962), p. 603.

2. Dimitri Obolensky, *The Byzantine Commonwealth: Eastern Europe. 500–1453* (New York, Washington, 1971), p. 75.

3. Speros Vryonis, Jr., *The Decline of Medieval Hellenism in Asia Minor and the Process of Islamization from the Eleventh through Fifteenth Centuries* (Berkeley and Los Angeles, 1971), p. 2.

4. See, among others, Bistra Cvetkova, "Influence exercée par certaines institutions de Byzance et des Balkans de Moyen Age sur le système féodal ottoman," *Byzantinobulgarica* I (1962), pp. 237–57.

5. Obolensky, p. 252.

6. H. A. R. Gibb and Harold Bowen, *Islamic Society and the West* (one volume in two parts, all published) (London, New York, Toronto, 1957), Part I, p. 289.

7. For the history of the Balkan city under

Ottoman rule see Nikolai Todorov, *The Balkan City, 1400-1900* (translator not given) (Seattle, London, 1983).

8. On the city structure see Peter F. Sugar, *Southeastern Europe under Ottoman Rule. 1354-1804* (Seattle, London, 1977), pp. 74-76.

9. On the *ayans* see ibid., pp. 237-241.

10. Halil Inalcik, *The Ottoman Empire: The Classical Age. 1300-1600*, Norman Itzkowitz and Colin Imber, trans., (New York, Washington, 1973), p. 100. I calculated 60 *do'num* = 1.55 acres and 150 do'num = 3.88 acres.

11. The value of the *akçe* varied from time to time. The best values I can give are:

>From Orhan to Murad II each *akçe* = 1.16 g silver;
>From Murad II to 1481 each *akçe* = .91 g silver;
>From Selim I to Murad III each *akçe* = .65 g silver;
>In 1584 the *akçe* was reduced to .325 g silver;
>In 1691 the *akçe* was reduced to .1625 g silver;

These are my calculations based in part on Gibb and Bowen, Part II, pp. 49-52 and on Sugar, n. 3, on pp. 37-38.

12. Unpublished paper prepared in the Woodrow Wilson Center in Washington, D.C., in 1989, Maria Todorova, *Myth-making in European Family History (The Zadruga Revisited)*.

13. Steven Runciman, *The Great Church in Captivity* (Cambridge, 1968), p. 379.

14. Vucinich, p. 604.

15. Ibid.

6
The Byzantine Artistic Tradition under Ottoman Rule*

John J. Yiannias
University of Virginia

With the consolidation of Ottoman rule over lands formerly held by the Byzantines and their Slavic neighbors, the art of Byzantium became the art of a politically subordinate but religiously and culturally self-regulating segment of Ottoman society. This "post-Byzantine" art, as we now call it,[1] helped to affirm and preserve the identity of the *Rum Millet*, the "nation" of Orthodox Christians subject to the sultan, by keeping alive the Byzantine visual language, with which Orthodox Christianity was so closely identified. Predicated on a respect for established types (although perhaps no more than Byzantine art itself had been), it was resistant to change. But it was not impervious to change. Over time, as the result of a process that ought someday to be explored in detail because of its deeper implications for the history of Balkan culture, post-Byzantine artists lost the incentive and concomitantly the ability to think, see, and create in a Byzantine mode.[2]

By the nineteenth century the Byzantine artistic tradition was reduced to a set of formulas employed by folk artists and a set of inhibitions displayed unconsciously in the work of painters whose sights were set elsewhere. It did not become a source of inspiration again in the Orthodox world until the twentieth century.[3] Yet throughout the Ottoman period, ironically, it was not the art of the Turkish conqueror that posed a threat to the Byzantine tradition, but the art of Western Christendom, in its Renaissance and Baroque phases. By the time the Ottoman yoke was lifted, the aesthetic tyranny, so to speak, of Western Europe over the visual arts of the Orthodox churches was an accomplished fact.[4]

The history of post-Byzantine art is the history of the survival of the Byzantine artistic tradition under conditions that brought it into somewhat strained coexistence with Western art and led ultimately to its tacit discreditation and virtual abandonment.[5] But it does not follow, just because it was the late phase of a tradition destined (as we now can see) to expire, or at least to go into hibernation, that post-Byzantine art was decrepit. No "species" of art, whether Byzantine or Gothic or Japanese, is a physical organism, subject to birth, maturation, and

Figure 1 Dragalevtsi (Bulgaria), monastery church. Sacrifice of Isaac by Abraham. 1476. (From A. Boschkov, *La peinture bulgare des origines au XIXe siècle* [Recklinghausen, 1974], pl. 101.

death. It is rather an aggregate of individual works, each to be judged on its own merits, even if certain traits can be predicated of them as a group; and some post-Byzantine images are of the highest aesthetic quality. If they have not received their due, this is because of an ingrained historiographic bias. In the Eurocentric scheme of history the "Tourkokratia" falls through the crack between the medieval and modern periods and must go begging for scholarly attention, at least in this country; and this is true also of its artistic achievements, which stand a bit outside the mainstream of the history of Western art as this is commonly perceived and studied.

How many works of art are we speaking of? Because artifacts in the part of the world under discussion have always had a precarious existence, the amount of artistic activity that took place there in any one period eludes precise measurement. Nevertheless it is clear that the Ottoman conquest did not put a permanent crimp in the artistic productivity of the Christian inhabitants of what had constituted the Byzantine world. Post-Byzantine icons can readily be seen in many museums or purchased in the art market, and any visitor to the Balkans who looks at inscriptions will have noticed that an impressive percentage of the churches, particularly in the rural areas, were built or painted between 1500 and 1800. Often an icon or a church building that passes for Byzantine to the casual viewer or is characterized as such in local oral tradition is, strictly speaking, post-Byzantine.[6]

Figure 2 Čučer (Yugoslavia), Church of St. Nikita. Archangel Gabriel. 1483/1484. (From G. Millet and A. Frolow, *La peinture du moyen âge in Yougoslavie*, fasc. 3 [Paris, 1962], pl. 50.1.)

A reliable estimate of the effects that the Ottoman conquest initially had on the production of monumental art would require a tabulation, to the extent possible, of the projects completed just before and after the imposition of Ottoman rule, region by region, a task made difficult by the accidents of preservation. Apparently the wars that had raged across the Balkans in the early and mid-fourteenth century had not stifled such projects: as if in defiance of the unstable social and political conditions, churches had been built and painted in considerable numbers. The situation does not seem to have changed drastically after the conquest, if we can take as representative the fair number of churches in Greek and Yugoslav Macedonia that preserve paintings from the first three quarters of the fifteenth century.[7] (Whether a slowdown in church painting had occurred in Anatolia over which Ottoman rule had been extended at an earlier date, and where conversion to Islam was more widespread than in the Balkans,[8] is uncer-

Figure 3 Kastoria (Greece), Church of St. Nicholas of the Nun Eupraxia. The Raising of Lazarus. 1485/1486. (From S. Pelekanidis, Καστορία, vol. 1, Βυζαντιναὶ τοιχογραφίαι: Πίνακες [Thessaloniki, 1953], pl. 184a.)

tain, since the post-Byzantine monuments there have not fared well in the political turmoil of modern times and have barely been studied.) Not least among the factors permitting the continuation of church art was the state of near *laissez-faire* in religious matters following the conquest. The Ottomans made no attempt, at least on any official level, to impose Moslem iconoclasm on the Orthodox Church. Nor did they deprive their Christian subjects of their places of worship, although the confiscation of churches for use as mosques, particularly in the cities, was not a rare occurrence.[9]

Whatever the true extent of the artistic activity in the Balkans in the first three quarters of the fifteenth century, we find signs of a modest efflorescence in the final quarter of the century. In Bulgaria, which had been subjugated in 1393 with the capture of Trnovo, wall paintings were executed in a series of monastery churches, beginning with Dragalevtsi (1476; fig. 1), Bobosevo (1488), and Orlitsa (1491). After the Turkish defeat of the Serbs at Kosovo in 1389, the center of Serbian culture had shifted northward to the still-free Morava region, where such churches as those in the monasteries of Manasija (1407–1408) and Kalenic' (1413–1417) were painted; but Macedonia, as already mentioned, was the site of continued activity. In the 1480s, paintings were commissioned there

Figure 4 Voroneţ (Rumania), monastery church. 1488. (Photo courtesy of Gary Vikan.)

for such churches as the Dormition at Treskavac (ca. 1483) and St. Nikita at Cucer, near Skopje (1483/1484: fig. 2). To the same decade belong some wall paintings in present-day Greece, in Thessaly (Meteora, Monastery of the Metamorphosis, 1483) and Macedonia, most notably the town of Kastoria (the Church of St. Nicholas of the Nun Eupraxia, 1485/1486: fig. 3). Several of these late fifteenth-century programs, as well as some others in Macedonia, have been attributed to a single itinerant workshop native to the region.[10]

The style of these and the other early post-Byzantine wall paintings in the Balkans indicates that, despite signs of some borrowing from fourteenth- and fifteenth-century Western sources, the artists were capitalizing on the last installment of the Byzantine inheritance—namely, Palaeologan art. They were using as their models the examples of Orthodox (i.e., Byzantine) art that were fairly recent and well preserved, rather than those of the greatest antiquity—many of which, in any case, had already been lost to view under successive renovations. Hence their work can be characterized as the extension of a living tradition.

Figure 5 Monastery of Philotheou (Mount Athos), trapeza, interior, east wall. Donor portrait with Alexander King of Kakhetia and his son Leo. 1539/1540. (After a photo by the author.)

Because Ottoman art had no associations with Christianity and no monumental figural tradition to compete with the Byzantine, it had very little effect, at this point or later, on post-Byzantine figural imagery, although some influence from Turkish-Persian miniatures has been detected.[11] The post-Byzantine reliance on Palaeologan models is not surprising. They were available in abundance, their expressiveness was unequalled, and their spiritual content was unimpeachable, indeed normative, to the Orthodox eye.

Ambitious artistic undertakings presuppose patronage. After 1453 the Ecumenical Patriarchate, which the sultan Mehmed the Conqueror himself had made directly responsible for the entire *Rum Millet*, exercised power over a far larger territory than in the Palaeologan period.[12] But although it enjoyed many of the prerogatives previously reserved for the Byzantine court and aristocracy and the lesser Balkan rulers of pre-Ottoman times, the patriarchate did not fill the void left by them as major patrons of the arts. In fact it was not, so far as we know, directly responsible for any of the important developments in art after the fall of Constantinople.[13] Other institutions and individuals took the lead.

The Orthodox voevods of the quasi-independent Romanian principalities of Moldavia and Wallachia undertook patronage on a grand scale, in keeping with their long-standing imperial—now necessarily "crypto-imperial"—ambitions.[14] The most spectacular examples of their benefactions in Rumania itself are the great monastery churches of the late fifteenth and the sixteenth centuries, immediately recognizable by their sweeping rooflines and the profusion of images covering their exteriors, as seen at Voroneţ (1488 and ca. 1547; fig. 4), Neamţ (1497), Arbore (ca. 1503), Humor (1530–1535), Moldoviţa (1532–1537), and Suceviţa (ca. 1582–ca. 1600). But the voevods also gave large sums (as well as extensive income-producing properties and precious liturgical objects) to the monasteries of Mount Athos until the mid-seventeenth century, and these donations made possible a variety of building and painting projects on the Holy Mountain and elsewhere.[15]

The rulers of Georgia, in the Caucasus, also came to the fore. On Mount Athos their largesse was not confined to the Georgian monastery of Iviron but extended also to Karakallou and Philotheou. A wall painting in the refectory of Philotheou depicts Leo, ruler of Kakhetia (a small inland kingdom independent from 1468 to 1762), and his son Alexander as the sponsors of the reconstruction of part of the monastery in 1539/1540 (fig. 5).[16]

Obviously those people gave the most money who were able to do so. But donors of lower than royal or princely rank, both clerics and laymen (among whom merchants become more and more conspicuous in the seventeenth and eighteenth centuries), were legion. Just as their assumption of this responsibility put all of these donors in the tradition of the aristocrats of the Palaeologan period who had taken the place of the destitute emperors as patrons,[17] the post-Byzantine images commemorating their contributions are close imitations of the traditional Byzantine donor portraits. These images, showing the donors presenting a model of the church to Christ, the Theotokos, or a saint, in compositions much like that in our figure 6, are found in countless post-Byzantine churches. Along with the customary painted inscriptions of donation, which employ time-honored verbal formulas, they express in conventional Byzantine fashion the benefactors' hope of a merciful last judgment.

As implied by the monuments named thus far, the sites of the major projects were most often the monasteries. Chief among these were the monasteries of the Holy Mountain, Athos. But hundreds of monastic establishments throughout the Balkans commissioned the building, renovation, and decoration of churches and other structures, and this demand was undoubtedly the major factor ensuring the survival of the Byzantine tradition in the visual arts. The monasteries were far more important in this connection than the cities, where in many cases

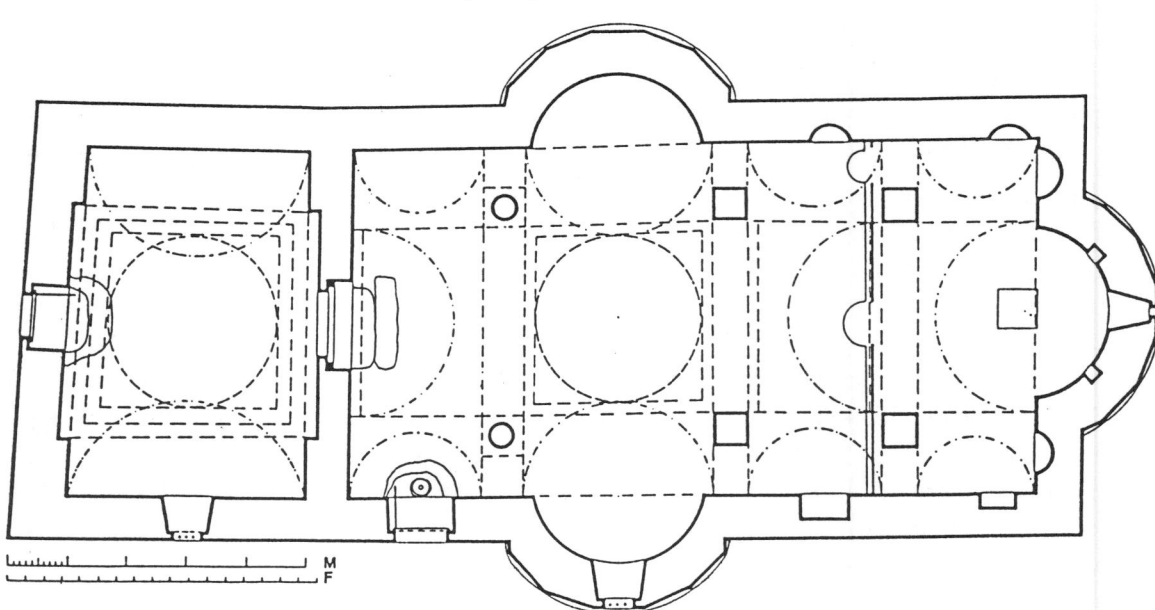

Figure 6 Church of St. Nicholas, Perivoli, Grevena (Greece). 1803. Ground plan. (From M. Polyviou, "The Church of Haghios Nicolaos at Perivoli in the Area of Grevena," *Churches in Greece 1453 - 1850* [Athens, 1979], fig. 3.)

the Orthodox population was severely depleted and where fewer and less imposing projects were undertaken.

Consequently the vast majority of the larger post-Byzantine churches were built primarily for monastic use. On Athos seven of the twenty major houses built new catholica in the sixteenth century, and another six were built or substantially renovated in the period between 1600 and 1812.[18] In Serbia many new monastery churches arose following the establishment of the Patriarchate of Pec' in 1557, which gave the Serbs (who for a century had been under the jurisdiction of the Archbishopric of Ohrid) both a large measure of ecclesiastical autonomy and the incentive to cultivate those elements of the Byzantine tradition that had taken root in Serbia before the Ottoman conquest.[19]

Post-Byzantine builders tended to repeat the forms they could see in the Byzantine structures of their respective vicinities, but certain characteristics of the churches of Athos were imitated because of their association with that great center of Orthodox monasticism. One finds throughout the Balkans, for instance, examples of the adoption by monasteries of the most salient feature of the Athonite plan, the semicircular "choir" added onto the north and south sides of the naos (fig. 6).[20]

Post-Byzantine churches occasionally incorporate Ottoman forms, such as pointed arches and low, windowless domes; but these borrowings are few and infrequent and do not significantly alter the character of the architecture.[21] There are even some cases of a reversal of influence, with Turkish mosques incorporating features found in churches of the same region.²² The Turkish presence made itself felt in other ways. The ringing of church bells was curtailed by law, and consequently old belfries were dismantled and the construction of new ones was prohibited or discouraged.²³ Theoretically a construction permit could be obtained only for badly needed restoration, corroborated as such by Moslem witnesses; and no church could be enlarged in the rebuilding. But there is evidence that these rules were occasionally circumvented.²⁴

Post-Byzantine church architecture was, on the whole, decidedly conservative, clinging to Byzantine solutions or to local traditions in which the Byzantine component was strong, and yielding to Western influences only where exposure to them was experienced for a lengthy period, such as on Venetian-controlled Crete and the Ionian Islands.²⁵ One notable departure from Byzantine church planning of the years before the Ottoman conquest, however, was the reversion, in northern Greece and on the Greek islands, to the construction of three-aisled, timber-roofed basilicas. The reasons for this turn, which began in the eighteenth century and resulted in churches somewhat reminiscent of Early Christian prototypes, are not yet fully understood. It is possible that post-Byzantine masons, faced at this time with the demand for more spacious churches, were not equal to the task of adapting the Byzantine system of vaults and domes to structures larger than those they had grown accustomed to building.²⁶

Figure 7 San Francisco, Greeley Coll., *Life of Joseph: Romance of Joseph and Aseneth*, fol. 22v: Joseph Receiving the Keys to the House of Pentephres. (Luke the Cypriot, ca. 1580.) (Photo courtesy of Gary Vikan.)

Book illumination, an art form in which the Byzantines had excelled, continued to be practiced in the *Rum Millet* for a long time after the invention of movable type. Although not strictly indispensable, illuminated manuscripts had for so long been identified with the Byzantine literary and liturgical traditions, that their continued production was felt to be an important part of the whole enterprise of preservation. Greek and Cyrillic books were printed in Venice by the early sixteenth century and were circulated throughout the Ottoman Empire, but Greeks, Slavs, and Romanians alike continued to write and illustrate manuscripts—most, though not all, intended for church use—well into the eighteenth century (fig. 7).²⁷

Figure 8 Monastery of Stavronikita (Mount Athos), trapeza, interior, apse. SS. John Chrysostom and Gregory the Theologian. Ca. 1546. Attributed to Theophanes the Cretan. (Photo by the author.)

We know the names of many illuminators and calligraphers, and the career of one of them, Luke the Cypriot (d. 1629), has recently been described in some detail.[28] Luke was a Greek bishop, born in Cyprus, who emigrated to Romania, and one of the manuscripts that he wrote, a lectionary inspired by Middle Byzantine examples, was transported at the end of the sixteenth century to the Holy Land after being provided with illustrations by Russian illuminators in Moscow.[29] The production and subsequent history of this manuscript, and the story of Luke's career as a whole, bring up an interesting and important fact that is amply corroborated from other quarters—namely, the international character of post-Byzantine art.

Some post-Byzantine artists were laymen, others monks, others priests or (as we have just seen) even bishops; and except for the icon painters and manuscript illuminators, most of them must have been itinerants, since in the Balkans their main market was the monasteries. Greek artists were very numerous: we know the names of over fifteen hundred from the period between 1454 and 1820.[30] The Slavs were also well represented, needless to say, although I am not aware of any estimate of their number. Above all, one is struck by how permeable were the ethnic boundaries. Even from a cursory review of the documentation, it emerges that Serbian artists were active in what are now Bulgaria and Romania; Bulgarians in Romania and Serbia; and Greeks in Bulgaria, Romania, Serbia, and Albania. Whether these artists, wherever they went, worked primarily for communities and/or patrons of the same ethnic or language background as their own is a pertinent question, but it may be impossible to provide an answer on the basis of the available evidence.

Speros Vryonis has shown that even the Byzantines were not oblivious to the concept of nationality;[31] and one should not pretend to minimize whatever ethnic feelings existed in the Ottoman period. But the remarkable uniformity of expression that characterizes post-Byzantine art, and the ease with which motifs circulated throughout the Orthodox territories, including Russia, suggests that Orthodox Christians everywhere, whatever their language or ethnic derivation, thought of themselves as partaking of a common religious and cultural tradition, one formed in the days of Byzantine sovereignty.[32] The political unity of the Ottoman Empire, the overarching authority of the still-Ecumenical Patriarchate, and the multiethnic character of that great *hestia* of Orthodox monasticism, Mount Athos, must have contributed to the strengthening of this consciousness, which lessened only with the growth of nationalistic sentiment in the eighteenth century.

If Constantinople, as noted earlier, was not the center of artistic patronage, it was also not the scene of the major developments in style. In fact the most important stylistic movement of the Tourkokratia did not germinate in the Ottoman Empire at all, but in Crete. Beginning in 1204, Crete was ruled by the Venetians for as long a time as the Balkans were later ruled by the Turks—over four hundred years; and in the latter half of its Venetian period it produced artists whose relatively well-documented activities in Italy and in the Ottoman Empire proved to be of central importance for post-Byzantine art. After its capture by the Turks in 1669, Crete lost its artistic preeminence, although the term "Cretan" continued to be associated with a specific painting technique, as we find done in the eighteenth-century "Painter's Manual" of Dionysius of Fourna.[33]

Even before 1453, artists from Constantinople had begun to take refuge on Crete, bringing with them the ideas and practices that were current in the metropolis. Cretan painters under Venetian rule, many of whom traveled to or took up residence in Italy, cultivated the Palaeologan legacy and developed a style that soon enjoyed a nearly monopolistic currency throughout the *Rum Millet* and exerted influence as far abroad as Muscovite Russia.[34] This style is typified by limited spatial recession, sharply defined contours, restraint in the expression of emotion and movement, an avoidance of "vulgar" physical types, and a linear articulation of drapery, with strictly controlled highlights. The "Cretan School" was represented by many painters of great talent, who in not a few cases were skilled in the execution of both icons and wall paintings, and who achieved a high reputation among Orthodox and heterodox alike.[35]

There were other styles, including that of the so-called school of Thebes, which is now thought to have originated in Epirus, and which combined older Macedonian traits with Cretan ones.[36] But the Cretan style became the most widespread and influential. Theophanes Strelitzas, or Bathas, a widower monk from Crete, who died in 1559 and is known as "Theophanes the Cretan," gave the style marked visibility and enduring prestige on the Greek mainland. Theophanes painted the monastery church of St. Nicholas Anapafsas at the Meteora in 1527, then the catholicon of the Great Lavra on Mt. Athos in 1535, and finally (with the help of two sons) the catholicon, chapel of St. John Prodromos, and trapeza (refectory) at Stavronikita, on Athos, in 1545–1546 (fig. 8). He may also have executed the trapeza paintings at the Great Lavra, which constitute one of the largest and most impressive refectory programs of the Holy Mountain.[37]

Theophanes was an icon painter as well. In his work one can discern assimilated Western motifs, but on the whole he concentrated on rephrasing and revivifying Palaeologan art, giving it new narrative clarity while observing its solemn character.[38]

It is this preservation of a genuine sense of solemnity, and an avoidance of banal sentimentality, that typifies the best post-Byzantine art, especially the examples that hew to the Byzantine models; and Western clients ordered icons in the Byzantine style from Orthodox painters for probably precisely this reason. The icon of the Virgin of the Passion painted by Andreas Ritzos (fig. 9), an iconographic type in which the angels accompanying the Theotokos and infant Christ hold the instruments of the Crucifixion, is firmly in the Byzantine stylistic tradi-

Figure 9 Virgin of the Passion, by Andreas Ritzos. Second half of the 15th century. Florence, Galleria dell' Accademia. (Photo Alinari.)

tion. Yet Ritzos probably painted it for a Roman Catholic patron, judging by the Latin inscription. Ritzos was also able to work in a Western style, however; and this dualism, or bilingualism, which may strike the modern viewer as equivalent to an abdication of artistic integrity, was practiced by many Cretan artists,[39] including one who, along with Theophanes, is one of the famous names in post-Byzantine art. He is Michael Damaskinos (ca. 1535–1592/1593).

A generation younger than Theophanes, Damaskinos spent eight years in Venice, where he acquired skill at copying paintings by such Italian artists as the Mannerist Parmigianino. He was renowned in the Orthodox world already in his lifetime. We have about a hundred icons by him, but no wall paintings (although we know that he was offered commissions for these as well).[40] Damaskinos could paint an icon as austere and ascetic as the one of St. John the Forerunner now in Zakynthos (fig. 10) or a picture as Western in spirit as the one depicting SS. Sergius, Bacchus, and Justina now on Corfu (fig. 11). What exactly was going on?

Although there is not time here in which to analyze any of the Western-style pictures painted by Cretan artists, I think it can be shown that in most instances they were executed in an old, and from one point of view an outmoded, manner. This is less true of the last-named painting by Damaskinos, perhaps, than of the many works modeled on fourteenth-century Western prototypes, in which Gothic taste predominates, and in which there was a brisk trade in the fifteenth century.[41] This reversion to an older style was of course intentional, and it suggests that the clients wanted pictures that would function as sacred devotional images, for which purpose the paintings done in the current "progressive" Western manner, with its celebration of corporeal reality and ready accommodation of secular themes, were unsatisfactory. Western clients probably ordered Western-style pictures from Cretan painters in the fifteenth century for the same reason that they ordered Byzantine-style icons from them: because the paintings had an aura of venerability and were intentionally out of step with current Western developments. Apparently those who were interested in acquiring a devotional image painted in the old style were willing to accept a painting done in either the Byzantine manner or a pre-Renaissance Western style.[42] And in the later sixteenth century, when some Westerners continued to prize it, the Byzantine style may have functioned for them as a viable alternative to the Western imagery inspired by the Counter-Reformation. It may have been welcomed as a counterstyle, so to speak. We shall return to this point, but first let us look, for purposes of contrast, at another post-Byzantine artist.

As mentioned above, the Cretan style gained acceptance throughout the Ottoman Empire and beyond. It made its appearance in Bulgaria in the late sixteenth century, first in churches painted by Greeks (or at the very least, by artists who inscribed their paintings in Greek), as in St. Stephen at Nesebar (Mesembria), of 1599.[43] Very shortly thereafter it was imported into Serbia, and

Figure 10 St. John the Forerunner. By Michael Damaskinos. Second half of the 16th century. Zakynthos, Museum. (From M. Acheimastou-Potamianou, ed., *From Byzantium to El Greco: Greek Frescoes and Icons* [Athens, 1987], fig. 66.)

Figure 11 SS. Sergius, Bacchus and Justina. By Michael Damaskinos. After 1571. Kerkyra, Museum of the Antivouniotissa. (From M. Acheimastou-Potamianou, ed., *From Byzantium to El Greco: Greek Frescoes and Icons* [Athens, 1987], fig. 65.)

one of the Serbian artists whose work reflects its strong influence was George Mitrofanović.

One of the great Serbian painters of the Ottoman period, Mitrofanović, who was a monk, flourished in the first quarter of the seventeenth century. He worked in the Serbian monastery of Chilandari (on Mount Athos) and in his homeland, where he painted several churches during the tenure of the Serbian Patriarch

Paisii (1614–1642), who was responsible for many cultural initiatives. Dozens of icons are also attributed to Mitrofanović. His output belongs to the period of expanded Serbian artistic activity that followed upon the establishment of the Patriarchate of Pec'. He was about a generation younger than Damaskinos. Yet whereas Damaskinos, an urbanite exposed to Western culture and trained in the copying of Venetian art, admitted Western motifs into his paintings when it suited him or his clients, Mitrofanović, a monastic working for uncompromisingly Orthodox patrons under Ottoman rule, found it possible and preferable to adhere to the Byzantine tradition. This is demonstrated by his paintings in the refectory of Chilandari, dated to 1622, which make no concession to the Western aesthetic values current in his day (fig. 12). The paintings that he executed in various monastery churches in Serbia, and his icons as well, demonstrate the same reliance on Byzantine models.[44]

Such comparisons as this one of Damaskinos and Mitrofanović could be multiplied many times over using other artists, to show that the Westernization of post-Byzantine art did not proceed at a regular pace and was not irreversible except over the long term. As we have known for some time, a later artist could be more Byzantine in his outlook than an earlier one, depending on such circumstances as place and patronage.[45] But eventually the Byzantine tradition lost its potency. It no longer seemed an option, either as a counterstyle or as a source to which artists could return after a flirtation with Western ways. The icon of the Virgin and Child painted in 1700 by Stephanos Tzangarolas can serve us as a symbol of the beginning of the final stage of this process (fig. 13). Earlier in his career Tzangarolas had worked in a more Byzantine manner. In this painting the only feature betraying the artist's background (aside from a certain lack of facility in the formal language he has committed himself to adopting) is the frame of small narrative scenes (in this case, the twenty-four stanzas of the Acathist Hymn) around the central image, which is a Madonna of a type made popular by Raphael.[46]

But notice: the date of the painting by Tzangarolas is 1700. Raphael had already been dead for 180 years. Assessing the relative importance of the Byzantine and the Western stylistic strains in Orthodox paintings of the Ottoman period should not lead us to ignore a telling fact. If a post-Byzantine work of any date and of either stylistic tendency is compared with Western art produced contemporaneously with it, it can usually be seen to be "old-fashioned." Initially Orthodox Christians who preferred the Byzantine style did so probably not only because it was more familiar and more evocative of Orthodox spirituality but also (and the difference between these motives is crucial) because it asserted their religious identity by force of contrast with Western art. But with the passage of time they became less concerned that the style be Byzantine; it was enough, for the purpose of maintaining a distance from prevailing Western fashion, that it be "old."

Figure 12 Monastery of Chilandari (Mount Athos), trapeza, interior, east wall. Above: Scenes from the life of St. Sava of Serbia. Below: SS. Anthony and Sabbas the Great. By George Mitrofanović. 1622. (Photo by the author.)

Figure 13 Virgin and Child, with The Twenty-Four Stanzas of the Acathist Hymn; by Stephanos Tzangarolas. 1700. Offices of the Metropolitanate of Argostolion. (From D. Konomos, ῾Η χριστιανική τέχνη στήν Κεφαλονιά, Athens, 1966], pl. 48.)

This may explain why most Westernized or Westernizing post-Byzantine artists (with the notable exception of Domenikos Theotokopoulos, or El Greco) did not work very creatively by the standards of their adopted aesthetic. The Western tradition in its classical Renaissance and Baroque exemplars became for them, ironically, what the Byzantine tradition had been for their predecessors, a repository of types. No other outcome was likely so long as post-Byzantine art was destined for liturgical use. The last serious resistance to this conversion in taste was put up in the early 1700s by such advocates of a return to Byzantine models as Dionysius of Fourna.[47] But the Western types, in their post-Byzantine renditions, were already on the way to receiving a kind of authentication through familiarity, and in the end they won popular acceptance.

The art of the Orthodox Church during the Tourkokratia was fueled to a great extent by the stored energy of the Byzantine tradition, but its course was deflected by forces that had arisen some generations earlier in Western art. Even under Ottoman rule, complete artistic isolation and self-sufficiency would have been impossible, had anyone thought them desirable. And the direction from which formative influences arrived was the predictable one. Artists living under Ottoman rule had little reason to look eastward, for the Islamic world lived by an alien religion and had quite different pictorial conventions; whereas they could see in the art of the sibling culture of the West, which shared with that of Byzantium an origin in late antiquity and a Christian (if heterodox) orientation, a repertory of subjects considerably like that of their own. At the same time, the underlying differences of outlook between the two religious traditions seriously compromised the attraction in the early phases of the encounter. Both in its acceptance of some Western features and in its compensatory rejection of others, post-Byzantine defined itself largely *in reaction to* the art of the West, something that would have been unthinkable to Westerners and Byzantines alike before, say, the thirteenth century. Until then, Byzantine art had enjoyed a unique reputation in the Christian world, Western no less than Eastern, and had undergone a development determined largely by its own inner dynamics.

The situation of church art in the Ottoman period was not unlike that which obtained in theology. Orthodox theologians living under Ottoman rule entered into a dialectical relationship with Western Christian, not Islamic, thought and thus became occupied—indeed, preoccupied—with problems that had received definition in the West and were by and large most amenable to solution on Western terms.[48] In the realms of both word and image, Orthodox Christianity found it necessary, given the historical exigencies, to assert its identity by dint of contrast, and in doing so it unconsciously shaped itself (some would argue) to the armature of Western preconditions.

The fading of the Byzantine artistic tradition is a highly interesting and instructive subchapter in the history of the global ascendancy of Western European cultural forms. As such it calls for investigation on different levels. The author of a recent study of the process as it manifested itself on the Ionian Islands has linked the acceptance of Western imagery there to the elements in the population that were most exposed to the socioeconomic influence of Venice.⁴⁹ Such connections must be established whenever possible. But they will raise other, contingent problems of interpretation, as we know from the study of the art of other societies and periods. No doubt these problems too will be addressed as historians of post-Byzantine art move beyond the task of recording and classifying the data to that of explaining them as symptomatic of broad cultural trends.

Notes

*This essay is a revised version of a talk delivered on January 13, 1990, at the conference on "Byzantium and the Slavic World."

1. This term may be, and often is, extended to refer to the art of all Orthodox Christians of the Balkans and the Near East after 1453, including those who, like the Cretans prior to 1669, were not living under Ottoman rule.

2. Unfortunately most histories of post-Byzantine art have been written almost exclusively from one or another national viewpoint. For the developments in the Greek world, which are unquestionably of special importance for the entire subject, see Andreas Xyngopoulos, Σχεδίασμα ἱστορίας τῆς θρησκευτικῆς ζωγραφικῆς μετὰ τὴν Ἅλωσι (Athens, 1957). For Serbia, see Svetozar Radojčić, *Majston starog srpskog slikarstva* (Belgrade, 1955), and for Bulgaria, Atanas Boschkov, *La peinture bulaare des au XIXe siècle* (Recklinghausen, 1974), pp. 185ff., and Machiel Kiel, *Art and Society of Bulgaria in the Turkish Period* (Assen and Maastricht, 1985). The last is contentious in tone but replete with information. Manolis Chatzidakis's magisterial Ἕλληνες ζωγράφοι μετὰ τὴν Ἅλωσι volume has appeared (Athens, 1987), containing a large bibliography and excellent historical conspectus, promises to become an indispensable reference work. See also his earlier but still valuable *Contribution `a l'étude de la peinture post-byzantine dans le cinq centième anniversaire de la prise de Constantinople* (Athens, 1953).

3. The Greek writer and artist Fotis Kontoglou (1896–1965), born in Asia Minor, stands out as the chief exponent of this revival. Excerpts from some of his polemical writings are presented in translation in Constantine Cavarnos, *Byzantine Sacred Art* (New York, 1957).

4. The influence of the Nazarene movement on Greek church art, beginning in the first half of the nineteenth century, which sealed this conversion to a Western aesthetic as far as the Greeks were concerned, is the subject of Demetrios Papastamos' *The Effect of the [sic] Nazarene Thought on the [sic] Modern Greek Church Painting* (Athens, 1977) (in Greek and English), which is furnished with excellent illustrations. Serbian church artists also fell under the spell of the Nazarenes: see Sonja Bogdanovic, "L'Orthodoxie dans la peinture religieuse serbe: À propos d'une ancienne polémique," *Zbornik za likovne umetnosti* 9 (1973), 229–42 (French resume: 241–42).

5. The negative or somewhat patronizing aesthetic judgments that underlie much of the scholarly writing on Byzantine art produced by Balkan archaeologists and art historians in the latter nineteenth century are indicative of the unquestioning acceptance by them of the assumptions of Western art criticism. When this criticism, under the influence of post-Impressionist apologetics, took a more favorable view of Byzantine art toward the end of the century, the scholars followed suit—as, in fact, did their colleagues in other parts of the world.

6. In modern Greek popular and even occasionally scholarly usage, the term "Byzantine," is applied loosely to all Orthodox art done in an "old," austere,

non–Western European style. While this usage may seem excessively liberal to some, it may be argued that restricting the term to works executed before, say, 1453 is arbitrary, since the lapsing of the Byzantine artistic tradition was gradual and cannot be charged to a single historical event.

7. Euthymios N. Tsigaridas, "Monumental Painting in Greek Macedonia during the Fifteenth Century," in Myrtali Acheimastou-Potamianou, ed., *Holy Image, Holy Space: Icons and Frescoes from Greece* (Baltimore, and Washington, D.C., 1988), pp. 54-60.

8. Speros Vryonis, Jr., "Religious Changes and Patterns in the Balkans, 14th-16th Centuries," in H. Birnbaum and S. Vryonis, Jr., eds., *Aspects of the Balkans* (The Hague and Paris, 1972), pp. 151-76; reprinted in Speros Vryonis, Jr., *Studies on Byzantium: Seljuks, and Ottomans: Reprinted Studies* (Malibu, CA, 1981).

9. For the practice in Serbia, see Andrej Andrejevic, "On the Transformation of Churches into Mosques," *Zbornik za likovne umetnosti* 12 (1976), 97-117 (English resume: 117). Kiel (pp. 167-84) goes into the subject of the Ottoman confiscation of churches in some detail. While his argument that the practice was not designed to stamp out Christianity is convincing, it does not follow that censure of the practice is unmerited.

10. Chatzidakis, Ἕλληνες ζωγράφοι, pp. 77-79; Svetozar Radojcic, "Une école de peintres de la deuxième moitié du XVe siècle: Contribution à l'histoire de l'art chrétien des Balkans sous la domination des turcs," *Zbornik za likovne umetnosti* 1 (1965), 67-104 (French resume: 103-4). The two authors' attributions differ in regard to several particulars.

11. Bojana Radojković, "Les influences turco-persanes sur les métiers d'art serbes au XVIe et XVII siècles," *Zbornik za likovne umetnosti* 1 (1965), 117-41 (French resume: 140-41).

12. The basic study in English of the Ecumenical Patriarchate during the Ottoman period is still Steven Runciman's *The Great Church in Captivity: A Study of the Patriarchate of Constantinople from the Eve of the Turkish Conquest to the Greek War of Independence* (Cambridge, 1968).

13. The closely related question of whether Constantinople was the scene of any significant post-Byzantine artistic activity has been debated: see D. I. Pallas, "Περὶ τῆς ζωγραφικῆς εἰς τὴν Κωνσταντινούπολιν καὶ τὴν Θεσσαλονίκην μετὰ τὴν Ἅλωσιν," Ἐπετηρὶς Ἑταιρείας Βυζαντινῶν Σπουδῶν, 42 (1976): 101-211, including further references. Chatzidakis has recently reaffirmed his view that "in no large Turkish-heldcity (Constantinople,Thessaloniki, Adrianople, Smyrna, Ioannina, and others) was religious painting cultivated," Ἕλληνες ζωγράφοι, p. 74; my translation).

14. For a discussion of these ambitions and the date of their emergence, and for further references, see Dimitri Nastase, "Imperial Claims in the Romanian Principalities from the Fourteenth to the Seventeenth Centuries: New Contributions," in Lowell Clucas, ed., *The Byzantine Legacy in Eastern Europe* (Boulder, CO, and New York, 1988), pp. 185-224.

15. For a detailed account of these benefactions, see Petre Ş. Năsturel, *Le mont Athos et les roumains: Recherches sur leurs relations du milieu du XIVe siècle à 1654* (=Orientalia Christiana Analecta, no. 227) (Rome, 1986).

16. The inscription accompanying this painting is published in G[abriel] Millet, J. Pargoire, and [Louis] Petit, *Recueil des inscriptions chretiennes de l'Athos*, pt. 1 (Paris, 1904), p. 99.

17. Andre Grabar notes this role of the Palaeologan nobility in his "The Artistic Climate in Byzantium during the Palaeologan Period," in Paul Underwood, ed., *The Kariye Djami*, 4 vols. (New York and Princeton, 1966-75), 4:4-5.

18. I base these numbers on the dates given in Paul Mylonas, "Ἡ ἀρχιτεκτονικὴ τοῦ Ἁγίου Ὄρους" *Νέα Ἑστία*, 54, no. 875 (Christmas 1963), fig. 3 (facing p. 192), where one may also find ground plans of these churches. The plans are reproduced more legibly in Paul M. Mylonas, "Le plan

initial du catholicon de la Grande Lavra au Mont Athos et la genese du type du catholicon athonite," *Cahiers archéologiques* 32 (1984), 108-9 (fig. 18).

19. Marica Šuput, *L'Architecture serbe pendant la domination ottomane 1459-1690* (Belgrade, 1984), pp. 21-32, 106-7.

20. Slobodan Ćurčić, "Byzantine Legacy in Ecclesiastical Architecture of the Balkans after 1453," in Clucas, p. 64, and Charalambos Bouras's forthcoming "The Byzantine Tradition in the Church Architecture of the Balkans in the Sixteenth and Seventeenth Centuries," in John J. Yiannias, ed., *The Byzantine Tradition after the Fall of Constantinople* (Charlottesville, VA and London, 1991 or 1992). For the origin of this plan, see Paul M. Mylonas, "Le plan initial," 89–112.

21. Šuput (p. 112) has written that "l'influence de l'architecture islamique sur la construction monumentale serbe à l'epoque de la domination turque était presque imperceptible." Ćurčić, writing about post-Byzantine church architecture in general (pp. 65–67), gives a less categorically negative assessment. Cf. Bouras, as cited above, n. 20.

22. Andrejević, p. 117, with reference to some mosques in Bosnia and Herzegovina. Of course, the influence of Byzantine church architecture on earlier Turkish and Islamic mosque architecture is another subject.

23. Ćurčić (pp. 68-72) invalidates the traditional view of scholars that Byzantine churches had no belfries prior to the thirteenth century.

24. On the subject of Ottoman regulations about churchbuilding and their effectiveness, see Kiel, chap. 6, esp. pp. 184-91.

25. Bouras, as cited in n. 20 above. For Crete, see Manolis Chatzidakis, "Essai sur l'école dite 'Italogrecque' précédé d'une note sur les rapports de l'art vénitien avec l'art cretois jusqu'à 1500," in Agostino Pertusi, ed., *Venezia e il Levante fino al secolo XV*, vol. 2 (Florence, 1974), pp. 70-71, with references.

26. Charalambos Bouras, "The Architectural Type of the Basilica during the Turkish Period, and the Patriarch Kallinikos," *Churches in Greece 1453-1850* (Athens, 1979–), 1:159-68 (English resume: 168).

27. Of the 178 illuminated manuscripts on Mount Athos published in Stylianos M. Pelekanides et al., Οἱ θησαυροὶ τοῦ Ἁγίου Ὄρους: Εἰκονογραφημένα χειρόγραφα, 3 vols. (Athens, 1973–1979), one third—about sixty-one—contain illustrations dating from the fifteenth century and later. The seventeenth century alone accounts for thirty.

28. Gary Vikan, "Byzance après Byzance: Luke the Cypriot, Metropolitan of Hungro-Wallachia," in Clucas, pp. 165-84; idem, "Walters Lectionary W535 (A.D. 1594) and the Revival of Deluxe Greek Manuscript Production after the Fall of Constantinople," in Yiannias, as cited above, n. 20.

29. Vikan, "Walters Lectionary."

30. Chatzidakis, Ἕλληνες ζωγράφοι, v 1:15. Almost half of the total number were active in the years 1700-1820.

31. "Byzantine and Turkish Societies and Their Sources of Manpower," in V. J. Parry and M. E. Yapp, eds., *War Technology and Society in the Middle East* (London, 1975), pp. 132ff.; reprinted in Vryonis, *Studies*.32. A revealing case in point, among the many that one could cite, is that of Božidar Vuković, a publisher in Venice, who regularly chose as models for the illustrations in his Serbian books icons in the Greek church of Venice, S. Giorgio dei Greci (of which he was for a time the "governor") and other Cretan icons: see Sreten Petković, "The Origin of the Illustrations in Serbian Books Printed in Venice," *Zbornik za likovne umetnosti* 12 (1976), 119-35 (English resume: 135).

33. A. Papadopoulos-Kerameus, ed., Διονυσίου τοῦ ἐκ Φουρνᾶ Ἑρμηνεία τῆς ζωγραφικῆς τέχνης (St. Petersburg, 1909), p. 34; for an English translation, see *The 'Painter's Manual' of Dionysius of Fourna*, trans. Paul Hetherington (London 1974), p. 12.

34. Chatzidakis, Ἕλληνες ζωγράφοι,, p. 131.

35. For an account of the careers of some of these artists, see Thalia Gouma-Peterson, "The Icon as Cultural Presence after 1453," in Gary Vikan, ed., *Icon: Four Essays*

(Washington, D.C., and Baltimore, 1988), pp. 48-64, to be reprinted in Yiannias (as cited in n. 20 above).

36. Chatzidakis, "Ελληνες ζωγράφοι, pp. 86–87; Myrtali Acheimastou-Potamianou, Ἡ Μονὴ τῶν Φιλανθρωπηνῶν καὶ ἡ πρώτη φάση τῆς μεταβυζαντινῆς ζωγραφικῆς (Athens, 1983) (with an English resume).

37. Manolis Chatzidakis, "Recherches sur le peintre Théophane le Crétois," *Dumbarton Oaks Papers* (1969-70), 311-52; John J. Yiannias, "The Refectory Paintings of Mount Athos: An Interpretation," in Yiannias, as cited above, n. 20.

38. Chatzidakis, "Recherches, " 330ff .

39. For a fuller discussion of this phenomenon, see Chatzidakis, "Essai, " pp. 108-16, who aptly refers to it as a "double capacite." Occasionally we also find both styles used in one and the same painting, a practice that Gouma-Peterson (p . 62) has likened to the Byzantine use of different stylistic "modes " in the same work .

40. Chatzidakis, "Ελληνες ζωγράφοι, pp. 90-91, 241-54 .

41. For example, the type of Pieta exemplified by a painting in the Benaki Museum, Athens (no. 3050): *Holy Image, Holy Space*, no. 56 *(pp.* 214-15). Maria Constantoudaki-Kitromilides, "Taste and the Market in Cretan Icons in the Fifteenth and Sixteenth Centuries," ibid., p. 52.

42. This generalization would seem to follow from the fact that we have documented examples of Western merchants ordering icons in both styles from the same Cretan workshop for the Western market, as noted in Constantoudaki-Kitromilides, p. 52.

43. Kiel, pp. 344-46.

44. See the well-illustrated monograph by Zdravko Kajmaković, *Georaije Mitrofanović* (Sarajevo, 1977). Mitrofanović was also influenced by Russian models, as Kajmaković points out; but this fact is only further indication of his adherence to the Byzantine tradition.

45. A reversal toward a more conservative style, for example, marked the work of many Cretan painters in the early seventeenth century, as Chatzidakis has observed ("Ελληνες ζωγράφοι) p. 92) .

46. The so-called Madonna della Seggiola, in Florence, of ca. 1514. See Dinos Konomos, Ἡ χριστιανικὴ τέχνη στὴν Κεφαλονιά (Athens, 1966), p. 18. Tzangarolas was an ordained monk of Cretan origin. For his career as an icon-painter, see Xyngopoulos, pp. 319-23.

47. Xyngopoulos, pp. 296-300;Chatzidakis, "Ελληνες ζωγράφοι pp. 105-7.

48. A considerable bibliography has grown up around this subject. I refer the reader only to the historical remarks in Christos Yannaras, "Theology in Present-Day Greece," *St. Vladimir's Theological Quarterly* 16 (1972), 195–214, and to Timothy Ware's less negative *Eustratios Argenti: A Study of the Greek Church under Turkish Rule* (Oxford, 1964), esp. chap. 1.

49. Demetrios D. Triantaphyllopulos, *Die nachbyzantinische Wandmalerei auf Kerkyra und den anderen Ionischen Inseln: Untersuchungen zur Konfrontation zwischen ostkirchlicher und abendlandischer Kunst (15.-18. Jahrhundert)*, 2 vols. (Munich, 1985); review by John J. Yiannias in *Speculum* 63 (1988), 726-29.

7
Russian Pre-Revolutionary Studies on Eleventh-Century Byzantium

Alexander Kazhdan
Dumbarton Oaks

Modern Byzantine studies were created in the last quarter of the nineteenth century, and they were created by giants: Karl Krumbacher, John Bagnel Bury, and Charles Diehl stood at the cradle of our discipline. Russian scholarship joined this trend, and here it was Basil (Vasilij Grigor'evič) Vasil'evskij (1838–1899) who was the founder of Byzantine studies. He published new sources, among which was one of the most interesting texts of the eleventh century, the *Admonitions* of Kekaumenos, and investigated various spheres of Byzantine history and culture; he studied, among other things, Byzantine relations with the Steppe in the eleventh century and the history of the Russian contingent on Byzantine service at the same time. Vasil'evskij's fame is connected primarily with his masterful analysis of texts: he moved gradually from one issue to another, amassing enormous quantities of data to comment on the issue in question—data from Greek, Latin, Slavic and Oriental sources, many of which were, in his day, unknown and unused by his contemporaries.[1] He also elaborated a general concept of Byzantine history presented in a concise form in the introductory chapter to his *Materials for internal history of the Byzantine State* that was published in 1879 and for many decades determined scholarly opinions of Byzantium.[2]

"The Byzantine state," begins Vasil'evskij, "inherited from the Roman empire two main features of social structure: the predominance of great landownership and colonate or serfdom." By the eighth century a radical upheaval occurred. Its causes, says Vasil'evskij the scholar, are not yet clarified, but right away Vasil'evskij the politician interlopes and adds: "By all the signs it was connected with the mass settlement of the Slavs on the Greco-Roman territory."[3] Later on, the Slavic foundation of the Byzantine countryside of the eighth through tenth centuries debouches without unnecessary reservations. The Slavs, he continues, were on the Byzantine land in no way numerically inferior to the Germanic tribes in the West, and the Iconoclastic movement, in its turn, contributed to the reduction of monastic properties and accordingly to the revival of the free peasantry. "At any rate, from the eighth century on, numerous peasant communities existed in Byzantium which possessed land on the principle of collective ownership."[4] But the great owners, weakened as they were, did not disappear into thin air: the texts of the tenth century know them as *dynatoi*, the powerful. Vasil'evskij describes them as consisting of two categories: the "local provincial aristocracy" claiming an ancient and noble origin, and the court and administration bureaucracy whose ranks were always being replenished by all kinds of arrivistes.[5] "This estate of the powerful, almost completely deprived of political significance, having lost all traditions of municipal self-government, feeble and slavish with regard to the central authority, comes up in the tenth century as a dangerous adversary of village communities, of the small peasant landownership."[6]

To such a point, continues Vasil'evskij, Byzantine development was parallel to that in the West, the chronological discrepancy being explained to the effect that the Slavic settlement in the East took place two centuries later than the Germanic occupation of western provinces. But here the similarity ends: the Byzantine state, owing to the uninterrupted Roman imperial tradition, was stronger than the western principalities. "The Byzantine emperors, armed with ancient state traditions, conceived in a clearer and more precise way of their duties to all their subjects and plainly announced that the monarch's authority was the common weal for everybody and that its first and foremost obligation was to defend the poor and the weak."[7] From these premises, Vasil'evskij investigated the agrarian legislation of the tenth century as a system intended to protect the peasantry from the "feudal tendencies" that in an incipient form, emerged among the Greek powerful.[8]

Here Vasil'evskij stops, and, I would say, stops in confusion. It was an agreeable task to eulogize the Macedonian dynasty of the tenth century for its protection of the "weak brethren"—anyhow, the emperors such as Nicephorus II Phokas, John I Tzimiskes, and Basil II could brag of their political achievements, and we may hypothesize that their agrarian legislation accounted for their military victories. But what happened afterward, in the eleventh century?

In a short chapter that concluded his article on the legislation of the Iconoclasts (published in 1878) Vasil'evskij gathered the data that indicated that after the tenth century, a peasant dependency reappeared that was similar to the pre-Justinianic patrocinium; the tithe was introduced, and the paroikoi emerged who paid heavy rent in kind and services.[9] Later, in the second part of his *Materials*, Vasil'evskij moved to the eleventh century: he meticulously investigated such texts as the *Peira* and the correspondence of Theophylaktos of Ochrid, and discovered that the principles of the Macedonian protection of the weak remained alive[10]—and nevertheless the empire was losing its political superiority and undergoing a political and military crisis.

The problem arose, in its full complexity, in the work of Nicholas (Nikolaj Afanas'-evič) Skabalanovič (1848–1918) who published in 1884 a book on eleventh-century Byzantium.[11] Professor of St. Petersburg Spiritual Academy and from 1886–1892 the editor in chief of the *Cerkovnyj vestnik* (Ecclesiastical Herald), he was much of a publicist while as Byzantinist he remained a *homo unius libri*. His book is a general survey of Byzantine history between the death of Basil II and Alexios I's ascent to the throne (1205–1281). It was based on an extensive array of sources, including two of the main chronicles for the eleventh century, by Psellos and Attaleiates, which were published shortly before his monograph, and its accurate expose of political events is valid even in our day. The political narrative is followed by characterization of the government, society, finances, army judicial court, and church, and of course these sections would now need substantial alterations due to numerous texts that became available after 1884; but for his time, Skabalanovič's book was a rare example of a minute analysis of Byzantine domestic structure, and I do not think we have similar surveys for other periods.

In his perception of Byzantine development Skabalanovič closely followed Vasil'evskij:[12] he emphasizes both the Roman legacy of three kinds *(municipium,* colonate, and the system of *precarium/beneficium)* and the Slavic settlement that played a part similar to that of the Germanic tribes in the West; that the central administration aquiesced with industrial corporations, whereas the provincial land-owning aristocracy, weakened by the Slavic invasion and restricted by the eighth century legislation, began to recover in the ninth century but met with strong resistance from the tenth-century emperors who effectively protected the small ownership. "The competition reached the point when the weak, using the unswerving support of the authorities, must get victory over the *dynatoi.*"[13] The *Peira,* says Skabalanovič, developing the idea of his predecessor, defended the interests of the peasantry against the powerful, and Psellos advised a *praktor* to back up the rural population.

And nevertheless the powerful did not lose their case despite the position of the supreme authorities and jurisprudence; Skabalanovič lists several phenomena that turned out advantageously for the *dynatoi:* first, some eleventh-century rulers (Romanos III, Constantine IX, Nicephorus III), by their origin and family links, were sympathetic to the landowning aristocracy and some—although against their own will—took sides with the powerful. Secondly, administrators and judges were often supportive to the *dynatoi* and overlooked their misdemeanors. Thirdly, the powerful knew how to use the country's "physical calamities"—earthquakes, droughts, flooding; Skabalanovič draws a comprehensive picture of these disasters from 1026 to 1063.[14] Skabalanovič ascribes particular importance in the final victory of the powerful over the peasants and the village communities to the system of *pronoia.* "The origin and the character of the *pronoia,*" so Skabalanovič, "may be understood only in connection with the ancient system of *precarium/beneficium.*"[15] In the West, Roman *precarium/beneficium* was assumed by the Germanic peoples and became one of the cornerstones of feudalism—in the East, ruminates Skabalanovič, it had to continue through the seventh to ninth centuries, even though there is no mention of such an institution in available sources; he thinks that without such an assumption we would be unable to comprehend its existence in the tenth century.

In the tenth century the Byzantine beneficiary system emerges "with clarity"[16]— in the form of the so-called *charistikion*, that is, the distribution of monasteries as grants conferred on clerics and lay persons. Skabalanovič boldly hypothesizes that *charistikion* must be linked to the secularization of monastic lands under the Iconoclasts of the eighth century. He goes even further and assumes that side by side with the distribution of monasteries among *charistikarioi,* in Byzantium a similar system of bestowal of private and state lands must have existed. By the eleventh century, a technical term for such a bestowal was established—*pronoia*. Various types of estate were conferred as *pronoia*—state lands, castles, arable fields, pastures, and so on. The evidence, he confesses, belongs to the next centuries. "Since we have no evidence concerning *pronoia* of this type (i.e. encompassing village communities and requiring the pronoiar's military service) we can come up with a tentative conclusion taking into consideration those elements of which the [later—A.K.] particularities of the pronoial estate have developed.[17] The system of *pronoia*, and this is Skabalanovič's final conclusion, contained a major threat for the peasant since it destroyed the village community and deteriorated the situation of the peasantry—but all this belonged to the future. "Despite all the disavantages for the peasantry, including pronoia, the basic principles which determined conditions of the peasantry and its legal status, have not changed in the eleventh century."[18] The riddle that startled and silenced Vasil'evskij remained unsolved: the basic principles of agrarian relations continued from the previous century; the supreme authorities cared about the peasantry, but nevertheless after the defeat at Mantzikert in 1071 the country was on the verge of catastrophe. Skabalanovič vividly describes the wrongdoings of numerous individuals on all rungs of the social ladder—but do individual transgressions suffice to suppress a healthy economic and social system inherited from the Romans and supported by Slavic communal traditions? The culprit had to be found.

It was Theodore (Fedor Ivanovič) Uspenskij (1845–1928) who suggested a clear-cut answer to the riddle of the Byzantine eleventh century. Uspenskij's heritage is enormous and varied[19]—from publications of Greek sources to his three-volume *History of the Byzantine Empire*, a pretentious book without any scholarly value. His works are very unequal in quality: the monograph on Niketas

Choniates is original and provocative and retains it significance now, more than a century after it had been issued. His doctoral dissertation, on the formation of the Second Bulgarian empire, met with severe criticism by Vasil'evskij, who crushed it into pieces in a review more than a hundred pages long. The articles on the agrarian history of Byzantium are probably the worst part of his oeuvre, second only to his history of the Byzantine empire—but by the strange irony of fate, these articles probably had the most significant impact on the further development of the scholarly perception of the Byzantine countryside and of the Byzantine eleventh century.

Like Vasil'evskij, Fedor Uspenskij accepted the theory of the Slavic settlement in Byzantium and accepted it with a greater consistency: even the Farmer's Law, from his viewpoint, was a document of Slavic customary law.[20] Like Vasil'evskij, he assumed that the Iconoclastic emperors promulgated crucial reform transforming the Slavic village community into the cornerstore of their taxation and army. Like Vasil'evskij, finally, he asserted that the emperors of the tenth century protected the village community. But unlike Vasil'evskij, Fedor Uspenskij put the emphasis not on the destruction of the village community but on its survival after the tenth century. In an article published in 1883 Uspenskij insisted that "the Slavic community and small free landownership survived the fourteenth century. The political role of the Slavic element in Byzantium was crucial in all times, especially during the momentous periods of its history."[21]

So far so good, but the riddle of the eleventh century was confused by the idea of the perennial Slavic community on Byzantine soil. If the healthy organization created by the Iconoclasts and protected by the Macedonians was still effective in the eleventh century and after, why did the empire fall? And so Uspenskij gradually began to demolish the building he had so energetically constructed.

In his article on peasant landownership (1883) he stressed that the system of *pronoia* was menacing the village community.[22] He developed this idea in another article published the same year and devoted to the problem of *pronoia*.[23] Starting with the Venetian documents of the fifteenth century for Dalamatia and moving then to the Greek acts of the proceeding period, Uspenskij suggested a picture of transformation of Byzantine *pronoia* from the conditional fief granted for military service and limited in time into *gonikon*, the seigniory that was to be transmitted to the heirs. Some years before that, Vasil'evskij quite cautiously admitted that the grants of monastic land given to the Byzantine knights may be considered as "actual embryo of feudal order."[24] By now with the theory of *pronia*-fief burgeoning on former peasant lands and heading toward inherited seigniory, the foundation was set for the full-fledged concept of Byzantine feudalism.

There was a contradiction in Fedor Uspenskij's concept of the development of *pronoia*. He considered Venetian documents "as the most signal and the most reliable material for the study of the historical significance of *pronoia*."[25] Let us leave alone the fact that they were Venetian documents regulating relations in the area long ago lost by the Byzantine authority. What matters much more is their chronological attribution—*pronoia* as fief appears in the fifteenth century; when Uspenskij turned to Byzantine acts of the previous century he discovered *pronoia* as hereditary ownership. If we stick to the documents as they were read by Uspenskij we should come to a strange conclusion: Byzantine *pronoia* evolved from hereditary ownership to conditioned fief.

This logical gap was, however, neglected by Uspenskij and his successor, and *pronoia* became for several decades the most striking example of a "feudal" or "westernized" institution of Byzantine society.

Two scholars contributed much to the development of the idea of Byzantine feudalism, although they were men of different scholarly temperaments and of dissimilar modes of investigation—Constantine Uspenskij and Peter Jakovenko. Peter Aleksandrovič Jakovenko (1870-1920), professor at Tartu University, produced two monographs relevant for our topic; the later of them, published in 1917, could have laid the foundation for modern Byzantine diplomatics had it not remained unnoticed, being written in Russian and published during a period of great turmoil. In this book Jakovenko elaborated principles for the categorization of Byzantine imperial acts of the eleventh century;[26] ten years later, Franz Dölger, evidently without knowledge of Jakovenko's book, came to similar conclusions. In the earlier monograph (1908), Jakovenko investigated the Byzantine institution of *exkousseia*. In the same way as *pronoia* was equated with western fief, *exkousseia* acquired, in Jakovenko's book, the features of western immunity. "In its core," says Jakovenko, "*exkousseia* amounts to medieval immunity."[27] The system of exemptions existed in the Roman world, but the decline of the municipal order led to the disappearance of immunity privileges even though the legal texts kept repeating obsolete statements. "The new institution grew up side by side with old immunity having inherited from it nothing but the name";[28] *exkousseia* developed in connection with the growing class of wealthy landowners and the dependency of the rural populaton, with the autonomy of monasteries and the prohibition that prevented the fiscal functionaries from entering privileged estates. The available texts describe *exkousseia* as an exemption from fiscal levies, but Jakovenko assumes that in the later centuries the privileged landowners could acquire judicial immunity as well.

Jakovenko was a very cautious scholar and his main interest lay in the minute analysis of formulas of Byzantine documents. He was satisfied with stating the fact that these formulas in Byzantine acts were similar to the formulas of western decrees. He was reluctant to define the role of *exkousseia* in the Byzantine social structure. "It is difficult to decide," he says in the concluding passage of the book, "whether *exkousseia* influenced the political and social order of Byzantium to the same extent that is acknowledged for immunity in history of Western Europe." Constantine Uspenskij had fewer scruples when he constructed his concept of Byzantine immunity.

Konstantin Nikolaevič Uspenskij (1874–1917), a student of Paul Vinorgradov, taught at the Superior Women's College in Moscow, and it was on the basis of his lectures there that his textbook of Byzantine history was produced.[29] The book comprises the first centuries of Byzantium with Iconoclasm having the place of honor (approximately, the last third of the book). Byzantine Iconoclasm, according to Constantine Uspenskij, was closely linked to the growth of feudalism in Byzantium. Feudalism, he asserts, was already entrenched in Byzantium by the seventh century and assumed primarily the form of "monasteries-princedoms." Monasteries played a double role: on the one hand, "they were the most powerful and viable organisms within feudalized society and state, the refuges for those who were oppressed and who lost expectations, for the weak elements"; on the other hand, they attracted "the strong elements of society which coveted for separation and carried into effect feudalization and decomposition of the great state into small political worlds."[30]

The main argument used by Constantine Uspenskij to prove his view was the institution studies by Jakovenko—Byzantine *exkousseia*=immunity. Constantine Uspenskij devoted to *exkousseia* a chapter in his textbook and an article published only in 1923, after the author's death.

In order to prove his thesis Constantine Uspenskij had to hurdle an evident difficulty: the acts conferring *exkousseia* are known only from the eleventh century onward, whereas Uspenskij needed them to be placed in the seventh century, before Iconoclasm, which he interpreted as the reaction of the state against the growth of feudal princedoms-monasteries. The solution he found was to see in the eleventh-century institution the peak of a long development. "We get an impression," he contemplates, "from this group of the eleventh-century chrysobulls granting *exkousseia* that we are dealing with an established, well settled institution, and not with the first experiments with the incipient *exkousseia*."[31] On the other hand, Uspenskij observes that immunity in twelfth-century grants is vaguer and less explicit, and it seems that the range of exemptions diminished and was vitiated. Then Uspenskij takes the next step: since the emperors of the second half of the eleventh and twelfth centuries (the period that bequeathed to us chrysobulls of exemption) were overtly antimonastic, we cannot expect them to introduce the system of *exkousseia*—it must precede their reigns. Uspenskij looked for the roots of monastic privileges in the legislation of the late Roman Empire and came to the following conclusion: "The period of the utter flourishing of monasticism in Byzantium was not the eleventh and twelfth centuries from which the available chrysobulls of exemption originate but the sixth and seventh centuries; then, in the conditions of the political disorder, social chaos, economic impoverishment, and cultural decay, monasteries acquired exceptional significance."[32]

Jakovenko and Constantine Uspenskij made Byzantine feudalism legitimate, and after them *pronoia* and *exkousseia* were conceived of as major feudal institutions of Byzantine society. In 1923, referring to Constantine Uspenskij's book, Alexander Vasiliev wrote, "The question about Byzantine feudalism is new and poorly investigated. But at any rate, now nobody except for a few extreme diehards, is confused by the possibility to speak of Byzantine feudalism and feudalizing processes, whereas not long ago the term 'Byzantine feudalism' would have seemed a paradox or a heresy."[33] Vasiliev regarded as feudal such institutions as *charistikion, pronoia* and *exkousseia*-immunity, as well as *prostasia*-patronage, and he accepted Constantine Uspenskij's theory concerning monasteries-princedoms. He also followed Vasil'evskij to the extent that the Macedonian dynasty took measures in defense of small landowners threatened by the growth of large estates. Vasiliev did not know what happened in "the troubled period of the eleventh century," but Alexios I emerges as "a representative of large landownership," and by the epoch of the Crusades "feudalizing processes in Byzantium had assumed so definite a shape that the westerners found nothing new to them in the general conditions of the Empire."[34]

Thus, in the works of Jakovenko, Constantine Uspenskij, and Vasiliev, the theory of Byzantine feudalism "assumed a definite shape." The general consensus was that from the late Roman Empire on, great landownership and some feudal institutions existed side by side with small landownership; the Iconoclastic emperors tried to destroy monasteries-princedoms and the Macedonian dynasty protected the little brethren from the assaults of the powerful; by the twelfth century, the feudal order succeeded, and Byzantine society became, at least in Vasiliev's perception, indistinguishably similar to that in the West. What impact did this development have on the fate of the Byzantine Empire?

Now we return to Feodor Uspenskij. For a long while he abstained from agrarian themes, the last article in this field being "Byzantine Agrimensors"—a paper read in 1884 and published in 1835;[35] thereafter he only accidentally touched on this problem, as in 1896 while publishing an act from the archive of the monastery of the Virgin the Merciful and in 1900, in his analysis of the decisions of the eleventh- and twelfth-century Constantinipolitan local councils on *charistikion*.[36] But these were publications of documents, without attempts to give any sweeping generalization. Uspenskij's interests seem to have shifted toward administrative history (the eparch, the table of ranks, the army), to history of culture (education, the trial of John Italos), to art history and archaeology. But he kept thinking over topics and started reconsidering his earlier views. In his short article for the Russian encyclopedia Brockhaus and Efron (vol. 24 [1898], pp. 199-201) the old concept appears concisely formulated: the Slavic village community was a predominant institution of the countryside that survived through the fourteenth century; the Macedonian dynasty protected the peasantry against the powerful; the system of *pronoia* contributed much to the dissolution of the community. But a quarter of a century later, writing on the legacy of the late Boris Pančenko (1872-1920),[37] Uspenskij was less certain about these points: without any criticism Uspenskij stated that Pančenko had defended the idea that communal landownership had not existed in Byzantium; Pančenko, he continued, refuted the concept of Zachariae von Lingenthal and Vasil'evskij—he did not mention that the same perception of the village community in Byzantium had been shared by Uspenskij himself, and he noted quite mildy that Pančenko's monograph did not offer a final solution of the problem.[38] I do not say that Uspenskij shrugged under Pančenko's influence, but he definitely carried on thinking about the village community and its linkage with the fate of Byzantium. And he came up with a coherent theory developed in both his *History of the Byzantine Empire* and in several articles produced at his advanced age.

As in his earlier articles, Uspenskij sought a solution to the problem of Byzantine history primarily in national interconnections. The difference, however, consisted in the shift of emphasis from the advantageous merge of Greek and Slavic elements to the damaging western influence on Byzantium. The successors of Constantine and Justinian, asserts Fedor Uspenskij, could not fulfill the major task—to transform the Roman empire into the Hellenic state, bound by the unity of faith and imperial power. If previously the Macedonian dynasty was praised for its protection of the Slavic village community that allegedly existed through the very end of Byzantium, now this praise is jettisoned: "This task was beyond the power of the Hellenic nation itself that in the Middle Ages was far from capable to appropriate close neighbors and extend Hellenic ideas beyond the limits of the direct authority of the Greek element."[39] The major blow was struck by the Latins, or the westerners, and their feudal order that thoroughly contradicted the principles of "the Orthodox monarchy." Uspenskij states: "One of the most momentous impacts of western civilizations on the Byzantine state was the transfer of the feudal system to the Eastern empire."[40] He considers *pronoia* and *charistikion* as feudal institutions and dates their introduction to the eleventh century, while under the Komnenoi the traditional Byzantine structures, substantially weakened, gave way to western-oriented feudalism. Uspenskij spared no paint to picture the corruption that overwhelmed the empire under the unhealthy western influence that brought Byzantium to its fall. "In order to secure the continuity of its political existence," wrote Uspenskij, "and to struggle successfully against the western and oriental enemies the empire must have to look for the means not in the assumption of feudalism and not in succumbing to the Latins but in domestic reforms and in according the interests of the ruling church and Hellenic nation with rejected dogmas and with peoples settled within the empire"[41] (he probably meant the Slavs, without specifying them). The attempt to carry out these reforms was exercised by Andronikos I Komnenos, the representative of the masses and the leader of the "national" reaction against foreign domination.[42] Later Uspenskij changed to some extent his attitude toward the last Komnenos: Andronikos, he said, claimed to be the peasant king; he was or at least seemed to be the king of the people, of the peasantry; Uspenskij expressed certain doubts concerning Andronikos's sincerity and treated him as a real villain on the royal throne.[43] But all these reservations refer to Andronikos's personality and were not supposed to cast any shadow on the program of radical reforms that "the national party" brought forth in the interest of the people.

We may summarize the Russian concept of Byzantine history in general and of the eleventh century in particular: while the Macedonian dynasty had a serious concern about the Slavic village community that formed the backbone of the Orthodox empire, in the eleventh century feudal institutions penetrated into Byzantium; even though the state, for a while, supported traditional policy, the westernized or Latinized empire neglected its weaker brethren and slid toward its ruin and ignoble end.

There was a difficulty in the concept of the horrible eleventh century that has never been clearly formulated by Russian Byzantinists but somehow was felt by some of them. This difficulty reveals itself in a strange contradiction: the beginning of the end in Byzantium coincided with an astonishing upsurge of intellectual life in the empire. Three works were especially signal for the study of Byzantine culture in the eleventh century: Vasil'evskij, in collaboration with Viktor Karlovic Ernstedt (1854–1902), published the *Admonitions* of Kekaumenos in 1896;[44] the next year, Fedor Uspenskij brought to light the documents on the trial of John Italos, who had been accused of heresy;[45] and finally, Paul (Paul Vladimirovič) Bezobrazov (1859–1918) produced in 1890 a monograph on Michael Psellos.[46] When Vasil'evskij characterized the *Admonitions* he mentioned the author's "purely Byzantine views on life and morale, on the family, society and state,"[47] but his attention was riveted primarily on Kekaumenos's unique evidence about wars and rebellions; Skabalanovič, in his monograph published three years after this article by Vasil'evskij, has not yet been able to use Kekaumenos's information.

Bezobrazov produced a good and comprehensive monograph on Psellos's life and activity as administrator and educator. Bezobrazov's judgement of Psellos is uncompromisingly negative. Psellos, according to Bezobrazov, was a typical Byzantine, who made a successful career; he achieved high rank by flattering and crawling before the bigwigs, by solicitation and by offering kickbacks; he was well read but he changed his opinions and sacrificed the truth in order to please the emperor. He had no principles, no ideals, he was capable of praising and berating the same thing, of whitewashing the crime and blackening the virtue, a genuine libertine, "the base child of the base time."[48] But what is the base time for Bezobrazov? Is the villainous functionary an offspring of the evil eleventh century made perverse by western and feudal poison, or is he a representative of the centralized empire that lately took care of its small landowners? The question had not been asked by Bezobrazov.

Fedor Uspenskij had much less data for his study of John Italos than Bezobrazov for his biography of Michael Psellos, and he did not reveal his like or dislike for the man. Moreover, his approach is far from coherent: while publishing the minutes of the trial of Italos he stressed, in the preamble, the existence of an unbroken system of higher education in Byzantium, dwelling at length on Constantine IX's *Novel on the Law School* published in the mid-eleventh century;[49] in his *Essays on History of Byzantine Education* issued in 1891 he devoted to Italos a long chapter linking his philosophical concepts to the western scholasticism of the eleventh through the thirteenth centuries. Was this linkage due to Italo's impact on inchoate scholasticism or may we speak of the parallel development of ideas in both parts of the Christian world of the time? Uspenskij raises the question but does not dare to offer a decisive answer. And he obviously did not consider the possibility that the similarity in ideological development and the similarity in social development of Byzantium and the West of the eleventh century have anything in common. The striking parallelism escaped his attention or seemed to him insubstantial.

Thus there were several interesting monographs and articles on Byzantine intellectual development in the eleventh century, but unlike social and economic history no general concept was developed, nor were the main problems formulated. Even though the same Byzantinists who studied the relations between the powerful and the village community (Bezobrazov also investigated sources for agrarian history, including some texts of the eleventh century)[50], they have never dared to trespass the borders between different fields and have never attempted to include cultural phenomena in the pattern of social development. It is worth noting that Russian western medievalists, especially Lev Platonovič Karsavin (1882–1952), attempted to create a "polyphonal," synthetic characterization of medieval culture[51]—long before their Byzantine colleagues.

Russian studies of Byzantine culture had little impact both in the West and in Orthodox Greece. But the Russian concept of Byzantine agrarian development became known by western scholars in part through Vasiliev's *History of the Byzantine Empire*, in part (an unquestionably larger part) because of George (Georgij Aleksandrovic) Ostrogorsky (1902–1976). Ostrogorsky was, as a matter of fact, the most representative member of the school founded by Vasil'evskij, whose ideas he accepted, cleansed, and elaborated—usually in conjunction with the tendencies of Russian historiography of the early twentieth century. His position vis-à-vis Vasil'evskij had already been expressed in his article to the anniversary of the founder of the Russian school of Byzantine studies.[52]

What Ostrogorsky had not accepted from the "Russian legacy" was the perception of the cardinal role of the Slavs in the Byzantine revival—the perception questioned already by some Russian Byzantinists, such as Pančenko; accordingly, Ostrogorsky restricted the significance of the Byzantine village community that he constructed as a fiscal rather than economic unit. He also moved the revival from the eighth to the seventh century, from the period of the Iconoclasts to that of the Heraklides. As for the further development he retained the main points of the Russian concept, which he presented with a brilliant clearness and accuracy that contrasted sharply with the confused and incoherent way of marshaling arguments that was typical of Fedor Uspenskij. Ostrogorsky believed that the restoration of a free countryside population (in the seventh century) had accounted for the reinforcement of the state finances and the army; that the Macedonian dynasty consistently defended the small landowners; that feudal institutions penetrated Byzantium in the eleventh century and—to this extent he refuted Constantine Uspenskij—invigorated the empire through the following centuries. Ostrogorsky meticulously analyzed the documents that demonstrated the growth of the estate and the development of *pronoia* and *exkousseia*. The eleventh century was for him the time when the state rejected traditional agrarian policy, began to neglect the peasantry's needs, reversed toward feudal elements, and by so doing unleashed decentralizing forces and prepared the decline and fall of the Byzantine Empire. The eleventh century acquired crucial significance in Ostrogorsky's theory of Byzantine feudalism.

Should the eleventh century be accursed, as Fedor Uspenskij and George Ostrogorsky suggested, as a period of westernization and feudalization, as a period of greedy and egotistic officialdom? Or does it deserve a rehabilitation? This is probably one of the most challenging goals that modern Byzantine studies may envisage.

NOTES

1. We have not yet a proper study of Vasil'evskij, except for some obituaries and memoirs, e.g., I.M. Grevs, "Vasilij Grigor'evič Vasil'evskij kak učitel' nauki," *ŽMNP* 324 (1899): 27-74; F.I. Uspenskij, "Akademik Vasilij Grigor'evič Vasil'evskij," *ŽMNP* 325 (1899): 291-342; P.Bezobrazov," V.G. Vasil'evskij," *VizVrem* 6 (1899) 636-58 (with a list of publications); E.K[urtz], V. Vasil'evskij, "BZ 9 (1900) 330-334; V.I. Modestov," V.Gr. Vasil'evskij," *ŽMNP* 339 (1902): 134-68. See below, n. 59

2. The first part of this work, especially pertinent for our purpose, was republished in the *Trudy* of V.G. Vasil'evskij, vol. 4 (Leningrad 1930) 250-331. This concept, based to some extent on the works of E. Zachariae von Lingenthal, was summarily developed already in an earlier article by

Vasil'evskij (see his *Trudy* 4: 230-35).

3. Vasil'evskij, *Trudy* 4: 250.

4. Vasil'evskij, *Trudy* 4: 251.

5. Vasil'evskij, *Trudy* 4: 252f.

6. Vasil'evskij, *Trudy* 4: 255.

7. Vasil'evskij, *Trudy* 4: 259.

8. Vasil'evskij, *Trudy* 4: 263.

9. See above, n. 2.

10. V. Vasil'evskij, "Materialy dlja vnutrennej istorii Vizantijskogo gosudarštva," *ŽMNP* 202 (1879): 386-438.

11. N. Skabalanovič, *Vizantijskoe gosudarstvo i cerko'v v XI veke* (St. Petersburg, 1884). See reviews of his book: P. Bezorbazov, *ŽMNP* 236 (1884): 153-74; T. Florinskij, *Universitetskie izvestija* (Kiev 1884), no. 8, pt. 2: 182-200.

12. Skabalanovič, *Vizantijskoe gosudarstvo*, 230-45.

13. Skabalanovič, *Vizantijskoe gosudarstvo*, 245.

14. Skabalonovič, *Vizantijsko gosudarstvo*, 250f. The catalog of the "people's ills" was reproduced without notable alterations and without reference to Skabalanovič in N.G. Svoronos, *Études sur l'organization intérieure, la société et l'économie de l'Empire byzantin* (London 1973) pt. 9: 12f.

15. Skabalanovič, *Vizantijskoe gosudarstvo*, 253.

16. Skabalanovič, *Vizantijskoe gosudarstvo*, 256.

17. Skabalanovič, *Vizantijskoe gosudarstvo*, 265.

18. Skabalanovič, *Vizantijskoe gosudarstvo*, 266.

19. See S.N. Kapterev, "Bibliographia Uspenskiana," *VizVrem* 1 (1947): 270-314. The survey includes not only the list of his works but also that of the works of Fedor Uspenskij. See also Z.V. Udal'zova, "K voprosu ob ocenk trudov akad. F.I. Uspenskopg," *Voprosy istorii* (1949) no. 6: 116-27.

20. F.I. Uspenskij, "Drevnejšij pamjatnik slavjanskogo prava," *Juridičeskij vestnik* (1886) no. 4: 700-13.

21. F.I. Uspenskij, "K istorii krest'janskogo zemlevladenija v Vizantii," *ŽMNP* 225 (1883): 360.

22. F. I. Uspenskij, "K istorii " (see n.21) 360. Cf. his "Materialy dlja istorii zemlevladenija v XIV v," *Učenye zapiski Novorossijskogo universiteta* 38 (1983): 23.

23. F. I. Uspenskij, *Značenie vizantijskoj i južnoslavjanskoj pronii, Sbornik statej po slavjanovedeniju, sostavlennyj i izdannj ucenikami V.I. Lamanskogo* (St. Petersburgh 1883), 1-32.

24. Vasil'evskij, "Materialy," (see above, n.10): 415.

25. F. Uspenskij, *Značenie* (see above, n. 23): 14.

26. P.A. Jakovenko, *Issledovanija v oblasti vizantijskich gramot. Gramoty Novog monastyrja na Chiose* (Juriev/Tartu 1917). On him see A.A. Vasiliev. *Pamjati P.A. Jakovenko, Annalyz* (1922), 258f.

27. P.A. Jakovenko, *K istorii immuniteta v. Vizantii* (Juriev/Tartu 1908), 38.

28. Jakovenko, *K istorii*, 48.

29. K.N. Uspenskij, *Očerki po istorii Vizantii, I* (Moscow 1917). On him see the obituary by Ju.A.I., *Byzantinoslavica* 1 (1929) 2120f. as well as E.F. Lipšic, Preamble to the posthumous publication of his "Očerki po istorii ikonoborčeskogo diviženija v Vizantijskoj imperii v VIII-IV vv," *VizVrem* 3 (1950): 393-96.

30. K. Uspenskij, *Očerki*, 207f.

31. K.N. Uspenskij, "Ekskussija-immunitet v Vizantijskoj imperii," *VizVrem* 33 (1917-22) (1923): 78.

32 K. Uspenskij, "Ekskussija-immunitet," 116.

33. A.A. Vasiliev, *Latinskoe vladyčestvo na Vostoke* (Petrograd 1923), 59. In the American edition (*History of the Byzantine Empire* [Madison, Wisc., 1952], 565) the sentence is shortened, reference to

Uspenskij deleted, and the polemical bathos considerably flattened.

34. Vasiliev, *Latinskoe vladyčestvo*, 72.

35. F. I. Uspenskij, *Vizantijskie zemlemery, Trudy VI archeologičeskogo s'ezda v Odesse v 1884g.*, 2 (Odessa 1988) 272-341. See also his "Nabljudenija po sel'sko-chozjajstvennoj istorii v Vizantii," *ŽMNP* 259 (1988): 229-59, and a review by P.V. Bezobrazov, *ŽMNP* 260 (1888): 272-80.

36. F.I. Uspenskij, "Akt otvoda zemli monasyrju Bogorodicy Milostivoj," *IRAIK* 1 (1896), 1-25; "Mnenija i postanovlenija Konstantinopol'skich pomestnych soborov XI-XII vv. o razdače cerkovnych imuščestv (charistikarii)," *IRAIK* 5 (1900), 1-48.

37. B.A. Pančenko, "Krest'janskaja sobstvennost' v Vizantii," *IRAIK* 9 (1904), 1-234. On him see M. Ja. Sjuzjumov, "Naučnoe nasledie B.A. Pančenko," *VizVrem* 25 (1964), 32-52. Close to Pančenko was A. P. Rudakov, *Očerki vizantijskoj kul'tury po dannym grečeskoj agiografii* (Moscow 1917), 176f. See also p. 50f. He thought, however, that Pančenko "headed to an opposing extreme."

38. F.I. Uspenskij, "Učenaja dejatel'nost' B.A. Pančenko, *VizVrem* 24 (1923-26): 97.

39. F.I. Uspenskij, *Istorija Vizantijskoj imperii* 3 (Moscow, Leningrad 1948.), 379.

40. F.I. Uspenskij, "Uklon konservativnoj Vizantii v storonu zapadnych vlijanij," *VizVrem* 22 (1915-16): 35.

41. F. Uspenskij, Istorija (see above, n. 39) 3: 383.

42. F.I. Uspenskij, Cari Aleksej II i Andronik Komniny, *ŽMNP* 219 (1880): 100.

43. F.I. Uspenskij, Poslednie Komniny. Načalo reakcii, *VizVrem* 25 (1927): 14-21.

44. *Cecaumeni Strategicon et incerti scriptoris De officiis regiis libellus* (St.Petersburg, 1896). Some fragments and translations from Kekaumenos appeared earlier: V.G. Vasil'evskij, "Sovety i rasskazy vizantijskogo bojarina XI v," *ŽMNP* 215 (1881): 242-99), 216 (1881): 102-71, 316-57.

45. F.I. Uspenskij, "Deloproizvodstvo po obvineniju Ioanna Itala v eresi," *IRAIK* 2 (1897) 1-66. On the analysis of the views of John Italos see F.I. Uspenskij, *Očerki po istorri vizantijsko obrazovannosti* (St. Petersburg, 1891), 149-89.

46. P.V. Bezobrazov, *Vizantijskij pisatel' i gosudarstvennyj dejatel' Michail Psell* (Moscow 1890).

47. Vasil'evskij, "Sovety" (see above n. 44), *ŽMNP* 215: 245.

48. Bzobrazov, *Vizantijskij psatel'*, 194. The same characterization Psellos received in another book: P.B. Bezobrazov, *Očerki vizantijskoj kul'tury* (Petrograd 1919), 76-86.

49 F. Uspenskij, "Deloproizvodstvo" (see above, n. 45) 19-29. On this novel see also E.A. Černousov, *Stranica iz kul'turnoj istorii Vizantii* (Khartkov, 1913).

50. P.V. Bezobrazov, "Patmosskaja piscovaja kniga," *VizVrem* 7 (1900): 69-106; Zaveščanie Voily, *VizVrem* 18 (1911-13): 107-15.

51. L.P Karsavin, *Kul'tura srednich vekov* (Petrograd, 1918).

52. G.A. Ostrogorskij, "V.G. Vasil'evskij kak vizantolog i tvorec novejšej russkoj vizantologii," *Seminarium Kondakovianum* 11 (1940): 232f.

8
The Greek and Arabic Sources on the Battle of Mantzikert, 1071 A.D.*

Speros Vryonis, Jr.
Alexander S. Onassis Center for Hellenic Studies
New York University

The Greek and Arabic Sources on the Battle of Mantzikert, 1071 A.D.

Any attempt at an analysis of the sources for the reconstruction of Byzantine culture in the eleventh century in a short article such as this would have to be reduced to an encyclopedic entry and so would be meaningless and uninteresting. Therefore, I shall attempt to approach this vast and crucial subject in a manner that I hope will introduce us to the nature of the problems presented by the sources and, also, to the linguistic, political, social, and religious variety that confronts the scholar who contemplates the momentous events and developments that Byzantine society faced in the eleventh century.

It will be useful, I think, and interesting as well, I hope, to focus on one of the most sensational events of the eleventh century, the battle of Mantzikert, August 26, 1071, in which the Seljuk sultan Alp Arslan defeated and captured the Byzantine emperor Romanus IV Diogenes. When I dealt with this event in 1971 I stressed two points that had not been sufficiently appreciated by either Byzantinists or Islamists: (1) The battle was more important as a symptom than as an undoubtedly sensational event; (2) It is obviously essential that the sources be analyzed more austerely and systematically, and that they be integrated into, or excised from, the reconstruction of events, according to their relative relevance. Not the least of the obstacles that stood, and still stands, in the path of the analyst is the rich linguistic variety of the sources: Greek, Arabic, Persian, Ottoman Turkish, Armenian, Syriac, and Latin.[1]

The Islamic historian Claude Cahen had, in his famous article published in *Byzantion*, in 1934, evaluated these sources, airily rejecting the Greek sources as secondary, and giving the place of honor to the Arab sources. Having satisfied himself that this was so, he then proceeded to the historical reconstruction of the complex events centering about the battle.[2] In 1971 I demonstrated the error of his methodology, his lack of linguistic understanding of the Greek texts, and the final inhistoricity of the entire undertaking.[3] Nevertheless, even after 1971 scholars continued to rely on a work that was fundamentally, and in great detail, historically unsound. The recent publication of Cahen's history of the Seljuks, in French, does not correct any of this.[4]

Twenty years later, after the error of Cahen's method and conclusions was pointed out, the conference on Byzantine Civilization in the Eleventh Century has forced me to go back to these sources and to attempt a new and critical analysis that will, I think, assist in a better historical understanding of the events associated with the battle. In this twenty-year interim the labors of Islamists and Byzantinists have not only made the task easier but have also made it possible to attain more satisfactory working conclusions.

On the Islamic side two publications have served to focus on the Islamic sources more clearly. In 1971, the nine hundredth anniversary of the battle, two Turkish scholars, F. Sümer and A. Sevim, reproduced nine Arabic and four Persian medieval texts that deal with the battle, adding useful introductions and Turkish translations of the texts themselves.[5] The Arab scholar Sohil Zakar published selections from Arab chronicles that dealt with the battle and accompanied them with critical commentaries that help to show more clearly on what sources these Arab chronicles relied.[6] In both cases the editors were much more careful than Cahen in accepting the data that the texts present.[7]

On the side of the Byzantinists we have new editions of Nicephorus Bryennius (by Gautier),[8] of the Continuator of Scylitzes (by Tsolakes),[9] and the promise of a badly needed new edition of Attaleiates (by Tsolakes). Just as important is the fact that Byzantinists have carried out a number of analyses of these texts that help us both to understand better the interrelations of the texts and to acquire fixed data, on the one hand, and also to comprehend the sociology of the authors, their thought and so their oeuvres, on the other. Much of this work has been surveyed in H. Hunger's fundamental work on Byzantine literature.[10]

I have over the years read and translated the six Greek, the eight Arab, the four Persian, and the one Ottoman texts. In addition I have familiarized myself with, but will not discuss here, the Gestae Roberti Wiscardi, the translations of the Armenian and Syriac sources.[11] They are all of secondary importance and will not basically affect our discussion of the Greek and Arab sources.

I shall begin with the obvious. To date there has been no overall analysis, no comparative study, of all the Greek sources among themselves. Carile demonstrated essentially the relation of the texts of Psellos and Nicephorus Bryennius to one another, and as important as his demonstration remains, it was marred by a serious misunderstanding of the texts in regard to the battle of Mantzikert.[12] Utilizing Carile's valuable examination, I have proceeded to reexamine the relation of Psellos to Nicephorus Bryennius and have examined the further relation of Nicephorus Bryennius to Attaleiates and of Attaleiates to

Psellos. Then within the second tier or category of Greek sources I have analyzed the relations of the Continuator of Scylitzes, Zonaras, and Manasses to one another and to the first category of Greek sources.

Though it is impossible to carry out a comparable analysis for the Islamic sources at present, I have carried out an analysis that reaches a preliminary stage of arrangement of these sources. They break down into three groups as to comprehension and content: (1) The first group consists of al-Qalanisi, Ibn al-Azraq, Ibn al-Adim and Ibn ad-Dawadari (all of which are useless); (2) An intermediate group of chronicles that is more extensive than the first, has variations, and can be explained only by further analysis. This includes the Akhbar, al-Bondari, and Ibn al-Athir. Of these, al-Bondari is an abbreviation of the longer work (now lost) of Imad al-Din Isfahani and so has peculiarities of its own; (3) The third group consists of the grandfather-grandson team Ibn al-Jauzi and Sibt ibn al-Jauzi who, though very similar to one another as to content, are at the same time different by virtue of the greater detail of the grandson, who seems to have plagiarized, verbatim, the work of Ghars an-Ni'me (d. 1088) for the events of concern to us here.

Finally, an effort has been made at a comparative analysis of these two groups of sources, Greek and Arab, in great detail and in an effort to investigate the following:

1. The chronological proximity of each author to the events;

2. The indirect chronological proximity of each author to the events, via older materials utilized or plagiarized;

3. The structure of the narrative in each author;

4. The specific details in each author;

5. The outlook and prejudices of each author;

6. Verbatim plagiarism, appearance of structure, relation of details to structure;

7. A comparison of the Greek and Arab works as to a) veracity, b) detail and extent, c) comprehension of events, d) aetiological understanding and sophistication and e) overlapping and identification of common data and themes.

Because of lack of space and time the conclusions of this research, based on a longer text of ninety-six typed pages, with appropriate notes, are summarized in what follows.

Greek Sources

The Greek accounts that were analyzed recount, with varying degrees of detail, the departure of Romanus IV Diogenes from Constantinople on the Day of Orthodoxy, March 13, 1071, for the eastern front, until the blinding and death of the emperor on June 29 and August 4, 1072, respectively. The separate versions break down into two basic divisions: (1) The departure of Romanus IV from Constantinople for the eastern front and the ensuing events through the battle of Mantzikert, Friday, August 26, 1071, and his captivity; (2) The events following his captivity until his death a year later, August 4, 1072.

The first division of the narratives is concerned primarily with Byzantino-Turkish relations, whereas the second has as its focal point the civil strife and political complications occasioned by the unexpected release of Romanus IV from captivity and the civil war between himself and the Ducas family now in control of Constantinople.

On the basis of a long, detailed analysis carried out within the framework of this basic twofold division, I reached the following conclusions as to the Greek sources for the events surrounding the battle of Mantizkert:

I concluded that the *Chronographia* of Psellos[13] displays a gross disproportion as to attention and details between the two divisions of his narrative, dealing with the events of the first division in little more than a page[14] and with the events of the second division more amply in nine and one-half pages.[15] The first section is, further, insignificant and has no independent value as a historical source for the events surrounding Mantzikert. When one considers the second division of his narrative one is struck by the rich detail of the philosopher's account. It is of particular importance for the intrigues and political upheavals in the capital itself, as in contrast to the military encounters in Asia Minor between Romanus on the one hand, and Michael VII Ducas and the Ducas family on the other. His is the longest, most detailed account for a reconstruction of the events in Constantinople. The strengths of Psellos, as a recorder of history, are also his weakness: intense political participation in the removal of Romanus IV from the throne, from the field, from the world of the visible, and finally from the very world of the living. One should note that Carile has demonstrated the fact that Nicephorus Bryennius has lifted practically all this second part of Psellos and incorporated it into his own work.[16]

The second source, and it must be restored to the place of honor (pace Cahen et Carile) as both the longest and the most detailed and reliable account of the events surrounding the battle of Mantzikert, was the history of Psellos's contemporary Michael Attaleiates.[17] What is the basis for the superiority of Attaleiates as a historical source?

1. The mere bulk and extent of his coverage[18] far outstrip the space and attention provided by the other five Byzantine authors (in the case of Nicephorus Bryennius by a ratio of 2:1, Continuator of Scylitzes 3:1, Psellos 4:1, Zonaras 4:1, Manasses 10:1).

2. He gives a more nearly balanced treatment of the two divisions of the

narrative (23 to 14 pages, respectively).[19] It is obvious that in terms of the emperor's march to the eastern front and accompanying episodes, conditions on the eastern frontier, the strategy and disposition of divisions of the army, the battle itself, and the defeat and captivity of Romanus IV, Attaleiates provides far and away the greater number of details, names, and places and has the most nearly coherent account. The same holds true for the second set of events commencing with the captivity and ending with the death of Romanus.

3. His superiority also lies in the features of veracity and reliability. These are the products of interrelated character traits, intelligence, experience, and access to written and oral sources.[20]

4. To what degree does he involve himself in his narrative? Though Attaleiates is not averse to referring to himself in the narrative, he intrudes only momentarily to indicate that he has either witnessed the event, or that he advised the emperor, that he took an active part in this or that action, or that he had been the recipient of an oral report.[21] In sharp contrast, Psellos is writing a personal memoir and is most often present in the narrative to praise himself and to criticize others. Above all, Psellos justifies his own political career, his political acts, and his political morality. Nicephorus Bryennius is often glorifying the roles of the Komnenos and Ducas families, and he exalts himself by praising his grandfather, who actually played an undistinguished role at the battle of Mantzikert. Of these three authors, Attaleiates comes closest to the truth, comes closest to balance of treatment, and though he was present at the battle he states specifically that others must judge whether or not his actions in the battle were appropriate.

5. Finally, his superiority resides on a unique historical fact: No other author (whose text survives)—Greek, Latin, Armenian, Syriac, Arab, Persian, or Turkish—who has left an account of the battle was present when the Christian emperor and the Moslem sultan disputed the field of Mantzikert on August 26, 1071. Only Attaleiates was an eyewitness to the famous battle and participated in it. He was present because he was one of the highest Byzantine officials, was supreme judge of the armies, and participated in the emperor's councils of war during the entire campaign, as well as during the battle.

The superiority of Attaleiates' account is immediately apparent even on the first reading of all the sources, but after detailed analysis and comparison, the sense of his superiority overpowers the historical and textual analyst.

On what basis, then, did Cahen and Carile base their rejection of Attaleiates? Why does Cahen prefer the Arab sources, and why does Carile judge Nicephorus Bryennius worthy of historical credence in preference to Attaleiates? It is clear from my detailed analysis that neither author has understood his texts correctly.

Cahen rejected Attaleiates because he relied on the mistaken Latin translation that appears at the bottom of the page in the Bonn edition. According to Cahen, Attaleiates accuses the emperor Michael VII of having betrayed Romanus IV on the field of battle at Mantzikert on that fateful August day of 1071, and Cahen charges that Attaleiates did this falsely in order to soil the character of Michael VII Ducas, who was the principal foe of Attaleiates' hero, Nicephorus III Botaniates. Cahen is thus the servant of the Latin translation of the original Greek text and was not able to check the translation against the original. Cahen therefore rejects completely the only eyewitness account. In effect the Latin translation of the Greek text is completely erroneous and can only be characterized as a schoolboy howler. In his Greek text Attaleiates says *none* of the things that his translator and Cahen say that he does. Further, Michael VII, as we know, was not present at the battle, not present at any part of the campaign, had never left Constantinople, and indeed was exiled to Asia Minor (Ephesus) only in 1078 by Nicephorus III Botaniates. So much for Cahen's "understanding" of Attaleiates, and indeed so much for his entire account of the battle of Mantzikert. This erroneously based rejection of Attaleiates' account is sufficient to discredit the entire work of Cahen on the battle.[22] But there are other reasons as well to judge Cahen's article unacceptable. To all these we shall return later.

Carile, who unlike Cahen knows the Greek text very well, has attempted to revindicate the veracity and reliability of the narrative of Nicephorus Bryennius and to attack the reliability of Attaleiates on the battle of Mantzikert. Indeed, he replaces the latter with Bryennius as the basic and true account of what happened. He does this by combining one presupposition with one interpretation of a passage in Attaleiates. The presupposition, like that of Cahen, has to do with the fact that the later emperor Nicephorus III Botaniates was Attaleiates' hero. Since during the battle another Nicephorus Bryennius (grandfather of the historian) took part in the battle, and years later had competed with Nicephorus III Botaniates for the imperial throne, it is natural, says Carile, for Attaleiates to blacken the memory of Botaniates' competitor Nicephorus Bryennius who had fought at the battle of Mantzikert. He feels that he has found this evidence in Attaleiates' account of the first skirmishes that finally ended in the battle. Carile asserts that in this passage Attaleiates has soiled the character of Bryennius the general by saying that Bryennius was a coward. Yet, Carile continues, Romanus IV appointed Nicephorus Bryennius as general of one of the wings of the army at the actual battle. Thus, he winds up his argument, Bryennius could not have been a coward or else Romanus IV would not have appointed him as one of the principal generals at the onset of the later battle. It follows, says Carile, that Attaleiates has besmirched the valor and reputation of Bryennius in order to heighten the moral stature of his own hero, the emperor Nicephorus III Botaniates. Given this alleged dishonesty, one cannot accept the historical account of Attaleiates on the battle of Mantzikert. It is prejudiced and mendacious.[23]

The only difficulty with Carile's rehabilitation of the historian Nicephorus Bryennius and the vilification of Attaleiates is that it is based, as was Cahen's argument, on a complete misunderstanding of what Attaleiates does in fact say. He asserts that the emperor Romanus IV charged the general Bryennius with cowardice, but Attaleiates in effect defends Bryennius against the charge. For, he says, "The emperor [Romanus IV], charging him [the general Bryennius] with cowardice, *for he was ignorant of the true state of affairs*, gave him no reinforcements."[24] Attaleiates is clear. Romanus IV charged Bryennius the general with cowardice. Attaleiates himself defends Bryennius against the charge, stating that Bryennius had asked for reinforcements because he was sorely pressed by the unexpected size of the Turkish contingents that suddenly attacked him. Attaleiates justifies this and defends Bryennius against the imperial charge of cowardice by stating clearly that Romanus was ignorant of the true state of affairs on the battlefront.

Thus we see that Cahen and Carile have argued on the basis of mistaken and questionable philological grounds and method. This being the case, their arguments are rapidly deflated and discarded, and Attaleiates remains unshaken as an extremely reliable authority on the events of 1071–1072.

What can we conclude about our three authors as historical sources for the battle of Mantzikert and for the events leading up to it and those which followed? There can no longer be any doubt as to the fact that Michael Attaleiates is the main Greek source for the events commencing with Romanus's departure from Constantinople and his progress through Asia Minor up to the battle of Mantzikert itself. He is also the primary source for the military strategy of Romanus at the battle of Mantzikert, and for the conditions of, and the actual release from, his Turkish captivity. Psellos has practically nothing to say about all these weighty and dramatic events. Nicephorus Bryennius is writing entirely a family and political pamphlet on the battle, has foreshortened everything, praises his grandfather beyond all belief, and the abridgement of his account is such that in the end it explains nothing. The sections of Nicephorus Bryennius which touch on these events have, however, historical interest precisely as a piece of family and dynastic propaganda. In the narration and construction of events that transpired after the Turkish captivity of Romanus IV, the *Chronographia* of Psellos is an important, though extremely prejudiced, source for the events in the court of Constantinople. Indeed, Nicephorus Bryennius lifts almost the entire body of these events in his own account from the *Chronographia* of Psellos, for the most part verbatim. Attaleiates remains, far and away, the most important, the principal source for the reconstruction of events in Asia Minor.

I shall finish the treatment of the Greek sources by summarizing in one sentence the relations of the second tier of sources to the first tier. The triad of the Continuator of Scylitzes, Zonaras, and Manasses constitute secondary sources as

ARAB SOURCES ON THE BATTLE OF MANTZIKERT

	Author	Date	Notes	Number of Lines
1.	Ibn al-Qalanisi	d. 1160	little value	11
2.	Ibn al Azraq	b. 1116	penurious oral tradition, written c. 1177	22
3.	Sadr ad-Din Alin al-Husayni Akhbar ad-Dawlat as Saljuqiyya	13th c.	depends on three sources: unknown, Imad ad-Din, source to 1193; detailed information on battle of Mantzikert	110
4.	Ibn al-Jauzi	1116–1200	chronicle ends at 1177; knew lost work of Gars an-Ni'me, d. 1088; detailed information on battle of Mantzikert	109
5.	al-Bondari	13th c.	abbreviated form of history of Imad ad-Din Isfahani; similar information on battle as Imad ad-Din, the Akhbar, Ibn al-Athir	93
6.	Ibn al-Athir	1160-1233	abbreviated version of battle that is found in Akhbar, Imad ad-Din; only one to mention that treaty AA,RD=50 years	51
7.	Sibt ibn al-Jauzi	1186-1257	very detailed account of Mantzikert; plagiarized work of Gars an-Ni'me verbatim; we do not know how to evaluate his work (Sumer-Sevim)	232
8.	Ibn al-Adim	d. 1260	utilizes 12th c. work of Abu Galib; his account of Mantzikert hardly differs from Akhbar, Imad ad-Din, Ibn al-Athir	148
9.	Ibn ad-Dawadari	14th c.	some parts of his text to be found in Sibt al-Jauzi	70

all are very highly derivative of Attaleiates, only secondarily derivative of Psellos, and Manasses has composed a short epic poem on the subject.[25]

Arab Sources

Let us now look, very briefly, at the nine Arab sources. The critical examination and study of these texts have remained in a far more primitive state than in the case of the Greek sources. In particular their interrelations are beset with thorny problems, a state to which von Rosen first drew attention in 1884 when he identified, published, and commented on the relevant sections of Ibn al-Qalanisi, the Akhbar ad-Daulat as-Saljuqiyya, and al-Bondari's abbreviation of the chronicle of Imad al-Din Isfahani.[26]

The weaknesses and difficulties of these texts, and they are very considerable, include the following:

1. All Moslem texts on the battle of Mantzikert are recorded by chroniclers *who were not contemporaries of the event*. They wrote their accounts much after the

events had taken place, from the mid twelfth through the thirteenth, fourteenth, and into the sixteenth century.²⁷

2. The Arab accounts are much shorter, on the events of 1071–1072, than is the narrative of Attaleiates.

3. It is difficult to evaluate and to give credence to the details of the Arab accounts, for legend rapidly replaced historical memory. a) The thirteenth century chronicler Ibn al-Athir, in his account of Mantzikert wrote:

و مدح الشعراء وذكروا هذا الفتح فأكثروا

"And the poets praised and mentioned this victory very frequently."²⁸

b) A century earlier the Greek chronicler Zonaras wrote, in describing Alp Arslan:

"Ἄξαν ἐκεῖνος ὠνόμαστο, οὗ πολλὰ ἐπὶ δικαιοσύνῃ καὶ μετριοφροσύνῃ ᾄδονται διηγήματα."

"He was called Axan (Arslan), of whom many tales are sung-narrated as to his justice and moderation."²⁹

Thus legend and the poets soon took over the events of Mantzikert with the result that the Arab sources, which are also later than Attaleiates, are full of exclamatory legend.

Though a majority of these Arab sources have some six common pieces of data, they are also characterized by great variety and by a diffusion of focus. Scholars have accordingly searched for elements that would justify the utilization of various parts of the Arab sources, given the fact that they are so greatly posterior to the events of the battle. These confirmatory elements scholars have found, variously, in the following:

1. Obviously some of these chronicles include extensive sections taken over from chronicles the texts of which are now lost, for example, Ghars an-Ni'me (1088) in Sibt ibn al-Jauzi, and Abu Ghalib and Imad al-Din Isfahani, also in Sibt ibn al-Jauzi.³⁰

2. There is the genre of the so-called Fatihname, a typical Islamic genre written by victorious rulers or generals to the caliph announcing their military victory in some given battle or war. The text referring to such a Fatihname sent by the victorious Alp Arslan to the caliph is mentioned in the chronicle of Sibt ibn al-Jauzi.³¹

3. There is reference to an exchange of correspondence between the sultan and the caliph.³²

These three types of sources were sufficient for Cahen to reject the contemporary Greek sources (Attaleiates) completely and to give preference and credence to the posterior Arab sources:

"This exposition [article] is essentially founded on them [Arab sources]. Of course it is to be understood that when the other sources agree or disagree with the [Arab] sources this is noted in regard to the details."[33] He does assert that the two principle sources for the battle are Imad al-Din Isfahani and Nicephorus Bryennius. By and large, for Cahen, the Christian sources, when relevant, serve basically to confirm the Muslim sources. It is these latter on which he bases his account of the battle. Unfortunately for Cahen, this has led him into the acceptance of a major portion of the Arab sources that are derived either from unreliable oral tradition, or else are so distant in time from the event that their authors cannot understand what original material they have incorporated. Cahen even accepts the ridiculously exaggerated numbers of the Byzantine armies that are reported by the Arab authors. More important, Cahen has not only handled the Arab materials in a gullible and uncritical manner, but he has rejected the Christian sources, especially Attaleiates, without understanding what is in them.

On the other hand the Turkish editors, translators, and commentators on these texts, F. Sümer and A. Sevim, are much more careful and caution that it is very difficult to know whether and to what degree one can give credence to this body of Arab and Persian sources since they were recorded so long after the event.[34]

In my analysis of the Arab sources I examined seven themes, and did so first in terms of the Arab sources alone and then in comparison with the Greek sources:

1. The date of the battle. The Arab sources give Friday as the day but gave different dates. A Byzantine source gives Friday also, but sets the date at August 26, 1071. The Byzantine source is to be preferred, since it is closest to the event and gives dates for other events that can be checked.[35]

2. The numbers of the armies as reported by the Arab sources are fantastic and unreliable. The Byzantines are said to have had, variously, between 200,000 and 600,000 troops, whereas Alp Arslan's army is minimized, between 5,000 and 200,000. Cahen accepts these notorious numbers in the Arab sources.[36] The Byzantine texts are much more cautious and conservative, and they are closer to the truth.

3. There is the matter of the immediate events leading up to the battle, and these are important as we cannot understand the battle in a vacuum. Writing from such a chronological distance the Arab chroniclers demonstrate clearly that they did not understand the flow of events, and consequently their narratives are jerky and highly disjointed. In contrast Attaleiates is far more detailed, he is completely coherent, and he helps us to understand the developments that led to the battle.

4. There is the embassy of peace that the sultan Alp Arslan unexpectedly and suddenly sent to Romanus IV. a) When the sultan offered peace to the emperor,

Ibn al-Azraq, Ibn al-Jauzi, and Ibn al-Athir relate that Romanus demanded as recompense for a peace treaty the cession of Ray, Hamadan, and Isfahan, famous cities in the heart of Iran and so in the distant domains of the sultan.[37] b) Attaleiates tells us what really was the content of Romanus's demand: that Alp Arslan remove his troops from the strategic situation, outside the city of Mantzikert, where they had the military advantage, controlling the surrounding heights and the only source of water, on which the Byzantine army relied for its needs.[38]

The account of the Arabs has given way to exaggerated sensationalism, whereas the eyewitness, Attaleiates, gives us a very realistic picture. Certainly the cities of Ray, Hamadan, and Isfahan had always been far beyond the military and strategic considerations of Romanus IV, who was so hard-pressed in his efforts to stay the devastating raids of the Turkish tribal groups into central and western Asia Minor. Further, his tactical situation at Mantzikert was a very difficult one, and quite naturally he was seeking to derive an important tactical advantage from the sultan's offer so as to give much needed relief to his harassed forces.

5. Most interesting, however, is the actual battle itself and the Arab accounts. a) Here Cahen relies overwhelmingly on the Arab accounts of which the longest is by Sibt ibn al-Jauzi. b) Of the Arab authors, al-Qalanisi, Ibn al-Azraq, Ibn al-Athir, and Ibn ad-Dawadari are worthless. This leaves the Akhbar, Ibn al-Jauzi and his grandson Sibt ibn al-Jauzi, al Bondari and Ibn al-Adim. These five authors generate five categories of data on the battle. i) Alp Arlsan's conversation with imam Abu Nasr Muhammad ibn Abdul Malik al-Buhari, after the failure of the sultan's peace embassy to Romanus IV;[39] ii) the prayer sent by the caliph to be read in the minbars on Friday, the day of the battle;[40] iii) the content of the prayer itself;[41] iv) the actual course of the battle[42] (we see that items i–iii are concerned with religion; item iv mentions briefly the preparations for battle) v) the description of the actual battle of Mantzikert, which the authors dispose of in two to three lines only. Attaleiates takes more than three pages to describe the evolution of the battle and the final rout and defeat of the emperor by the sultan.[43]

Thus, Attaleiates is the most detailed, by far more detailed than the Arab sources, and it is his narrative alone that allows us to follow the development and the phases of the battle. None of this is to be found in the Arab sources. The Arab sources are severely limited as to detail, development, and etiological explanation of the various happenings and phases of the battle.

But, and this is unexpected, there is a sixth source of fascinating data generated by the Arab sources, and these data seem to be confirmed by Attaleiates. This has to do with the capture of the emperor Romanus IV and his captivity for some days in the camp of the sultan Alp Arslan. Here, in contrast to all other points and data about the battle of Mantzikert, the Arab sources seem to be superior to the Greek sources, and it is here basically, and only in this section, that the Greek and Arab sources converge.

The principal source for Romanus's captivity and sojourn in the sultan's camp in the Byzantine sources (here essentially Attaleiates and Psellos) seems to be the letter that Romanus sent to Constantinople after his release from captivity by the sultan, in which he recounts his adventures during the eight-day captivity in the sultan's camp. It is Attaleiates[44] who gives much of the contents of this letter, and Psellos mentions it specifically.[45] But there is no evidence that the Arab chroniclers had access to this letter.

It is not clear what the origins of details in the Arab sources on this sensational event were. Some of the details seem to be preserved in the Fatihname which Alp Arslan sent to the caliph in Baghdad. Certainly the most detailed account of the captivity is in Sibt ibn al-Jauzi, who presents a verbatim copy from the lost chronicle of Ghars an-Ni'me (d. 1088).[46] The account of Romanus's captivity takes up some fifty-eight lines in this chronicle. And it is here that we see the one unique overlap between the Greek and Arab sources, so that we actually know that they are talking about one and the same thing. Sibt's account is confirmed by that of Attaleiates not only in a general sense but also by a passage that is common to both the Arabic and Greek sources. In this common passage the sultan is reported to have treated the emperor magnanimously, comforting and healing him. Then in a postprandial conversation he is reported, by both the Greek and Arab sources (Sibt ibn al-Jauzi and Attaleiates) to have asked his vanquished foe, "What would you have done with me had you taken me captive?" And both sources agree on what the emperor replied: "I would have inflicted bodily punishment on you etc."

Thus we conclude that on the episode of the emperor's captivity, for the first and only time the Arab sources are superior and preferable to the Greek. They give greater detail on the purported discussions and negotiations of the two rulers, and Sibt ibn al-Jauzi is confirmed by the independent report of Attaleiates.

7. The seventh and last category of data generated by the Arab sources deals with the fate of the emperor Romanus IV after his release from captivity. Here the Arab sources lose interest, and what they do mention is highly confused, erroneous, and penurious.[47]

Notes

*This paper was presented at the conference "Byzantine Society and Civilization in the Eleventh Century," sponsored by the Alexander S. Onassis Center for Hellenic Studies, New York University; the Center for Medieval and Renaissance Studies, University of California, Los Angeles; and the Speros Basil Vryonis Center for the Study of Hellenism, Sacramento, California. The conference, which took place at

U.C.L.A., March 8, 1991, constitutes a preliminary introduction to a much larger conference, to take place in 1993, which will have as its scope a reinterpretation and evaluation of this crucial period. I wish to thank Mrs. Seka Allen of Dumbarton Oaks, Washington, D.C., for her great kindness in supplying me with photocopied materials of works unavailable to me in New York.

1. S. Vryonis, *The Decline of Medieval Hellenism in Asia Minor and the Process of Islamization from the Eleventh through the Fifteenth Century* (Berkeley-Los Angeles-London, 1971), reprinted in 1986, pp. 96-103. For a detailed analysis of the reviews of this book, see Vryonis, "The Decline of Medieval Hellenism in Asia Minor and the Process of Islamization from the Eleventh through the Fifteenth Century: The Book and its Reviews Ten Years Later," *The Greek Orthodox Theological Review* 27 (1982), 225-285.

2. C. Cahen, "La campagne de Mantzikert d'après les sources musulmans," *Byzantion*, 9 (1934), 613-642.

3. Vryonis, *The Decline* (see n. 1 above), pp. 100-101.

4. Cahen, *La Turquie Pré-Ottomane* (Istanbul-Paris, 1988). Unfortunately this work is almost completely the same as the earlier English version, *Pre-Ottoman Turkey* (London, 1968). Only a very few bibliographical references have been added and as a result the French edition is badly dated.

5. F. Sümer and A. Sevim, *Islam Kaynaklarına gore Malazgirt savaşı (metinler ve çevirleri)* (Ankara, 1971).

6. Sohil Zakar, *Muhtarat min kitabat al-mu'arihin al-Arab*, n.d., n.p., pp. 105-161.

7. The bibliography on the battle of Mantzikert is very considerable and of unequal value. I list below, aside from materials already mentioned in the above notes, the following. The 900th anniversary of the event was celebrated in Turkey as a national holiday and was accompanied by a plethora of publications as well as by a modern reenactment of the event. The Türk Tarih Kurumu, under the direction of its then General Director U. Igdemir, issued a volume entitled *Malazgirt Armaganı* (Ankara, 1971) to celebrate the event. The Milli Egitim Basimevi published a substantial, though not comprehensive, bibliography on the subject, carrying the title, *Selçuklu tarihi. Alp Arslan ve Malazgirt bibliografyası* (Ankara, 1971). Other studies include: Ş. Baştav, "La bataille rangée de Malazgirt et Roman Diogène," *Cultura Turcica*, 9-10 (1971), 132-152; F. Dirimtekin, *Malazgirt meydan muharebesi* (Istanbul, 1943); S. Eyice, "Malazgirt savaşına kaybeden Romanos IV Diogenes (1068-1071)," (Ankara, 1971); A. Friendly, *The Dreadful Day. The Battle of Mantzikert 1071* (London, 1981), is completely derivative of other secondary works and has no independent value; I. Kafesoglu, "Malazgird," *Islam Ansiklopedisi*, 242-248; J. Laurent, "Le duc d'Antioche Khatchatour 1068-72," 30 (1919-20), 405-411; J. Laurent, "Byzance et les Turcs seldjoucides en Asie Mineure. Leurs traités anterieurs à Alexis Comnène," Βυζαντίς 2 A-B (1911), 101-26; A. Sevim, "Malazgirt meydan savaşı ve sonuçları," in *Malazgirt Armagani* (Ankara, 1972), Türk Tarih Kurumu, 219-30; J. Shepard, "Byzantinorussica," *Revue des Etudes Byzantines*, 33 (1975), 211-25, on Russians at Mantzikert and the problem of the allagion; O. Turan, *Selçuklular zamanında Türkiye. Siyasi tarih Alp Arslan'dan Osman Gazi'ye (1071-1318)*, (Istanbul, 1971), 21-37 (especially 27-32), is all taken from Turan's earlier book, *Selçuklular tarihi ve Türk-Islam medeniyeti* (Ankara, 1965), 115-140;

For some extended considerations one can consult, S.G. Agadzanov and K.N. Yuzbashian, "K istorii tiurskich nabegov na Armenija v XI v.," *Palestinskij Sbornik* 13 (76), (1965), 144-159; A. Hamdani, "A Possible Fatimid Background to the Battle of Mantzikert," *Ankara Üniversitesi DTC Fakültesi, Tarih Araştırmaları Dergisi*, 6 (1968), 1-59; "Byzantino-Fatimid Relations before the Battle of Mantzikert," *Byzantine Studies* 1 (1974), 169-79; R. Guseynov, "La conquête de l'Azerbaijan par les Seldjoucides," *Bedi Karthlisa* 19-20 (1965), 99-109; *Siriiskie istochnik ob Azerbaidzhane* (Baku, 1960); M. A. Köymen, "The Importance of Malazgirt Victory with Special Reference to Iran and Turkey," *Journal of Religion Culture Institutions* (1972), 5-12; J.C. Cheynet, "Mantzikert un désastre militaire," Byzantion 50 (1980): 410-38

8. *Nicephori Byrennii historiarum libri quattour*, ed. P. Gautier (Brussels, 1975) (hereafter Bryennius-Gautier).

9. E. Th. Tsolakes, Ἡ Συνέχεια τῆς Χρονογραφίας τοῦ Ἰωάννου Σκυλίτση (Thessaloniki, 1968), reviewed by H. Thurn, *Byzantinische Zeitschrift*, 63 (1970), 75-79. The Tsolakes edition is referred to, hereafter, as Scylitzes-Continuator-Tsolakes. The older edition is in Georgii Cedreni, *Ioannis Scylitzae Opera*, ed. I Bekker (Bonn, 1939) (hereafter Scylitzes-Bonn).

10. H. Hunger, *Die hoschsprachliche profane Literatur der Byzantiner* (Munich) I, 372-422.

11. Guillaume de Pouille, *La Geste de Robert Guiscard*, édition, traduction, commentaire et introduction par M. Mathieu avec une preface de M. H. Grégoire (Palermo, 1961); Aristakes de Lastivert, *Récit des malheurs de la nation arménienne*. Traduction française avec une introduction et commentaire par Marius Canard et Haig Berberian d'après l'édition et la traduction russe de Karen Yuzbashian (Brussels, 1973); Aristakes de Lastivert, *Histoire d'Arménie*, tr. E. Prud'homme (Paris, 1964); *Povestovanie Aristakesa Lastivertsi*, ed., introd., K.N. Yuzbashian (Yerevan, 1963); *Chronique de Michel le Syrien Patriarche Jacobite d'Antioche (1166-1199)*. Editée pour la première fois et traduite en française par J-B. Chabot (Paris, 1905), reprinted Brussels, 1963, vol. III; Bar Hebraeus, *The Chronography of Gregory Abu'l Faraj the Son of Aaron, the Hebrew Physician, commonly known as Bar Hebraeus, being the First Part of his Political History of the World*, translated from the Syriac by E.A. Wallis Budge (London, 1932), vol. I. R. Guseynov, "Sirijskie istochnikov po istorii Vizantii XI-XII vv," *Vizantiiskii Vremennik*, 33 (1972), 120-128. E. Merçil, ed., "Türkçce Selcuknâme'ye göre Malazgirt savaşı," Tarih Enstitüsü Dergisi, II (1971): 17-49

12. A. Carile, "Il Cesare Niceforo Briennio," *Aevum*, 42 (1968), 429-454; "La Ὕλη ἱστορίας del Cesare Niceforo Briennio," *Aevum*, 43 (1969), 56-87, 235-282.

13. For the account in Psellos, Michel Psellus, *Chronographie*, texte établie et traduit par E. Renauld (Paris, 1928), II, 161-172. On Psellos: Hunger, as in n. 10 above, I, 372-382; Y. N. Ljubarski, *Mihail Psell.: Lichnost i tvorchestvo* (Moscow, 1978); A. Gadolin, *A Theory of History and Society with Special Reference to the Chronographia of Michael Psellus. Eleventh Century Byzantium* (Stockholm, 1970), and the second edition; E. Kriaras, "Μιχαὴλ Ψελλός," Βυζαντινά" 4 (1972), 55-128; P. Speck, *Die kaiserliche Universität von Konstantinopel* (Munich, 1974).

14. Psellus-Renauld, II, 161-162.

15. Psellus-Renauld, II, 162-172.

16. Carile, as in n. 12 above.

17. Michaelis Attaliotae, *Historia*, ed. I. Bekker (Bonn, 1853) (hereafter Attaleiates-Bonn), 142-179.

18. Attaleiates-Bonn, 142-179.

19. Attaleiates-Bonn, 142-165, 165-179.

20. Hunger, as in n. 10 above, I, 382-388; E. Tsolakis, "Die Geschichtswerk des Michael Attaleiates und die Zeit seiner Abfassung," Βυζαντινά 2 (1970), 253-268; "Aus dem Leben des Michael Attaleitates (Seine Heimstadt, sein Geburtstag-und Todesjahr," *Byzantinische Zeitschrift*, 58 (1965), 3-10; ῾Ο Μιχαὴλ Ἀτταλειάτης ὡς κριτικὸς τῶν ἐπιχειρήσεων καὶ τῆς τακτικῆς τοῦ πολέμου" Βυζαντινά, 1 (1969), 189-204; H. Thurn, "Textgeschichtliches zu Michael Attaleiates," *Byzantinische Zeitschrift*, 57 (1964), 293-301; E. Janssens, "Michail Attaliates en die slag bij Mantzikert," Zeteis, ed. E. Strijcker (Amsterdam, 1973), 585-596; "La bataille de Mantzikert (1071), selon Michel Attaleiate," *Annuaire de l'institut philologique et d'histoire orientales et slaves*, 20 (1968-72), 291-304;

A.P. Kazhdan, "The Social Views of Attaleiates," in Kazhdan and Epstein, *Studies on Byzantine Literature of the Eleventh and Twelfth Centuries* (Cambridge, 1984), 23–86.

21. Attaleiates-Bonn, 151, where he intercedes in the narrative, justifying the emperor, in the face of criticism, for his tactical decision to divide the army into two and for sending the major portion off to Chliat. On p. 152 he says that he witnessed the surrender of the Turks of the town of Mantzikert, and he criticizes the unarmed emperor for receiving the armed Turks in his presence; p. 153, he witnessed, and criticized the emperor for, the immoderate punishment that Romanus inflicted on a Byzantine soldier for stealing a Turkish donkey; p. 154, he censured Romanus for having charged the general Nicephorus Bryennius for cowardice, and defends the honor of the general; Attaleiates is present at the imperial council of war where the gospel was read and ominously interpreted, p. 154; pp. 156–157, he witnessed, and comments on, the confusion of the Byzantine camp as it underwent a Turkish night attack; pp. 158–159, in the midst of the emperor's preparations for the battle, Attaleiates tells us that he advised Romanus to ensure the loyalty of the "Scythian" mercenaries, and so Attaleiates executes the oath of loyalty; pp. 159–160, he was present at the emperor's reception of Kilidj Arslan's ambassadors who had come to sue for peace, and the historian criticizes the emperor for having handed over to them the religious/military standard of the Byzantine Empire; pp. 162–163, Attaleiates aske the reader to judge his conduct during the course of the disastrous battle; p. 167, Attaleiates informs us that he heard the rumors of the fate of Romanus IV after he, Atteleiates, had fled to Trebizond where he was awaiting ship for Constantinople.

22. For the detailed analysis of Cahen's concatenation of errors, Vryonis, as in n. 1, above, 100–101 and specifically n. 109, where the completely erroneous Latin translation of the Greek text is analyzed along with its subsequent, blind adoption by Cahen in his reconstruction of the battle.

23. Carile, as in n. 12 above, passim.

24. Attaleiates-Bonn, 154.

25. E. Th. Tsolakes, as in n. 9, above; S. Mauromate-Katsougiannopoulou, ʽΗ Χρονογραφία τοῦ Μιχαὴλ Γλυκᾶ καὶ οἱ πηγές της (περίοδος 100 π.Χ. – 1118 μ. Χ.) (Thessaloniki, 1984). Hunger as in n. 10, above, I, 416–419. This has been worked out in detail and will appear in my book on Mantzikert.

26. V. R. Rosen, "Arabskie skazanija o porazhennii Romana Diogena Alp-Arslanom. I. Ibn al-Athir," 189–22; "II. Imad ed-Din Isfaghani," 189–202; "Sadr ed-Din al-Huseini," 243–252. All three studies and editions appeared in *Zapiski Vostochnago. Otdelenija Imperatorskago Russkago Arkheologicheskago Obshchestva*, 1, 1886 (St. Petersburg, 1887).

27. Though this factor is completely ignored by Cahen, the Turkish editors and translators of the Arab sources underline this fatal flaw and caution the readers to beware of reliance on them, Sümer and Sevin, as in n. 5 above, especially p. IX of the Introduction.

28. This is reported in Ibn al-Athir, al-Kamil fi't-tarih, Vol. X, 67, as reproduced in Sümer and Sevim, as in n. 5, above, p. 24 of the Arabic texts.

29. *Ioannis Zonarae Epitome historiarum* (libri I-XVIII), ed. Th. Buttner-Wobst (Bonn, III, 702).

30. Rosen, as in n. 26, above, passim. Sümer and Sevim, as in n. 5, above, XIV–XV. Sadr al-Din, *Ali al-Husaini Akhbar ad-Dawlat as-Saldjukija (Zubdat at-tewarih)*, ed., tr. Z.M. Bunjatova (Moscow, 1980), 8–9, on the lost chronicle of Ghars an-Ni'me.

31. For comments on the Fatihname, Sibt ibn al-Jauzi, in Sümer and Sevim, as in n. 5 above, XIV–XV of the Introduction, and the reproduction of the Arabic text on p. 34. A. Sevim, *Mir'atu-zaman fi tarihi'l-ayan (Selçuklularla ilgili kısımları)* (Ankara, 1968).

32. Sümer and Sevim, as in n. 5 above, XI,

and pp. 6, 10.

33. Cahen, as in n. 2 above, 621, n. 1.

34. Sümer and Sevim, as in n.5 above," Introduction" (Giriş).

35. Sümer and Sevim, as in n. 5, IX. P. Gautier, "Monodie inedite de Michel Psellos sur le Basileus Andronic Doucas," *Revue des Etudes Byzantines* 24 (1966), 156–57, has shown that August 26 is the actual date, thus correcting the estimate of D. Polemis, "Notes on Eleventh Century Chronology (1059-1081)," *Byzantinische Zeitschrift* 58 (1965), 63.

36. Sümer and Sevim, as in n. 5 above, 3, 4, 6, 12, 19, 22, 29–30, 33–34, 37 of the Arabic texts.

37. Sümer and Sevim, as in n. 5 above, 4, 12, 22, of the Arabic texts.

38. Attaleiates-Bonn, 159–160.

39. Sümer and Sevim as in n. 5 above, 8, 22, 46 of the Arabic texts. Ibn al-Jauzi has nothing on this.

40. Sümer and Sevim, as in n. 5 above, 6, 18, 22, 43–44 of the Arabic texts.

41. Sümer and Sevim, as in n. 5 above, 7–8, 43–44. Some of the Arab authors (Ibn al-Athir, Ibn al-Jauzi, al-Bondari) do not give the contents of the prayer.

42. Sümer and Sevim, as in n. 5 above, 3, 4, 8–9, 11, 13, 16–17, 23, 30, 41, 46 of the Arabic texts .

43. Attaleiates-Bonn, 160–164.

44. Attaleiates-Bonn, 164–167, gives details of its contents.

45. Psellus-Renauld, II, 164.

46. Sümer and Sevim, as in n. 5 above, 31–33 of the Arabic texts. This sensational encounter is also recorded, in less detail, by Ibn al-Qalinisi, 3; The Akhbar, 9, 10; Ibn al-Jauzi, 13–15; al-Bondari, 17, 18, 19–20; Ibn al-Athir, 23; Ibn al- Adim, 47–48. All pages refer to Sümer and Sevim, as in n. 5 above, to the Arabic texts.

47. The most detailed Muslim account, that of Sibt ibn al-Jauzi, is of some interest as a measure of what the Muslim world knew of the internal events of Byzantium in this particular case. It is, of course, far inferior to the copious reports of Attaleiates and Psellos. Ibn al-Athir and Ibn al-Jauzi say a few things, of no independent value, and the remaining Arab authors report very little or nothing at all.

9
The Economy: A Brief Survey*

Michael Hendy
Harvard University

It is a matter of very considerable pleasure to be invited, at a preparatory conference such as this, to speak on a topic with which—for better or for worse—one seems over the years and in some degree to have become identified. Although it is of course extremely dangerous to proclaim premature victory on matters scholarly and intellectual—as on any other kind of matter—nevertheless it has to be confessed that it is also very good to be able to feel that (whether by luck or by judgment) one has been in on a campaign involving really major change, in this case involving the state and development of the Byzantine economy during the eleventh (and indeed twelfth) century, from the very beginning.

For when, over twenty years ago (actually 1969–1970) one began to publish on eleventh- and twelfth-century economic and monetary affairs, the subject bore a stamp very different from that which it does today. In other words, since then a radical shift in scholarly opinion has come about: not necessarily an unanimous one, of course, but—so it may be hoped—an increasing and probably irrevocable one. At that time, both centuries in question—that is, eleventh and twelfth—were uniformly regarded as forming a period of ever deepening economic crisis and contraction, the supposed processes of which, and causation behind which, it is no longer necessary to expend much detail, time, and space, while noting that they took on both an external and an internal aspect. I now think, and have pointed out elsewhere, that such supposed external factors (for example, Seljuk destruction and dislocation and Italian commercial competition), while real enough up to a point, nevertheless also need to be cast a particularly skeptical eye upon, for they tend to provide scholarly and intellectual cop-outs, in order to explain eventual Byzantine weaknesses and failures that actually had internal—and deeper, that is, more complex and inherent—causes.

The historiographical background to this shift in opinion runs more or less as follows. In 1969–1970, the only somewhat skeptical voice that had already been raised against the traditional view of increasing decline was that of Alexander

Kazhdan, who as long ago as 1954 had suggested that the Byzantine city (obviously at least likely to have been paradigmatic for the economy as a whole) had declined/changed drastically—indeed had all but disappeared—in the course of the seventh century and that it had only recovered progressively over the tenth and eleventh centuries: thus in effect reversing the traditional schema.[1]

This revisionary pattern of development, based to a large extent on archeological/numismatic evidence, had not met with general professional approval—witness, as a single example, the proceedings of the Dumbarton Oaks Symposium on the Byzantine City, held in 1957 and published in *Dumbarton Oaks Papers* for 1959, with the late George Ostrogorsky leading the traditionalist attack.[2] There then followed my own economic/monetary studies of 1969–1970,[3] and shortly after that Clive Foss's confirmatory archeological/historical studies of Sardis (1976) and Ephesus (1979) as well as of other Anatolian sites (e.g., 1977),[4] thus complementing preexisting—but hitherto supposedly defective or a typical—studies of the Balkan sites of Corinth and Athens and of others. Most recently (1989), we have had a further "vicennial" study of my own and, more extensively, Alan Harvey's book *Economic Expansion in the Byzantine Empire 900–1200,* the title of which well stands for its contents and which came as a particular personal pleasure to me as a former supervisor of its doctoral origins, the revisionary programmer therefore now stretching across three academic generations.[5]

The case is as yet by no means complete, and—with hindsight—one has, for example, distinct reservations as to the somewhat simplistic interpretation of the seventh-century archeological evidence and its historical reconstruction that has now become orthodox (which I have elsewhere christened the "Humpty-Dumpty" paradigm) and as to the details of the way we have all at some stage utilized the crucial numismatic evidence (based on traditionalist assumptions regarding the basis of coin production and its subsequent archeological appearance).[6] But even so, the result now seems to be that the developmental sequence of mid-Byzantine economic history has been decisively reversed: from apogee in the tenth century and decline and nadir in the eleventh and twelfth, to continuing expansion over the period as a whole. Even the late Paul Lemerle signalled at least a partial withdrawal from the full traditionalist position in his *Cinq Études sur l'Onzième Siècle Byzantin* (1977), itself based largely on the Parisian *table ronde* in the eleventh century that had taken place shortly before.[7] In effect, he declared that century sanitized and fit for scholarly study, while still firmly attaching a surgeon-general's warning to the twelfth. Why he came to this curiously divided conclusion remains obscure, but in any case it seems clear that few—if any—scholars seriously interested in Byzantine economic history would now dissent from at least the main lines of the new perception.

How so many scholars got it so wrong and for so long remains another mystery, which I will forbear to pursue in any detail, while at least strongly suspecting that the problem arose from a set of prevalent but parachronistic general assumptions, each of which was more or less fallacious: that the political/military situation must necessarily be closely reflected in the economic one; that economic matters (concerning the exploitation of available material resources) and fiscal ones (concerning the revenue and expenditure of the state) were essentially the same undifferentiated thing; and that the Byzantine economic/fiscal model, overwhelming involving the extraction of a surplus from a territorially extensive but strongly accentuated and technically primitive agricultural base, so as to support a relatively massive state superstructure, operated in much the same way as a modern capitalist one. Each of these assumptions—it has long seemed to me—is at least seriously questionable, without having previously been seriously questioned.[8]

This, then, in however simplified and truncated a format, is historiographically more or less how we have arrived at the present situation. Now we turn to a more structured or layered analysis of the economy as a whole, commencing with the more general and proceeding to the more particular.

The starting point here must be, as always, the extent and nature of the territorial base involved, for it was this that directly dictated a whole range of economic—and therefore indirectly fiscal—parameters. Between c.800 and c.1200, the empire relied in essence upon two large and peninsular landmasses, although at different stages of the period, different territorial balances obtained: during the ninth and tenth centuries it relied essentially on Anatolia, with the Balkans as something of a makeweight; during the twelfth it relied on the Balkans with Anatolia as makeweight. During the eleventh century alone it possessed, and was therefore able to exploit, both peninsulas, in theory giving it an exploitative maximum. But, as pointed out elsewhere in detail, in fact each of these peninsulas possessed a different—but highly accentuated—physical structure, necessarily entailing quite radical contingent consequences in matters such as climate, predominant forms of landuse, and density of population. In other words, mere extent of landmass is not everything. In this case, the largely mountainous interior of the Balkans, and the predominant raised plateau of inner Anatolia, will have favored—possibly even ensured—the existence of a largely pastoral-based economy, and relatively light population density. In contrast, the sporadic—and largely alluvial—plains of the peripheries, will have permitted a more varied cultivation and a denser—more urbanized—population. This basic economic/social distinction will have been reflected in the fiscal resources available to the state: it is on the whole easier—and more profitable—to tax a sedentary/agricultural population, than an at least potentially movable/pastoral one.[9]

But, in addition to all this, one must necessarily also take into account various inherent technical constraints imposed on such economies and societies. For example, as again pointed out elsewhere, the high cost of land transport would (in any case) have militated against the commercial movement of agricultural surpluses off the peninsular centers toward the peripheries. Pastoral surpluses in the form of livestock on the hoof or trotter would clearly have been less affected, but in terms of straight profitability (whether to individual owner or to state taxation), they were almost certainly of lesser impact. Familial economic autarky—selfsufficiency—would thus in many cases not have been a simple conceptual option, but even a living necessity: the existence of anything more than a very basic and heavily circumscribed market was in no way a matter of ensured promiscuity, particularly in the centers. As it happens, we do have two eleventh-century descriptions, by metropolitans Leo Synnada (c.1000) and John of Euchaita (c.1050), of conditions in their Anatolian sees (both intermediate between plateau and plain), and indeed both approximate closely to what might be expected in what—as I have consistently emphasized elsewhere—was essentially a historical/geographical continuum.[10]

As already mentioned, we do have some general idea as to where the population ought to have been relatively light, and as to where it ought to have been relatively heavy: interiors and peripheries respectively. This is very much confirmed by study of such matters as subscription lists to the ecclesiastical councils of 680–681 and 691–692, of 787, and of 869–871 and 879. These, for all their theoretical limitations (they rely on the essential equation between episcopal see and city; they tell us *where* cities were at those dates, but not *what* they were then; and only actual participants' sees are represented), nevertheless again suggest a very basic continuity of population pattern stretching from late antiquity, through Ottoman times (via, e.g., maps of the sixteenth-century Friday mosques), and up to the present.[11] Now, on this broad continuum, we are in a position to impose certain more particular and changing items of evidence. For the cities there is, for instance, the very occasional literary mention and, much more important, an ever-increasing amount of archeological evidence for both Balkans and Anatolia. This shows the medieval city to have been (despite an overwhelming continuity of site, nomenclature, and ecclesiastical status) simply very different from its antique predecessor: uniformly smaller and defensive rather than larger and monumental, the difference clearly denoting substantial interim economic and social change. Within the medieval period as a whole, there is a now quite clear increase in economic activity between c.900 and c.1200 on almost every site—with perhaps more in the Balkans than in Anatolia. This can no longer be simple ascribed to freak conditions or incompleteness of excavation, and must now I think be accepted as normative. Again, the evidence of dated or datable churches conveys much the same message.[12] For the massively predominant rural population (much more difficult to analyze, because of the evidential bias) we nevertheless have the evidence of several cadastral documents of different status, and that of monastic archives—both of these pertaining mainly to the Balkans, with exploration of the latter being dominated by Athenite materials and by French scholars such as Jacques Lefort. Here, once again, we have both an apparently increasing density of population and exploitation, and a parallel (and surely connected) increasing complexity in the nature and extent of landholding.[13] Urban and rural conditions therefore seem consistent—and expanding.

A further item that has assumed an enhanced significance over the past number of years has been what might loosely be termed prosopographical studies. By this I do not necessarily mean the detailed study of particular people in their careers (although that—via such subdisciplines as sigillography—is of deservedly increasing importance). I refer rather to studies concerning such matters as where members of the dominant class originated or owned estates or both; analysis of the geographical/professional (and/or other) nature of family names; and the possible information to be derived from any or all of these: in other words, to matters of socioeconomic interest and significance by way of the family.[14]

The ramifications of such study are complex and as yet by no means fully explored—and one can therefore do no more than summarize and simplify. The "military" sector of the dominant class, also predominant in regional administration, was overwhelmingly connected with central and noncentral Anatolia (the "plateau"), whereas the "civil" sector of that class, predominant in the metropolitan bureaus, was to a similar degree derived from the capital, the islands, and the coastal areas (the "plain") of Anatolia and the Balkans. This division may therefore well have possessed not only a geographical but also a cultural and professional basis and may have lain at the base of east-west and military-civil tensions that are, in however complex and blurred a fashion, observable sporadically in the history of the eleventh century.[15]

This brings one inevitably to the subject of Constantinople itself, overwhelmingly the greatest single source of economic accumulation and consumption within the empire, and the provisioning of which (now normally private, if strictly regulated, since the cessation of state-provided and state-subsidized foodstuffs during the seventh century), undoubtedly represented a critical economic and political factor in itself. The developmental history of the city—recently the subject of treatment by, for example, Cyril Mango—clearly reflected (as indeed might be expected) the general trends apparent in the wider rural-urban economy.[16] We have no single and major source of information on its everyday eleventh-century life, such as is represented by the four fascinating Ptochoprodromic poems of the mid-twelfth century, themselves the object of several recent studies, but there is no reason to doubt that the two situations were very different.[17] What we do have, however, to be cobbled together from sporadic comments and descriptions made by the leading historians and writers of the period is something quite else: the process through which the metropolitan populace gained increased political power and social status, including access to the chief civil body, the senate, not simply on dramatic or exceptional occasions of crisis as generally in the past, but normatively, as exemplified through the senatorial representation of its members by the professional and even artisanal guilds. Such developments had previously and long been resisted by the state and its personnel, fearing among other things the social "contagion" involved. The phenomenon represents perhaps the single most interesting and significant of all the socioeconomic features of the period and also has a distinct fiscal aspect to it, for the largely decorative offices and ranks through which such access was granted tended to carry with them an annual salary—and, ominously, salaries formed a major, overall the major, item in the imperial budget. An increased expenditure on salaries in combination with an essentially inflexible revenue therefore provided an at least potential source of trouble.

The process in question (early on the object of study by Speros Vryonis) commenced not long after the death of that statist paragon Basil II in 1025, and it was to most intents and purposes at least severely curtailed shortly after the accession of the family-oriented military magnate Alexius I (Komnenus) in 1081. Thus, it was in some real sense an eleventh-century phenomenon. Between these dates, and particularly during the critical reigns of Constantine IX (Monomachus, 1042–1055), Constantine X (Ducas, 1059–1067), and Nicephorus III (Botaniates, 1078–1081), the populace and its representatives achieved an impact that remained unparalleled. There are, of course, a number of possible or probable reasons for this: several of the emperors of the period actually derived from the artisanal classes (Michael IV, 1034–1041; Michael V 1041–1042) or from the metropolitan—that is, civil—bureaucracy (Romanus III, Argyrus, 1028–1034; Michael IV, Bringas, 1056–1057; and indeed others). The common interest of both groups, now strongly based on the senate, and whether conscious or not, lay in attempting to curb the resurgent power and influence of the regional—that is, military—magnates. But, as the bottom line to all this, it does seem inconceivable that the phenomenon would, or could, have taken place if the populace in general had been gripped in a state of economic constriction, and there are indeed some clear indications that it was rather in a state of continuing expansion.[18] In any case, the eminent western historian Georges Duby has reckoned that, in the West, the period c.1050–c.1080 represented economically a critical period of preparatory growth, with c.1080 representing the point of "take-off". If this were to prove to be the case, then the parallel with these eastern/metropolitan developments would be highly suggestive, and it may well have been that the effective check to the Byzantine process with the accession of Alexius (1081) and the century-long maintenance of such restrictions (to c.1185), formed a decisive factor in the failure of the Byzantine mercantile classes to develop beyond a certain economic and social point.[19]

One must now turn to the questions of trade and coinage before moving toward a conclusion. Again one has to be brief and in effect to confine oneself to the odd features that have figured in recent debate. There seem to me to be three such features necessitating mention.

In the first place, and as already noted, the eleventh and—admittedly even more—the twelfth centuries have traditionally been seen as forming a period when, because of foreign competition resulting from the imperial grant of favorable rates of taxation (or even complete exemption from taxation) and of independent legal status and physically separate quarters to the Italian trading states of Venice, Pisa, and Genoa, the Byzantine commercial classes entered into swift and irreversible decline, and the state thereby forfeited an important item of its revenue.[20]

Now, as demonstrated elsewhere, there are very good—indeed decisive—empirical reasons for supposing that the presence and operation of the kind of numbers of foreign traders, and the size and extent of their individual and collective investments, have been grossly exaggerated and that their uniformly malignant effect on both the condition of Byzantine commerce and the collection of state revenue are simply mistaken.[21]

The assumption involved has throughout been that the Byzantine economy operated essentially as a modern one, where the terms and balances of trade are indeed of extreme importance and are calculated and published on a monthly or annual basis, and if necessary consciously manipulated, by the government of the day.

But this begs the absolutely fundamental question as to the nature and mode of operation of a medieval economy such as the Byzantine and even to the degree to which contemporaries were conceptually aware of its components and of the various interactions between them that went to make up the economy as a whole. It has to be said that the evidence in favor of such an assumption and of its contingent requirements is at present showing utterly and damningly negative, on virtually all—probably even all—counts. And it should in particular be stressed that privately based (and especially long-distance) trade, while of course always present and evidenced (indeed, probably because of its largely metropolitan focus and somewhat exotic nature, proportionaly overevidenced), nevertheless will have inevitably remained of marginal importance in the economy as a whole, still dominated as it was by primitive agriculture operating within the territorial context of large landmasses, with all that this will have entailed.[22]

In the second place, and indeed very largely as a corollary of the above, the debasement of the gold coinage that marked the middle and second half of the eleventh century has been—and in certain quarters still is—viewed above all as the inevitable result of an economic problem: the decline of Byzantine production and commerce in the face of privileged foreign activity, and so on.[23]

The phenomenon of debasement is in itself an undoubted one—not least because it is not only provable through modern technical means but, and particularly in its later heavily accentuated phase, it is also dramatically visible to the naked and unspecialized eye. The salient facts are as follows. Between c.1040 and c.1070, the gold content of the coinage fell from a theoretical (but rarely actual) 24 carats fine to about 16 carats—a drop of one-third over some thirty years, therefore representing what one might call (perhaps unwisely) controlled debasement. Between c.1070 and c.1080, its gold content fell to virtually nil—a drop of two-thirds over some twenty years, certainly representing precipitate debasement. All this was accompanied, more or less, by parallel developments in the silver and copper coinage.[24]

Now, on the face of it, one might conclude the traditional "economic" view to be upheld by the overall pattern of monetary events, with economic decline and military disaster/political confusion providing the determinant factors—the former dominating the first phase of debasement, and the latter increasingly dominating the second.

But even here, there are severe problems, and these again derive ultimately from the same set of parachronistic assumptions mentioned above.

For it is clear that the Byzantine coinage was not—at least until quite late on—in any direct sense a general economic phenomenon, but rather a particular fiscal one: providing, that is, a standardized means of collecting state taxation and distributing its expenditure. Moreover, the fiscal system depended overwhelmingly on the state's ability to collect the land tax and to a minor extent only on such items as trade tax. Coinage was therefore produced pretty rigidly according to the currently prevalent pattern of fiscal administration and marginally only—if at all—to reflect such matters as private trade: it consequently entered the equation not in such primary factors as production and distribution but in the secondary one of subsequent circulation only.[25]

If this is indeed the case (and it most assuredly is), then it follows inexorably that the basic causation behind debasement is unlikely to have been—possibly even could not have—"economic" or trade related. Leaving aside the possible significance of the fact that Michael IV had been a moneychanger suspected of forgery prior to his accession, and that is was apparently under him that the whole process began, it now seems much more in keeping with the wider evidence to seek a fiscal solution to the problem—probably involving an increasing budgetary imbalance, quite possibly connected with the increasing grant of senatorial offices and ranks (and, with them, salaries) that has already been mentioned, and later also most certainly reflecting the disastrous military and political situation of the seventies and eighties when members of the dominant class are known to have successfully, and in a wholesale fashion, evaded their full tax liabilities.[26]

For, at the end of the period, and as a severe embarrassment to the traditional case, there lies a fact that was only just beginning to be fully appreciated in 1969–1970: that the whole coinage system underwent fundamental reform during the reign of Alexius I in 1092. This involved the reintroduction of a high-quality coinage at twenty and one-half carats fine, and the establishment of a complex and much more flexible series of subordinate denominations according to a new pattern. This reform was backed by a whole series of fiscal reforms involving administrative reorganization and the reestablishment of a uniformly based taxation structure. The evident conundrum is thus as follows: if the debasement of c.1040–c.1090 reflected "economic" and largely trade-related difficulties, then what did the reform of 1092 reflect—a miraculous and sustained "economic recovery"? For the coinage system of 1092 remained operative and reasonably stable throughout the twelfth century.[27]

It was, at least one suspects in part, the half-submerged presence of this conundrum that led to the evolution of the third of the features mentioned above as due for discussion. This involved the attempt by my old friend Cécile Morrisson to interpret the first and less dramatic phase of debasement (c.1040–c.1070) in terms of a conscious, preemptive, and manipulative act on the part of the state to effect an increase in the money supply in the face of an essentially static volume of precious metal and an increase in population. Now this, on the face of it, may sound impressive, but it yet again immediately begs a question of fundamental significance with regard to the nature and functioning of the Byzantine monetary economy: To what extent were the Byzantines (and indeed most or all of their contemporaries) capable of this kind of predictive maneuver, relying as it must have been on some conceptual and integrative awareness of the economy as an autonomous entity and of the operation of at least the basics of the Quantity Theory of Money (if not of the details of Fisher's Equation, $MV\text{-}PT$), within the economy?[28]

This was, after all, a period when a number of individuals, both rulers and others, are identified as having possessed "economic" expertise: Michael IV perhaps, Constantine X and Michael XVII certainly; and in addition John the Eunuch under Michael VII. Yet in not one of these cases is there the slightest evidence that the expertise involved was other than fiscal, even in the case—that of Michael Psellos's description of Michael VII—where the material is presented in some detail. The conclusion must be that the Byzantines did not possess such conceptual and manipulative capacities—but then it is highly likely that nobody else at this stage of history did either.[29]

This survey has had—of necessity—to be a brief one, but the general message is I think clear: we have now finally established the general developmental course of Byzantine economic history as one in which the eleventh century (and indeed the twelfth) stands "rehabilitated". What remains is to continue study of that course, but this time always within the conceptual, technical, and other constraints of the time. We may then arrive at some useful and pertinent conclusions capable of bearing a wider and comparative significance. Above all, however, the traditional view of the economy is dead: it ought to be buried resolutely, if inevitably metaphorically, at the crossroads and with a stake through its heart, lest it ever rise again.

NOTES

* This stands very much as delivered on March 8, 1991. I have, in the notes below, as seems appropriate to such a brief and preparatory survey, given basic references and included in general minimal critical discussion only.

1. A.P. Kazhdan, "Vizantiiski goroda v VII–XI vekakh," *Sovetskaya Arkhelogoiya* 21 (1954), pp. 164–83

2. G. Ostrogorsky, "Byzantine Cities in the Early Middle Ages," *Dumbarton Oaks Papers* 13 (1959), pp 47–66

3. M.F. Hendy, "Byzantium, 1081–1204: An Economic Reappraisal," *Transactions of the Royal Historical Society*, ser. 5, 20 (1970), pp. 31–52—now reprinted in idem, *The Economy, Fiscal Administration and Coinage of Byzantium* (= Variorum Collected Studies Series, CS305; Northampton, 1989)—hereafter Economy no. II. Idem, *Coinage and Money in the Byzantine Empire 1081–1261* (=Dumbarton Oaks Studies, 12; Washington, D.C., 1969).

4. C.F.W. Foss, *Byzantine and Turkish Sardis* (= Archaeological Exploration of Sardis, 4; Cambridge, Mass/London, 1976). Idem, *Ephesus after Antiquity: A Late Antique, Byzantine and Turkish City* (Cambridge, 1979). Idem, "Archaeology and the 'Twenty Cities' of Byzantine Asia," *American Journal of Archaeology*, 81 (1977), pp. 469–86.

5. M. F. Hendy, "'Byzantium, 1081–1204': The Economy Revisited, Twenty Years On," in *Economy*, no. III, pp. 1–48. A. L. Harvey, *Economic Expansion in the Byzantine Empire 900–1200* (Cambridge, 1989).

6. For the Humpty-Dumpty paradigm at its most accentuated see, e.g., C.F.W. Foss, "The Persians in Asia Minor and the End of Antiquity," *English Historical Review*, 90 (1975), pp. 721–47. As I have pointed out several times elsewhere, while the general archeological phenomenon can no longer be doubted, the historical causation behind it is likely to have been much more complex than Foss would allow. Again, e.g., it remains invalid to compare twelfth-century Anatolian and Balkan coin series for simple historical information: in Anatolia the basic subordinate denomination in circulation was the billon *trakhy*, still of quite high value; in the Balkans it was the copper *tetarteron*, of much lower value. The Anatolian series are therefore numerically much weaker than the Balkan ones: the *trakhy* was lost less, the *tetarteron* much more. As for the basis of coin production, see below, n. 25.

7. P. Lemerle, *Cinq études sur l'onzième siècle*

byzantin (Paris, 1977). See also several of the articles deriving from the *table ronde* in *Travaux et Mémoires*, 6 (1976)—"Recherches sur l'onzième siècle."

8. Such questioning, lacking almost entirely for the nature and functioning of the Byzantine economy, is a well established feature for that of the ancient one. See, e.g., and with particular regard to the role of trade, P. Garnsey et. al. (eds), *Trade in the Ancient Economy* (Berkeley and Los Angeles, 1983). See also, M. F. Hendy, "Economy and State in Late Rome and Early Byzantium: An Introduction," in *Economy*, no. I, pp. 1-23.

9. M. F. Hendy, *Studies in the Byzantine Monetary Economy c. 300-1450* (Cambridge, 1985)—hereafter Studies—pp. 21-68.

10. Hendy, *Studies*, pp. 554-69. For Synnada and Euchaita, with trans. and refs., see ibid, pp. 138-45. The existence of a continuum is the constant burden of the whole first section of *Studies*. C. F. W. Foss (in a review of the book in *Speculum*, 64 [1989], at pp. 966-69) somehow contrives to misunderstand or deny this—one can only assume from an utterly careless reading of the section in question or for disingenuous reasons presumably best known to himself.

11. Hendy, *Studies*, pp. 69-85, 90-100.

12. For Anatolia see, e.g., Foss in n. 4 above; for the Balkans, Harvey, *Economic Expansion*, pp. 213-25. See also, M. J. Angold, "The Shaping of the Medieval Byzantine 'City'," *Byzantinische Forschungen* 10 (1985), pp. 1-37; Hendy, "Byzantium, 1081-1204", pp. 35-36, 45-48; idem, "The Economy Revisited", pp. 12-19.

13. Harvey, *Economic Expansion*, pp. 35-79. For a list of Lefort's main works see ibid, p. 283.

14. A. P. Kazhdan, *Sotsial'n'ii Sostav Gospodstvuiushchego Klassa Vizantii XI-XII vv.* (Moscow, 1974), usefully summarized by I. Sorlin, "Bulletin byzantino-slave: publications soviétiques sur le XIe siècle," *Travaux et Mémoires*, 6 (1976), pp. 367-98. S. Vryonis, "The Internal History of Byzantium during the 'Time of Troubles' (1057-81)" (PhD. thesis, Harvard University, 1956). See also n. 15, below.

15. Hendy, *Studies*, pp. 85-90, 100-07, 136-38.

16. C. A. Mango, "The Development of Constantinople as an Urban Centre," *The 17th International Byzantine Congress, Major Papers* (New Rochelle, N.Y., 1986), pp. 117-36.

17. Hendy, "The Economy Revisited, " pp. 23-24 and n. 85.

18. Hendy, *Studies*, pp. 570-90; S. Vryonis, "Byzantine Demokratia and the Guilds in the Eleventh Century," *Dumbarton Oaks Papers*, 17 (1963), pp. 287-314; J.-C. Cheynet, "Dévaluation des dignités et dévaluation monétaire dans la seconde moitié du XIe siècle," *Byzantion* 53 (1983), pp. 453-77.

19. G. Duby, *The Early Growth of the European Economy, Warriors and Peasants from the Seventh to the Twelfth Century* (London, 1974), pp. 157-270.

20. See, e.g., Hendy, "Byzantium, 1081-1204, " pp. 31, 39-41.

21. Hendy, *Studies*, pp. 590-602. See also n. 20, above.

22. M.F Hendy, "East and West: Divergent Models of Coinage and its Use," *Settimane di studio del Centro italiano di studi sull'alto medioevo, 38, Il secolo di ferro: mito e realta del secolo X, Spoleto, 19-25 aprile 1990* (Spoleto, 1991), 2, pp. 638, 640-47.

23. Hendy, "Byzantium, 1081-1204," p. 31; idem, "The Economy Revisited, " p.2.

24. Hendy, *Studies*, pp. 508-10, 511-12, 513.

25. This is the constant message of Hendy, *Studies*, esp. pp. 371-447. See also articles nos. IV-VIII in idem, *Economy*.

26. Hendy, *Studies*, pp. 233-36, 580. See also Cheynet, above, n. 18.

27. Hendy, *Coinage and Money*; idem, "The Economy Revisited, " pp. 34-41.

28. C. Morrison, "La dévaluation de la

monnaie byzantine au XIe siècle: essai d'interprétation," *Travaux et Mémoires*, 6 (1976), pp. 3–48. I have taken issue with this proposition on a number of occasions and in a number of places: simply an indication of the potential significance of the problem involved. See also, Hendy, above, n. 22.

29. For Psellos's description of Michael VII see, e.g., Hendy, *Studies*, p. 241. For Nicephoritzes see, e.g., J. Karayannopoulos, "Ho hypsōsis tēs timēs tou sitou epi Parapinakē," *Byzantina* 5 (1973), pp. 106–109. See also Lemerle, *Cinq études*.

10
Religion and Religious Life in Eleventh-Century Byzantium

Gerhard Podskalsky
Frankfurt-am-Main

To address the stated theme for an entire century first requires acknowledging the complexity of the question. Researchers from France, Russia, Italy, and other countries have devoted decades to the study of relevant authors, texts, and events from this period without reaching a conclusive statement. How, then, is an individual to master the subject on a first attempt and in a limited amount of space? However he phrases his arguments, he is best advised to brace himself for criticism rather than agreement.

After careful consideration as to how one might best combine factual, if necessarily incomplete, information with an independent analysis, I have hit on the following solution: in part 1, I would like to introduce the most important subthemes and cite the accompanying literature that has appeared in the last twenty years (based on the bibliography of the *Byzantinische Zeitschrift*, 1971–1989). Obviously, it will not be possible to develop further, in any systematic way, any of the problems mentioned here, some of which represent wholly divergent issues. In part 2, in a manner that is to represent and prove exemplary for the general theme, I would like to present and critically elucidate a topic that until now has been virtually ignored: namely the theological position of the mystic Symeon, the New Theologian, as well as that of his pupil, biographer, and editor, Niketas Stethatos. This position, which, with verve and consistency, Symeon presents and defends against the ex-metropolitan and teacher Stefan of Nikomedeia, anticipates many elements of the theological conception of Gregorios Palamas without the benefit of being understood and discussed in its range during the lifetime of its authors.

I. Overview of the Research of the Last Two Decades (1970–1990)

By research is understood here all general scholarly work, from critical text editions to individual and complete studies (monographs) to simple but occasionally arduously prepared lexicon articles. Because of a number of overlaps, the subcategories (themes) are organized in order of importance rahter than chronologically. A brief overview of most of these areas can be found in the handbooks on Byzantine church history by H.-G. Beck and J. M. Hussey.[1] As far as the number of authors of the eleventh century to be addressed here is concerned, the Tusculum Lexicon (Munich, 1983) lists barely forty names to which one or two others might be added.[2]

If one takes the appraisal of broad public opinion in east and west as a standard, then the so-called Great Schism (July 1054) certainly occupies the foremost position of religiously significant themes.[3] Although in the first dogmatic polemical treatises, the quarrel over the Azyma[4] and/or the Filioque was foregrounded, the most difficult complaints actually involved the differing assessments concerning the mode of election and the competency of the popes that were fully thematized in the twelfth century. The fact that they were repeatedly stricken from the Byzantine diptychs is simply a symptom of a smoldering conflict.[5] On the other hand, it ought to be kept in mind that the Patriarch Michael Kerullarios, who was dismissed by the emperor in 1058, was only formally defended by the Eastern Church and, in fact, in contrast to Photios, was neither canonized nor judged a theologian.[6] In addition, his dispute with Michael Psellos, who also received promotion under Emperor Constantine IX, a dispute that concerned not only the classical curriculum but also had something to do with his opposition to the course of church politics pursued by the patriarch, was not likely to garner him scholarly glory or worldly recognition.[7] Nonetheless, for some length of time, he was able to block the path of fellow officials, themselves intent on conciliation (e.g., Petros III of Antiocheia[8]), to the proscenium of history.

In the person of Psellos, a second inner-Byzantine subcategory is addressed, one whose significance can hardly be overestimated: namely, the relationship of classsical education to Christian faith, which is also often treated using the lapidary terms of "faith and knowledge." Psellos's teacher, Johannes Mauropus, who later became metropolitan of Euchaita,[9] managed, if only because of his personal piety, to continue to use traditional educational methods, maintaining a system that later threatened to disintegrate under the leadership of Psellos's pupil and his successor as headmaster, John Italos, as well as the Metropolitan Eustratios of Nikaia. Even if Psellos's curriculum—together with his temporary friend John VIII Xiphilinos who later became patriarch—corresponded to the desires of his eager students,[10] his predisposition for the "higher wisdom" of the neo-Platonic philosophy (Proklos), the tendency toward the irrational, and the defense of immanent philosophical perception and argumentation, as much as predicted clashes for the future[11] in spite of his basic conviction that Greek thought and Christian theology were compatible. Even if Psellos managed to escape[12] the dispute by spending some time at the Monastery of the Fair Source in the Bithynian Olympias (after January 1055), his pupil and successor, John

Italos, who was neither theologically (patristically) nor diplomatically decorated, was twice condemned by the Synod.[13] As one of the pupils of Italos, Eustratios was indeed spared by the excommunication ruling (1082), but later on, as a result of the rigorous application of dialectics in theology, he too suffered the same charge and, despite an unequivocal retraction of his errors (ἐξομολόγησις/1117),[14] was suspended for life from the office of bishop (most likely, purely by coincidence, his treatises against the Armenians—apparently forged by another hand—were the direct cause). Theodoros Smyrnaios, the successor of Italos as Hypatos of the philosophers (beginning in 1082), was spared a confrontation with the church authorities. An exact sequencing (of the events), however, must yet be awaited in L. G. Benakes' forthcoming edition of his primary works (Περὶ φύσεως καὶ τῶν φυσικῶν ἀρχῶν· ὅσα τοῖς παλαιοῖς διείληπται).

But problems for the church did not only result from the new school headmasters, who were neo-Platonites and dialecticians, but also with almost the same intensity from the heretical movements that not only rejected the institution of the church as a primary sacrament but also the individual sacraments and cults. That means here especially the Bogomils (bearing various group names) who moved into Byzantium, as well, after the end of the first Bulgarian Empire (1018). Their actual area of origin continues to be a matter of dispute: southwestern Bulgaria (Macedonia) or the central region around Preslav and/or Plovdiv (Thracia).[15] In the eleventh century, Byzantium contributed two documents that described and rejected the new heretical movements: the polemical treatise of Euthymios of Peribleptos Monastery (Constantinople ca. 1050)[16] and the synodal letter of the Ecumenical Patriarch Kosmas I (1075-1081)[17] which, with its twelve anathemas, was later introduced into the Synodik of Boril (1211). The writings of Euthymios Zigabenos (or Zigadenos),[18] especially the antiheretical "Panoplia," perhaps belong to the beginning of the twelfth century.

Formerly unknown opponents arose against the church, one being Islam that, since 1048, began advancing into Asia Minor (and especially after 1071) as well as the new wave of immigrants, the Monophysites (Syrian Jacobites and Armenians) fleeing before the Islamic advance. Against the Armenians, Emperor Alexios I Komnenos himself took up pen and paper.[19] Relations toward Islam,[20] which were at first in part informed by the spirit of tolerance, soon yielded to hard-line polemics/apologetics.[21]

But within the Byzantine Church as well, tensions developed, short-lived though they may have been, including, among other things, the confiscation of church fixtures, relics, and icons for the enrichment of state coffers under Emperor Alexios I Komnenos (1081/1082 and 1087), a practice initially condoned by the synod. The opposition party, which had at its head the Metropolitan Leon of Chalkedon, associated the conflict between state and church with a new discusssion of icon theology (*Bildertheologie*), which, however, ended with the defeat of the bishop.[22]

Over against this, in the same period, an over-all positive, in fact, glowing development occurred in Byzantine monachism. This is demonstrated not only by the fact that the new order of the Holy Mountain, set down by Athanasios Athonites (after approximately 1000), was confirmed and inscribed by means of the Hypotyposis for the Great Laura (ca. 1020) and the Typikon of Emperor Constantine IX Monomachos (1045)[23] for centuries, that is, up to the beginnings of idiorrhythmic monasticism (*Idiorrhythmie*). In addition, the eleventh century distinguished itself with a wealth of newly founded monasteries (according to J. Darrouzès's list, fifty-seven) throughout the empire[24] constructed out of a variety of motivations. Many of the founding figures known to us summarized their ascetic and practical conceptions by corresponding Typika. Of greatest importance here is Patriarch Alexios Studites (1025–1043) whose Reformed Studite Rule (1034) preserved to this day only in a Slavic version, supposedly experienced its greatest influence in the newly converted Rus' (the Caves Monastery of Kiev and since ca. 1065 other affiliates). Similar influence was experienced by the Typikon (after 1084) of Nikon of the Black Mount (Syria), whose critical complete edition is still lacking to this day.[26] What had a more enduring effect on the monasticism of the capital city were the various foundings by Lazaros of Mount Galesios (d. 1054). His vita,[27] rich in traditional themes (caves, hesychia, demons, crosses, holy sites in Jerusalem, heretics/paulicians, etc.), contains as well the summary of a Typikon (Hypotyposis). The Diataxis (1077) of Michael Attaleiates attributes great significance to a small monastery and poorhouse in Constantinople.[28] The exact, predictory remarks of the founder testify his firm and personal engagement in the matter. The Typikon of Gregorios Pakurianos (1083) for the Georgian Monastery of Petritzos (forbidden for the Greeks only from the beginning of the 16th century under Greek-Bulgarian management: Backovo) holds a special place.[29] In contrast to the monastery mentioned above (seven monks) it was supposed to lodge fifty-one monks. Of stronger religious significance for the existing cloister of Saint John the Evangelist,[30] famous to this day, is the Typikon of the Abbot Christodulos of Patmos (with a spiritual testament: 1091/1093). With these we have mentioned only the best known, especially reform-minded typika of the century, but by no means all of them (compare, e.g., those of the latter Bishop of Strumica [Manuel] for a Mother of God monastery[31] or the rhymed typikon of the Patriarch Nikolaos III Grammmatikos for a Protos of the Holy Mountain [1096?][32]).

The theme of monachism, however, by no means receives complete treatment with a discussion of the founders of monasteries. An important person to mention at this point is a critic like Patriarch Johannes Oxeites of Antiocheia

(1089-1100) who spared neither the Emperor nor bishops his critiques and especially attacked the institution of the Charistikariat.[33] The topic includes many well-read moral writers such as Philippos Monotropos, excerpted by Niketas Stethatos, with his dialogue between body and soul,[34] or compilers of sayings, maxims, and quotes such as Antonios Melissa, Johannes Georgides, and Paulos Euergetinos, known only by their names. Finally there is the exegesis of the Holy Scripture itself, which cannot be separated from spirituality and which though in the eleventh century no longer considered as creative work, aspired to a broad influence with its catenae in a fashion similar to the compiled maxims. Especially deserving of mention here are the multi-faceted writers Niketas of Herakleia[35] and Niketas Seides[36] who came out in opposition to Eustratios of Nikaia. The Archbishop Theophylaktos of Achrida[37] with his New Testament commentaries—a final illumination of the allegorical exegesis of the fathers—could be designated as "Chrysostomus redivivus." Almost as timeless as the Holy Scripture, of course, the monastic "classic," the edifying novel *Barlaam and Josaphat*, has been passed down in a century rich in literature of edification.[38]

A further, important complex that can only be touched upon here but whose repercussions upon Byzantine Christianity can hardly be overestimated, not to mention the even stronger influence upon post-Byzantine Christianity, is the mission of the Rus',[39] supported as it was, by the hierarchy of Greek descent (only one of the Kiev Metropolitans of the eleventh century was Slavic!). Was there a direct connection between the Bogomilian sentence condemned in 1143 by Byzantium that a Christian could only be saved as a monk and the thesis in the Kievan Rus', presented by Kirill, the Kievan monk of the caves and later Bishop of Turov, that a true Christian was only imaginable as a monk?[40] Among the Kiev Metropolitans of the eleventh century, Ioann(es) II. (Prodromos) is the most prominent; his descent and biography are still insufficiently illuminated.[41]

There are still other movements, events and individuals worthy of mention that played an influential role on eleventh century Byzantium. Some of these include the crusade movement that was just being constituted toward the end of the century (1096) and that presented the Greek Church with an essentially foreign and, in part, threatening conceptual perspective; the reconstitution of the Bulgarian Church (Archdiocese of Ochrid and/or "Bulgaria") following the defeat of the first Bulgarian Empire that then intensified the direct Byzantine influence amont the Slavs; the Proclus expert and editor (in the sense of Christian terminology/theology) Isaak Sebastokrator,[42] the still-contested author of the "Timarion";[43] and the numerous, industrious canonists (primary area of activity: questions of marriage) such as Demetrios of Kyzikos, Niketas of Ankyra, Patriarch Nikolaos III Grammatikos,[44] and others who have already been mentioned in a different context.

What was it in this colorful, confusing multiplicity of currents and ideas that was decisive for religious life in the eleventh century? Proceeding from the intensity of the influence, one could say with certainty that of foremost importance are the "Great Schism," the confrontation of the culture of antiquity with Christian faith (problem: humanism; theological method and the by no means uniform diffusion of monasticism.

To this latter chapter belongs as well the subject that until now has remained unmentioned owing to the fact that its significance in terms of its consequence to theology has been scarcely noticed and certainly not given its proper due; namely, the first postpatristic flowering of mysticism embodied in Symeon, the New Theologian, and his pupil, biographer, and editor, Niketas Stethatos.

II. (Pars pro toto): The Light Mysticism of Symeon the New Theologian. A Predecessor to Palamism and His View of Theology as a Science

In the last twenty years, a lot of work has been done on Symeon, the New Theologian (949–1022), and his propagator, Niketas Stethatos (= stout-hearted; ca. 1005–ca. 1090). The unusually numerous, in some cases, doubled, editions of his works[45] are not the only cause of this; studies on the spiritual experience of the Studite Monks, sometimes scientific, sometimes vulgarizing,[46] can also be attributed to the current faddishness of mysticism and esoteric studies. The aspect of interest to us here, however, especially as a counterpoint to the scientific and theological conception of Michael Psellos and Johannes Italos,[47] has formerly, as far as I can tell, received scant recognition or treatment.[48] Symeon, who after a basic education (grammar/calligraphy) had already received a vision prior to his entry into the Studios Monastery (977), remained somewhere between sceptical and deprecatory toward schools and school education[49] all his life despite the fact that, without literary skills, his writings (especially the hymns) would have been unthinkable. The inner discord, however, only came to light by means of the attacks of the ex-Metropolitan Stephanos of Nikomedeia who, out of jealousy for the visionary's great resonance, hoped to cast Symeon as ignorant with his cunning question on the type of distinction between Father and Son.[50] Flaunting his erudition, Stephanos, who had been promoted to court theologian and vested with supervisory powers, attempted to force Symeon to make the entire weight of potential knowledge of God dependent upon inner enlightenment and/or the vision of light. This later allowed Monk Nephon Hypopsephios (=Ps.-Demetrios Kydones) to combine an attack on Palamas with a cutting remark against Symeon who had supposedly written much that was "unholy and blasphemous" (βέβηλα καὶ βλάσφημα).[51] The French Hellenist F. Combefis OP (1605–1679) for the same reasons tended to exclude Symeon's *vita* from inclusion into the "*Acta Sanctorum*";[52] similar as to the case of Palamas, Symeon's orthodoxy and saintliness were doubted in the West.[53] On the Eastern Orthodox side, in contrast, Symeon was one of the most widely read authors on Athos[54] and viewed as an inspirator of Palamas.⁵⁵ For his part, Symeon very much followed in the footsteps of his spiritual father, Symeon Eulabes, whose private cult (together with his biography, now lost) was made the subject of an additional charge against the famous adept.⁵⁶ Among the church fathers Basilios, Gregorios of Nazianz, and Johannes Chrysostomos are occasionally named or cited.⁵⁷ Spiritually, however, Symeon also perceived himself as heir of the monk fathers of Sinai (Johannes Klimax, Diadochos of Photike),⁵⁸ especially in the cultivation of a not yet methodically standardized hesychasm.

Every reader of the formerly edited writings of Symeon soon notices their thematic cohesiveness that, in part, extends to parallel word choice. Although their time of composition⁵⁹ can be approximately determined in only a few cases (the controversy with Stephanos of Nikomedeia apparently occurred in the years prior to Symeon's exile; hence from about 1003 to 1009), it has been ascertained that Niketas Stethatos, foreseen by Symeon himself as the publisher of his works, edited the writings posthumously, that is, revised them several times for a larger audience (monks and laymen). This explains the striking similarities between the (monk's) sermons⁶⁰ and the theological-ethical treatises. Obviously the tangled path of the text's transmission cannot be documented in detail here.

With these introductory remarks, let us now return to our central question. Stephanos of Nikomedeia (d. after 1011) whose works unfortunately were not edited⁶¹—in addition to doctrine of the trinity, they included several logical-dialectical writings—and which would possibly be useful in illuminating the exact points of dispute, was a man who, according to Symeon's judgment of him, was found lacking in ἀπάθεια!,⁶² a quality so necessary to intellectual-spiritual ascension. What appeared to be intellectual superiority and wisdom ascribed to him by the people were in actuality only a delusion produced by evil.⁶³ With a certain degree of sarcasm, Symeon later called the engineer of his exile his "benefactor, gentleman and true friend."⁶⁴ In actuality, however, nobody could trust someone not familiar with the heart of man and whose knowledge does not extend beyond sensory experience (sight and hearing).⁶⁵ Symeon set the incomprehensibility of God's nature as well as the majority of its works over and against the apparently unlimited thirst for learning of his opponent. Symeon felt that his incomprehensibility could only be ameliorated by means of God's actions (energies) that were accessible to human knowledge.⁶⁶ The above-mentioned maliciously intended trick question by Stephanos about the distinction between Father and Son was answered by Symeon with the assertion that between two divine persons no special distinctions could be made (in similar fashion to the distinction of reason and language in humans).⁶⁷

But what did Symeon have to oppose to this, let us say, purely academic theological conception as his own contribution, that would be more than a polemic thesis? The turntable of his basic thesis is the statement that the only thing important to Christian action was conscious experience of the spirit, while the supposed unconscious possession of the spirit and/or the affirmation concerning the impossibility of experiencing the spirit while on earth supposedly represented a hollow argument.[68] This sentence implies the fundamental distinction, often presented by Symeon, between receiving the sacrament of baptism and possession of spirit (i.e., a real life in Christ). According to Symeon the two are only comparable if the baptism is preceded by a period of preparational cleansing or if a form of confirmation of faith were to follow.[69] He, then, who continues to experience himself as a prisoner of the world, not entirely transformed by the spirit, ought best be silent in church rather than speak empty words.[70] Teachers, abbots, and hierarchs of the church not standing in the light of Christ or the Holy Ghost were therefore usurpers, Simonists and spiritually ignorant. Knowledge was not identical with inner light, but first made possible by this light.[71] Nobody, then, should instruct others, unless they themselves first observed the commandments and were granted the vision of light, which gave them the authority to instruct other.[72] Symeon did not thereby wish to diminish the value of the sacrament of baptism or exclude it (as did the Bogomils); rather (in correspondence with the teachings of the Apostle Paul as well as everyday life experience), he only wanted to point to the necessity of a second baptism that was related to the first as it is the truth to an omen (τύπος).[73] In any case, up until then, at most, less than one among a thousand, or even among ten thousand of his followers had received this second spiritual baptism.[74] Niketas Stethatos himself, in his foreword to the hymns, was quite clear on this point: that his theological conception (τὸ ὕψος τῆς θεολογίας καὶ τὸ βάθος τῆς τούτων ἄντικρυς γνώσεως) would not be understandable or accessible to all people.[75] Symeon's basic thesis can be summarized in his conviction of the absolute indispensable primacy of experiencing the view of light (on the basis of the sacraments: baptism and eucharist) prior to study and/or preceding grace before every discursive thought for all those who wished to call themselves a "theologian."[76] The prototype of a theologian was for Symeon quite plainly the oft-quoted Apostle Paul.[77] It was his example that showed that the divine was not recognizable and/or utterable either by means of words alone or via exact proofs for teachers or pupils. Rather, this was only possible by means of the mystagogy of Christian life.[78]

One proof that Symeon was not totally alone in his convictions but instead lent expression to a certain tendency of the period, is provided by a singular observation made by a layman, the general and statesman Kekaumenos (second half of the eleventh century), in giving the following advice to his son: "If you are accepted into the hierarchy, perhaps as a metropolitan or bishop, do not accept your election if you have not yet, by means of fasting and night vigil, received a revelation from on high and a complete certainty of God. Should the appearance of God be not forthcoming, be of good spirit, persevere and humble yourself before God and you shall come to see him. Only this: your life must be pure and free of restrictive passions. But why even speak of a metropoly? If you should be elected Patriarch, do not dare to take the tiller of God's holy church in your hand if God has not first shown himself unto you."[79] Unfortunately nothing is known about the person of Kekaumenos or of his potential familiarity with the figure and writings of Symeon. Even the degree to which Konstantin Chrysomallos, who was posthumously condemned by a synod, shared Symeon's conceptions can no longer be exactly ascertained because of the fact that his writings were almost completely destroyed.[80]

But how does the theological conception of Symeon relate to that of Palamas as whose predecessor and fellow traveler he is often considered? Where do the similarities lie? What are the differences? In approaching this question it is of course necessary to limit ourselves exclusively to Symeon's conception without taking up the problematic of the Palamite position.

As is well known the effect of uncreated grace, namely, of divine energies in Palamism, has extensively taken the place of the turn of phrase frequently employed in early Christianity, that is to say the Holy Ghost (Christ's Spirit) indwelling the human soul.[81] According to this premise, the trinity can only be comprehensible to people in its unified, no longer person-specific activity directed to the creation. The rays of Tabor light then remain the sole witness to the inaccessible essence of the sun (=God), from which these rays emanate, but are also in reality simultaneously separated. In this closed system, theology is only conceivable in the form of divine illumination, the effectiveness of which is not necessarily bound to the receiving of church sacraments. In opposition, Symeon spoke candidly of the life and work of Christ and the Holy Ghost in us.[82] At the same time, however, he also knew of the view of divine light with the spiritual eyes of mankind (not sensory as was the case with Palamas).[83] Elsewhere he himself designates God as inexpressible and inaccessible light who supposedly only revealed himself to the worthy according to the measure of their faith.[84] The paradigm of the Tabor-happening as well (i.e., the view of Christ[!] in his divine light) is not foreign to Symeon without attributing a monopoly function to him.[85] Furthermore the metaphor of the Holy Ghost as a "form of lighted swimming pool" (κολυμβήθρα φωτοειδής) occurs frequently.[86] Symeon's quite fluent terminology betrays itself in one location in the hymns, for example, when "the sole light of the Holy Trinity," is characterized as "inseparable and yet three-parted, subsisting as unique in three persons."[87] He is even able to maintain that God lives essentially (οὐσιοδῶς) in humans.[88] He then speaks with the same certainty once again of the "energies of light"[89] without being aware of even the slightest contradiction in his manner of expression. One comes upon a similar broad palette of statements and experiences on divine life in man in the (shorter) *vita* by Symeon's pupil Niketas Stethatos.[90]

In this way we can ascertain that Symeon anticipated many elements of the theology of Palamas but that he neither totally systematized it as a whole nor considered individual elements of it to be absolutes. It was not until the arguments over the correct and solely legitimate way to practice theology that the two mystics came together in a narrowed concept of theology that is only tolerant of those results of research that directly and exclusively lead back to the divine effects existing within man. Both theologians designate certain criteria that define who is able or permitted to undertake a definitive evaluation of the results. However, neither theologian's criteria are satisfactory. In the final analysis, each theologian proposes either himself (throught critical self-analysis) or else someone else, whose qualifications, however, are determined by the theologian himself.[91] A doctrine department in the institution of the church would either be declared as incompetent, or would have to legitimize itself via self-identification as a circle of mystics. Theological research in connection with the older "wordly" sciences necessarily leads, according to this view, to "double truth" (empirical/transcendental) and, in its mystical components remains totally inobjectifiable. Symeon's position purposefully limits theology to mysticism while centuries later, and not without some justification, the opposing method of Barlaam of Seminara faced the charge of agnosticism.

An aspect that is entirely missing in Symeon in respect to the Hesychasm of the fourteenth century, both in its pre-Palamitic and its Palamitic form, is the recommendation of the Jesus prayer and especially the breathing technique accompanying its performance: in any case it is not be found among Symeon's prayer instructions for an adept.[92] Corresponding to an earlier Sinaitic Hesychasm, Symeon further rejected the conception of a sensual light (intended for the nonbelievers!)—in favor of a purely intellectual-spiritual one.[93] Toward this end he defended the conformity to the fathers like a dogma against the heretics.[94]

One of the most important themes of Symeon's that lay entirely outside his main theological thesis was the repeated allusion to the seven days or periods (millennia) of the life of the world that would be followed by an eighth eternal day of peace:[95] this frequently employed calculation is a fixed component of Byzantine eschatology. That Symeon came to speak of it may have had some connection to the expectation, around the year 1000, of an imminent end of the world.[96] At one point the Eucharist is referred to as *viaticum*, that is, as provisions for the heavenward migration of the soul.[97] This view is consistent with early monasticism.

It remains for us to take a brief look at Niketas Stethatos,[98] the pupil, biographer, and editor (i.e., interpreter as well) of Symeon, the New Theologian. The middle phase of his life as cocombatant of Kerullarios against the Latins can be ignored. His mystical writings are the work of elderly years. Italos's[99] accuser was himself no speculative theologian, but rather only sought to defend the orthodox creed against all heretical attacks. His themes resemble those of Symeon but are independently treated. In his "Κεφάλαια" for example, he sets out four preconditions for a mystical theologian who, however, would never be able to manage without the "φυσικὴ θεωρία."[100] Without the Holy Ghost, with only profane knowledge (ἔξω μαθήματα), there can be no understanding of the Holy Scripture.[101] For this reason, laymen should not put themselves forward as teachers of dogma.[102] On the other hand, however, a spiritually gifted individual (such as the Apostle Paul) stands above an individual who has only received a bishop's ordination.[103] Niketas heeded patriarchs, metropolitans, and archbishops as members of the church hierarchy and expressly bound himself to the normative doctrine of the fathers.[104] The relationship of essence and energies in God is (in comparison to Symeon) not yet more closely determined in his writings: he speaks of the intellectually perceivable, light-radiating "energies of the Holy Ghost."[105]

After Niketas Stethatos, it appears that none developed the theological position of Symeon any further. Because of this, a gap remained in the monastic light mysticism until Gregorios Palamas in the first half of the fourteenth century (that is if one ignores the so-called Palamism prior to Palamas in the thirteenth century that in fact, does refer earlier to the Filioque problem). A similar fate is suffered by dialectical theology, whose main representative was condemned in the eleventh century. It experienced a revival with Barlaam and others of like mind before being definitively branded "unorthodox" (which a post-Byzantine lingering could not entirely hinder). Symeon, the New Theologian, and his theology seem, therefore, to have temporarily earned a type of "right to sole representation in the Orthodox Church." For this reason alone, his theology had to be clearly presented. A further aspect could be the comparison of the eleventh century in Byzantium with the West or the Christian-Arabic culture of this time.[106] In both of these cultures, this period is referred to as a period of blossoming. But this comparison can only be recommended here, not investigated further.

Notes

1. H. G. Beck, *Geschichte der orthodoxen Kirche im byzantinischen Reich* (Göttingen, 1980), 134–47, 164–67; J. M. Hussey, *The Orthodox Church in the Byzantine Empire* (Oxford, 1986), 114–66.

2. Cf. H. G. Beck, *Kirche und theologische Literatur im byzantinischen Reich* (Munich, 1959; repr. 1977) (hereafter *Kirche*), 531–663.

3. On the different stages of the Schism before and after the mutual excommunications that were effectively irrevocable, although they were intended to have a limited effect, see V. Grumel and J. Darrouzès, *Les Regestes des actes du patriarcat de Constantinople* (hereafter *Les Regestes*), 1:2–3 (covering the years 715 to 1206), (Paris, 1989): 327–454 (nos. 815–998b). This source also deals with all official church procedures

relating to educational discipline.

4. One example out of many is: J. Darrouzès, "Nicolas d'Andida et les azymes," *Rev. Et. Byz.* 32 (1974): 199-210.

5. From the less recent literature see, e.g., V. Grumel, "Les préliminaires du schisme de Michel Cérulaire ou la question romaine avant 1054," *Rev. Et. Byz.* 10 (1952): 5-23.

6. See the recently published critical appraisal of his biography by F. Tinnefeld, "Michael I. Kerullarios, Patriarch von Konstantinopel (1043-1058): Kritische Überlegungen zu einer Biographie," *Jahrbuch Öst. Byz.* 39 (1989): 95-127.

7. See the essays by Ja. N. Ljubarskij, "Michail Psell i Michailj Kirularij," in *Klio* 54 (1972): 351-60; idem, "Psell v otnošenijach s sovremennikami (Psell i semja Kirulariev)," *Viz. Vrem.* 35 (1973): 89-102; idem, " Psell v otnošenijach s sovremennikami (Opyt charakteristiki ličnosti)," ibid. 37 (1976): 98-113. Two further editions are pertinent here: U. Criscuolo, *Michele Psello: Epistola a Michele Cerulario* (Naples, 1973); K. Snipes, "A Letter of Michael Psellos to Constantine the Nephew of Michael Cerularios," *Greek, Roman and Byzantine Studies* 22 (1981): 89-107.

8. On Peter III of Antioch, see J. Liébaert, "Pierre III, patr. d'Antioch," *Cathol.* 11 (Paris, 1988): 369.

9. See the following editions of, and essays on, Johannes Mauropus, see R. Anastasi, "Su tre epigrammi di Giovanni di Euchaita," *Siculorum Gymn.* ns. 25 (1972): 56-60; Ja. N. Ljubarskij, "K biografii Ioanna Mavropoda," *Byz.-Bulg.* 4 (1973): 41-51; D. Stiernon, "Jean Mauropous, métr. d"Euchaîte, 11e siècle," *Dict. de Spir.* 8 (Paris, 1973), 624-626; J. Shepard, "John Mauropus, Leo Tornicius and an alleged Russian Army: The Chronology of the Pecheneg Crisis of 1048-1049," *Jahrbuch Öst. Byz.* 24 (1975): 61-89; J. Lefort, "Rhétorique et politique: trois discours de Jean Mauropous en 1047," *Trav. et Mém* 6 (1976), 265-303 [see p. 303 for a rejection of Shepard's chronology, cf. previous ref.]; R. Anastasi, "Su Giovanni D'Euchaita," *Siculorum Gymn.* ns. 29 (1976): 19-49; A. Karpozelos, ʼΙωάννης Μαυρόπους. Συμβολὴ στὴν μελέτη τοῦ βίου καὶ τοῦ ἔργου τοῦ ʼΙωάννου Μαυρόποδος, Jannina, 1982); N. G. Wilson, *Scholars of Byzantium* (London, 1983), 151-53; R. Anastasi, "Giovanni Mauropode e Platone," *Siculorum Gymn.* ns. 40 (1987): 183-200; idem, "Giovanni d'Euchaita" (Epistola 40, p. 77 Lagarde), *Studi ital. di filol. classica* 3:5 (1987): 224-26; idem, "Michele Psello al Metropolita d'Euchaita" (Epistola 34, pp. 53-56 K.D.), *Studi di filol. biz.* 4 (Catania, 1988): 105-120.

10. See W. Wolska-Conus, "Les écoles de Psellos et de Xiphilin sous Constantin IX Monomaque," *Trav. et Mém.* 6 (1976): 223-43; idem, "L'école de droit et l'enseignement du droit à Byzance au 11e siècle: Xiphilin et Psellos," ibid. 7 (1979): 1-107; P. Lemerle, "Le gouvernement des philosophes: Notes et remarques sur l'enseignement, les écoles, la culture," *Cinq études sur le 11e siècle byzantin* (Paris, 1977), 193-248; D. G. Dakouras, "Die Rehabilitation der griechischen Studien im 11. Jahrhundert und Michael Psellos," in Θεολ. 49 (1978): 185-98, 392-411; C. Niarchos, "The Philosophical Background of the Eleventh Century Revival of Learning in Byzantium," in *Byzantium and the Classical Tradition* (Birmingham, 1981), 127-32; R. Browning, "Courants intellectuels et organisation scolaire à Byzance au 11e siècle: Résumé," *Trav. et Mém.* 6 (1976): 219-22.

11. Several editions and essays can be provided as references on this subject: P. P. Joannou, *Démonologie populaire–démonologie critique au 11e siècle: La vie inédite de S. Auzence par M. Psellos* (Wiesbaden, 1971); Ja. N. Ljubarskij, "Psell v otnošenijach s sovremennikami: Ioann Mavropod, Ioann Ksifilin, Konstantin Lichud," *Palest. sborn.* 23 (86) (1971), 125-43; J. Gouillard, "La religion des philosophes," *Trav. et Mém.* 6 (1976): 305-24, specifically 315ff. (also in idem, *La vie religieuse à Byzance* 3 [London, 1981]); J. Grosdidier de Matons, "Psellos et le monde de l'irrationnel," *Trav. et Mém.* 6 (1976): 325-49; D. G. Dakouras, "Michael

Psellos' Kritik an den alten Griechen und dem griechischen Kult," in Θεολ. 48 (1977): 40–75; L. G. Benakes, "Χρόνος καὶ αἰών. Ἀντιπαράθεση ἑλληνικῆς καὶ χριστιανικῆς διδασκαλίας στὸ ἀνέκδοτο ἔργο τοῦ Μιχαὴλ Ψελλοῦ" in Φιλοσοφία 10/11 (1980/1981), 398–421; U. Criscuolo, "Tardoantico e umanesimo bizantino: Michele Psello," in Κοινωνία 5 (1981): 7–23. Two works that in future will no longer be ascribed to Psellos are also pertinent to this issue: P. Gautier, ed., "Le De Daemonibus du Pseudo-Psellos," Rev. Et. Byz. 38 (1980): 105–94; idem, "Pseudo-Psellos: Graecorum opiniones de daemonibus," ibid. 46 (1988): 85–107.

12. See U. Criscuolo, ed., *Michele Psello: Epistola a Giovanni Xifilino* (Naples, 1973); idem, "Sui rapporti tra Michele Psello e Giovanni Xifilino" (epistola 191 K.-D.), *Atti Accad. Pontiniana* n.s. 24 (1975): 1–8 (this is a commentary on the above in the form of an amicable discussion about monastic life); Ja. N. Ljubarskij, "Vizantijskij monach XI v. Ilija: P materialem perepiski Michaila Psella," *Anticnaja drevnost' i srednie veka* 10 (1973): 198–202; P. Gautier, "Éloge funèbre de Nicolas de la Belle Source par Michel Psellos, moine à l'Olympe," in *Βυζαντινά* 6 (1974): 9–69, esp. 15–22 [Michael Psellos on Olympus]; for German translation of the above see G. Weiß, "Die Leichenrede des Michael Psellos auf den Abt Nikolaos vom Kloster von der Schönen Quelle," ibid.: 219–322; M. L. Agati, "Due epistole di Psello ad un monaco del monte Olimpo," in *Studi albanologici, balcanici, bizantini e orientali in onore di G. Valentini* (Florence, 1986), 177–90; see also P. Gautier, "Précisions historiques sur le monastère Ta Narsou," *Rev. Et. Byz.* 34 (1976): 101–110. Although no complete edition of Psellos's works exists at this time, there is no end to the list of editions of individual writings (esp. letters) and of shorter miscellanea (we owe a great deal to the planning and work of the philologists L. G. Westerink and P. Gautier, both now deceased): J. D. Baggarly, "A Parallel between Michael Psellus and the *Hexaemeron* of Anastasius of Sinai," *Or. Chr. Per.* 36 (1970): 337–347; G. Weiß, "Forschungen zu den noch nicht edierten Schriften des Michael Psellos," in *Βυζαντινά* 4 (1972), 11–52; Ja. N. Ljubarskij, "Psell v otnošenijach s sovremennikami (Psell i femnye sud'i)," *Rev. Et. Sud-Est eur.* 10 (1972), 1:17–32; idem, "Psell v otnošenijach s sovremennikami," *Viz. Vrem.* 34 (1973): 72–87; G. Karakalios, "Michael Psellos on man and his beginning: A philosophical interpretation of man's creation and fall by a Byzantine thinker in the 11th century," *The Greek Orthodox Theol. Rev.* 18 (1973): 79–96; S. Ebbeson, "Ὁ Ψελλὸς καὶ οἱ σοφιστικοὶ ἔλεγχοι," in *Βυζαντινά* 5 (1973): 427–44; A. M. Guglielmo, "Un maestro di grammatica a Bizancio nell' XI secolo e l'epitafio per Niceta di Michele Psellos," *Siculorum Gymn.* n.s. 27 (1974): 421–63; Ja. N. Ljubarskij, "Literaturno-estetičeskie vzgljady Michaela Psella," *Antičnost' i Vizantija*, 1975:114–40; R. Anastasi, "Psello e giovanni Italo," *Siculorum Gymn.* n.s. 28 (1975): 525–38; R. Browning, "Enlightenment and repression in Byzantium in the 11th and 12th centuries," *Past and Present* 69 (1975): 3–12; J. Whittaker, "Proclus, Procopius, Psellus and the scholia on Gregory Nazianzen," *Vig. Chr.* 29 (1975): 309–313; L. G. Benakes, "Μιχαὴλ Ψελλοῦ περὶ τῶν ἰδεῶν, ἃς ὁ Πλάτων λέγει," in *Φιλοσοφία* 5/6 (1975/1976): 391–423; P. Gautier, ed., "Michael Psellos et la Rhétorique de Longin," *Prometheus* 3 (1977): 193–203; E. G. Kriaras, "Μιχαὴλ Ψελλός. Ὁ ἀνθρωπιστὴς—ὁ Χριστανός," in *Φιλολογικὴ πρωτοχρονιά* 34 (1977): 181–186; O. Musso, ed., *Michele Psello: Nozioni paradossali* (Naples, 1977); A. Jacob, "Un opuscule didactique otrantais sur la liturgie eucharistique: L'adaption en vers, faussement attribuée à Psellos, de la Protheoria de Nicolas d'Andida," *Riv. Studi Biz. e Neoell.* n.s. 14–16 (1977/1979): 161–78; P. Gautier, ed., "Monodies inédites de Michel Psellos," *Rev. Et. Byz.* 36 (1978): 83–151; M. D. Spadaro, ed., "Un inedito di Psello del cod. Par. gr. 1182," Ἑλληνικά 30 (1977/1978): 84–98; Ja. N. Ljubarski, *Michail Psell. Ličnost' i tvorčestvo: K istorii vizantijskogo predgumanizma* (Moscow, 1978);

M. L. Agati, ed., "Tre epistole inedite di Michele Psello," *Siculorum Gymn.* n.s. 33 (1980): 909-16; A. Karpozelos, "Δύο ἀνέκδοτες ἐπιστολὲς τοῦ Μιχαὴλ Ψελλοῦ," in *Δωδώνη*, 9 (1980): 299-310; P. Gautier, ed., "La défense de Lazare de Philippoupolis par Michel Psellos," *Trav. et Mém.* 8 (1981): 151-69; U. Criscuolo, "Πολιτικὸς ἀνήρ: Contributo all pensiero politico di Michele Psello," *Rendic. Acc. Lett. Belzantium* n.s. 57 (1982): 129-63; N. G. Wilson, *Scholars of Byzantium* (London, 1983), 156-66; M. Angold, "The intellectual currents in 11th century Byzantium," in *The Byzantine Empire, 1025-1204: A political history* (London, 1984), 76-90; Č. Milanović, "Psel ij Grigorije, Nona e Teodota," *Zborn. rad. Viz. inst.* 23 (1984): 73-87; M. D. Spadaro, "Un chrysobullon Pselliano" (no. 1023 Dölger), *Orpheus* 5 (1984): 335-56; P. Gautier, ed., "Quelques lettres de Psellos inédites ou déjà éditées," *Rev. Et. Byz.* 44 (1986), 111-97; G. Vergari, "Michele Psello e la tipologia femminile cristiana," *Siculorum Gymn.* n.s. 40 (1987): 217-25; E. V. Maltese, "Epistole inedite di Michele Psello, I-II," *Studi ital. filol. class.* vol. 3, no. 5 (1987): 82-96, 214-23; idem, *Cultura e politica nell' XI seculo in Bizanzio: Versioni di testi di M. Psello e di G. di Euchaita* (Catania, 1988); J. M. Duffy and D. J. O'Meara, *Michaelis Pselli Philosophica Minora* (Leipzig, 1989), vol. 2, *Opuscula psychologica, theologica, daemonologica* (ed. D. J. O'Meara).

13. For the more recent literature on John Italos, see the lexicon article: G. Podskalsky, "Johannes Italos," in *Lex. MA, V* (Munich and Zürich, 1991), 583; in addition to the literature listed in the above, see also: P. Joannou, "Zwei vermißte Traktate aus den 93 Quaestiones quodlibetales des Johannes Italos: 'de iconis' und 'de duobus naturis' in Christo," in *Silloge Bizantina in onore di S. G. Mercati* (Rome 1957), 233-36; K. G. Niarchos, " Ὁ Ἀριστοτέλης γιὰ τὴ φύση καὶ ἡ κριτικὴ τοῦ Ἰωάννου τοῦ Ἰταλοῦ," in *Ἀριστοτέλης. Πρακτικὰ Παγκοσμίου Συνεδρίου "Ἀριστοτέλης,"* Θεσσαλονίκη 7-14 Αὐγ., vol. 2 (Athens, 1981): 40-49; J. Gouillard, "Léthargie des âmes et culte des Saints: Un plaidoyer inédit de Jean diacre et maistor," *Trav. et Mém* 8 (1981): 171-86; N. G. Wilson, *Scholars of Byzantium* (London, 1983), 153-56; J. Gouillard, ed., "Une lettre de (Jean) l'Italien au patr. de Constantinople?" *Trav. et Mém.* 9 (1985): 175-79; A. P. Kazhdan and A. Wharton Epstein, *Change in Byzantine Culture in the 11th and 12th Centuries* (Berkeley and Los Angeles, 1985), 127f., 248f.; J. H. Erickson, "John Italos (ca. 1025-after 1082)," in *Dict. of the Middle Ages*, 7 (1986), 131f. For background on Latin-Greek relations, see H. Hunger, *Graeculus perfidus. ΙΤΑΛΟΣ ΙΤΑΜΟΣ.: Il senso dell' alterità nei rapporti greco-romani ed italo-bizantini* (Rome, 1987).

14. For the more recent literature on Eustratios, see G. Podskalsky, "Eustratios von Nikaia," in *Theol. Realenz* 10 (Berlin and New York, 1982), 550f., also in *Lex. MA* 4 (Munich and Zürich, 1989), 117. The following titles (editions and essays) are an incomplete listing: P. Joannou, "Les sort des évêques hérétiques réconciliés: Un discours inédit de Nicétas de Serres contre Eustrate de Nicée," *Byz.* 28 (1958): 1-30; S. A. Gukova, "Kosmografičeskij traktat Evstratija Nikejskogo," *Viz. Vrem.* 47 (1986): 145-56; K. Alpers, ed., "Die 'Definition des Seins' des Eustratios von Nikaia: Kritische Neuausgabe," in *ΦΙΛΟΦΡΟΝΗΜΑ. Festschrift für Martin Sicherl zum 75. Geburtstag* [festschrift for Martin Sicherl on his 75th birthday] (Paderborn, 1990), 141-59.

15. On heresy and the study of heresy in Byzantium, both in general and in the eleventh century in particular, see J. Gouillard, "L'héresie dans l'Empire byzantin des origines au 12e siècle," *Trav. et Mém.* 1 (1965): 299-324 (also in idem, *La vie religieuse à Byzance* [London, 1981], vol. 1); idem, "Le Synodikon de l'orthodoxie," *Trav. et Mém.* 2 (1967): 1-316; M. Loos, "Certains aspects du bogomilisme byzantin du 11e et 12e siècles" (hereafter "Certains aspects"), *Byz. Slav* 28 (1967): 39-53; E. Werner, *Häresie und Gesellschaft im 11. Jahrhundert*, (Berlin, 1975) (mostly on the Western point of view); G. Cankove-Petkova, "Zu den Nachrichten der byzantinischen Quellen

über die Ketzerbewegungen in Bulgarien und den bulgarischen Gebieten während des 11. und 12. Jahrhunderts," in J. Dummer and J. Irmscher, eds., *Byzanz in der europäischen Staatenwelt* (Berlin, 1983), 200-204.

16. On Euthymios, see J. Darrouzès, "Euthyme, moine de Péribleptos," in *Dict. d'Hist. et de Géogr. Eccl.* 16 (Paris, 1964): 63f.; Loos, "Certains aspects."

17. Even Patriarch Kosmas II (1146/1147) cannot be completely ruled out as [Abdender?]: J. Gouillard, ed., "Une source grecque du Sinodik de Boril: La lettre inédite du patr. Cosmas," *Trav. et Mém.* 4 (1970): 361-74 (also in idem, *La vie religieuse à Byzance* [London, 1981], vol. 15).

18. On Euthymios Zigabenos (Zigadenos) see A. N. Papabasileiou, Εὐθύμιος –' Ιω άννης Ζυγαδηνός. Βίο ς–Συγγραφαί (Athens, 1977); G. Podskalsky, "Euthymios Zigabenos [Zigabenos], 11.-12. Jahrhundert)," in *Theol. Realenz* 10 (Berlin and New York, 1982): 557f.

19. See Sp. Vryonis, Jr., *The Decline of Medieval Hellenism in Asia Minor and the Process of Islamisation from the 11th to the 15th century* (Berkeley, 1971), esp. 55-68; E. Janssens, "La bataille de Mantzikert (1071) selon Michel Attaleiate," *Annuaire Inst. Phil. et Hist. Orient. et Slav.* 20 (1968-1972): 291-304; G. Dagron, "Minorités ethniques et religieuses dans l'Orient byzantin à la fin du 11e et au 12e siècle: L'immigration syrienne," *Trav. et Mém.* 6 (1976): 177-216.

20. On relations towards Islam, see, e.g., Michael Psellos's letter to a sultan (1073/1074): P. Gautier, ed., "Lettre au sultan Melik-Shah rédigée par Michel Psellos," *Rev. Et. Byz.* 35 (1977): 73-97. See also G. Makdisi et al., *La notion de liberté au Moyen-âge: Islam, Byzance, Occident* (Paris, 1985), esp. 239-55 (L. Clucas).

21. The dispute of a monk named Euthymios with a Moslem (before the 12th century) may possibly have originated with Euthymios of Peribleptos as well: see E. Trapp, ed., "Die Dialexis des Mönchs Euthymios mit einem Sarazenen," *Jahrbuch Öst. Byz.* 20 (1971): 111-32.

22. The charge instigated in 1085 by Eustratios of Nikaia led in 1086 to [the bishop's] condemnation and divestment, that was not lifted until 1094/1095 after a reconciliation. See P. Gautier, "Le synode des Blachernes (fin 1094): Etude prosopographique," *Rev. Et. Byz.* 29 (1971): 213-84; A. A. Glavinas, ʹΗ ἐπὶ ʹΑλεξίου Κομνηνοῦ (1081-1118) περὶ ἱερῶν σκευῶν, καιμηλίων καὶ ἁγίων εἰκόνων ἔρις (1081-1095), (Thessaloniki, 1972); D. Stiernon, "Léon de Chalcédoine, métr. byz., fin du 11e siècle," in *Dict. de Spir.* 9 (Paris, 1976): 626.

23) Ph. Meyer, ed., *Die Haupturkunden für die Geschichte der Athos-Klöster* (Leipzig, 1894; repr. Amsterdam, 1965), 130-40, 151-62.

24. See A. P. Každan, "Vizantijskij monastyr' 11-12 vv. kak social'naja gruppa," *Viz. Vrem.* 31 (1971): 48-70; P. Charanis, "The monk as an element of Byzantine society," *Dumb. Oaks Pap.* 25 (1971): 61-84 (from the 7th to the 15th century); A. Failler, "Le monachisme byzantin aux 11e et 12e siècles: Aspects sociaux et économiques," *Cah. d'Hist.* 20 (1975): 279-302; J. Leroy, "Monachisme oriental aux 10e-13e siècles," ibid., 303-331; J. Darrouzès, "Le mouvement des fondations monastiques au 11e siècle," *Trav. et Mém.* 6 (1976): 159-76.

25. On editions of their work and some of the more recent essays: G. Podskalsky, "Der heilige Feodosij Pečerskij: Historisch und literarisch betrachtet," *Harv. Ukr. Stud.* 12/13 (1988/1989), 719f. (nn. 19-25).

26. On the status of research, see J. Nasrallah, "Un auteur antiochien au 11e siècle: Nicon de la Montaigne Noire (vers 1025-début du 12e siècle)," *Proche-Or. Chrét.* 19 (1969): 150-61; A. Solignac, "Nicon de la Montaigne Noire, moine antiochien, 11 siècle," in *Dict. de Spir.* 11 (Paris, 1982): 319f.

27. "Vita S. Lazari auctore Gregorio monacho" (BHG 979), *ASS Nov.* 3 (Brussels, 1910), 508-588 (an incomplete text), (Hypotyposis: 585, no. 246).

28. For a critical essay, see P. Gautier, "La Diataxis de Michel Attaleiate," *Rev. Et. Byz.* 39 (1981): 5-143. On the status of research, see A. P. Každan, "Social'nye vozzrenija Michaila Attaliata," *Zborn. rad. Viz. inst.* 17 (1976): 1-53; idem., "The social views of Michael Attaleiates, in A. Každan and S. Franklin, *Studies of Byzantine Literature of the 11th and 12th Centuries* (Cambridge and Paris, 1984), 23-86; P. Lemerle, "La Diataxis de Michel Attaliate (mars 1077)," in *Cinq Études sur le 11e siècle byzantin* (Paris, 1977), 65-112; E.Th.Tsolakes, "Κάποια προβλήματα τῆς "διατάξεως" τοῦ Μιχαήλ 'Ατταλειάτη," in "'Αφιέρωμα στὸν 'Εμμανουὴλ Κριαρά." Πρακτικὰ 'Επιστημονικοῦ Συμποσίου ('Απριλίου 1987), (Thessaloniki, 1988), 29-36 (up to the year of his death: after 1085).

29. For a critical essay, see P. Gautier, "Le typikon du Sébaste Grégoire Pakourianos, *Rev. Et. Byz.* 42 (1984): 5-145. See also P. Lemerle, "Le typikon de Grégoire Pakourianos (décembre 1083)," in *Cinq Études sur le 11e siècle byzantin* (Paris, 1977), 113-91; K. Mamone, "Παρατηρήσεις ἐπὶ τοῦ Τυπικοῦ τῆς Μονῆς Πετριτζοῦ (Μπατσκόβου)," in *'Επ. 'Ετ. Βυζ. Σπ.* 43 (1977/1978): 329-44; I. M. Konidares, *Τὸ τυπικὸν τοῦ Πακουριανοῦ καὶ ἡ "'Ιερατικὴ σχολὴ" τῆς μονῆς Πετριτζοῦ*, in festschrift for G. Konidares (Athens, 1984), 156-169.

30. A new critical edition is badly needed; until such is available, see F. Miklosich and J. Müller, *Acta et diplomata graeca medii aevi* 6 (Vienna, 1894, repr. Aalen, 1968), 59-90. The article by H. M. Biedermann, "Christodulos von Patmos," in *Lex. MA* 2 (London and Zürich, 1983), 1920f., unfortunately does not take into account the following essay: P. Gautier, "La date de la mort de Christodule de Patmos (mercredi 16 mars 1093)," *Rev. Et. Byz.* 25 (1967): 235-38.

31. On all the typica (approx. 40), see K. A. Manaphes, *Μοναστηριακὰ τυπικὰ—Διαθῆκαι. Μελέτη φιλολογική*, (Athens, 1970); I. M. Konidares, *Τὸ δίκαιον τῆς μοναστηριακῆς περιουσίας ἀπὸ τοῦ 9ου μέχρι καὶ τοῦ 12ου αἰῶνος*, (Athens, 1979).

32. See Grumel and Darrouzès, *Les Regestes*, 982 (975).

33. See P. Gautier, "Diatribes de Jean l'Oxite contre Alexis Ier Comnène," *Rev. Et. Byz.* 28 (1970): 5-55; idem, "Réquisitoire du patr. Jean d'Antioche contre le charisticariat," ibid. 33 (1975): 77-132; D. Stiernon, "Jean V (IV), dit l'Oxite, patr. d'Antioche (avant sept. 1089-1100), in *Dict. de Spir.* 8 (Paris, 1973): 641-45. On the Charisticariate, see H. Ahrweiler, "Le charisticariat et les autre formes d'attribution de couvents aux 10e-11e siècles," *Zborn. rad. Viz. inst.* 10 (1967): 1-27 (also in idem, *Etudes sur les structures administratives et sociales de Byzance* [London, 1971], vol. 7).

34. On Philippos Monotropos, see G. M. Prochorov, "Dioptra Filippa Pustynnika," and "Dušezritel'noe zercalo," in *Russkaja i gruzinskaja srednovekovye literatury* (Leningrad, 1979): 143-66; A. Solighac, "Philippe le Solitaire, moine grec ou byzantin, fin 11e-début 12e siècle," in *Dict. de Spir.* 12, 1 (Paris, 1984): 1323-25; W. Hörander, "Notizen zu Philippos Monotropos," in *Βυζαντινά* 13 (1985/escr. 1986): 2, 815-831.

35. On the work of Niketas of Kerakleia, see Ch. Th. Krikones, *Συναγωγὴ πατέρων εἰς τὸ κατὰ Λουκᾶν Εὐαγγέλιον ὑπὸ Νικήτα Ἡρακλείας*, (Thessaloniki, 1973); for public information, see J. Reuss, "Ein unbekannter Kommentar zum 1. Kapitel des Lukasevangeliums," *Biblica* 58 (1977): 224-30; D. Stiernon, Nicétas d'Heraclée, metr. byz. (fin 11e-début 12e siècle), in *Dict. de Spir.* 11 (Paris, 1981): 219-21; idem, "Nicétas d'Heraclée, écrivain et metr. byz. (seconde moitié du 11e siècle-première moitié du 12e siècle)," in *Cath.* 9 (Paris, 1982): 1206-8.

36. On the work of Niketas Seides, see P. N. Simotas, Νικήτα Σείδου, Σύνοψις τῆς Ἁγίας Γραφῆς κατὰ τὸ ὑπ' ἀριθ. 483 κώδικα τῆς Ἐθνικῆς Βιβλιοθήκης τῆς Ἑλλάδος, (Thessaloniki, 1984); for biographical information, see D. Stiernon, "Nicétas Seidès, controversiste byz. (11e-12e siècle), *Cath.* 9 (Paris, 1982): 1216f. On his dispute

with the Latinists (esp. Archbishop Grossolano of Milan), see R. Gahbauer, *Gegen den Primat des Papstes: Studien zu Niketas Seides* (Munich, 1975).

37. On Theophylaktos' complete works, which are still of great importance to the Southern and Eastern Slavs (Klimentvita et al.), see G. Podskalsky, "Théophylacte d'Achrida, archevêque (+ vers 1120-26?)," in *Dict. de Spir.* 15 (Paris, 1991): 542-46. See also R. Katičić, *Vizantijski izvori na istorija naroda Jugoslavija* 3 (Belgrade, 1966); B. Panov, *Teofilakt Ochridski kako izvor za srednovekovnata istorija na makedonskiot narod* (Skopje, 1971); idem, "Ochrid vo krajot na 11 i početakot na 12 v. vo svetlinata na pismata na Teofilakt Ochridski," *Zborn. Archeol. Muzej na Makedonija* 6/7 (1967-1974), (Skopje, 1975): 181-95; R. Anastasi, "Sul Logos basilikos di Teofilatto per Alessio Comneno," *Orpheus* n.s. 3 (1982): 358-62; S. Antoljak and B. Panov, *Srednovikovna Makedonija* 2 (Skopje, 1985); B. Panov, "Teofilakt Ochridski kako izvor za srednovekovnata istorija na makedonakijot narod" (see above).

38. See B. L. Fonkič, "Un 'Barlaam et Joasaph' grec daté de 1021," *An. Boll.* 91 (1973): 13-20.

39. See note 25 above; see also A. Poppe, *Panstwo i koscio na Rusi w 11 wieku* (Warsaw, 1968); idem, "Das Reich der Rus' im 10. und 11. Jahrhundert," *Jahrbuch für Geschichte Osteur.* 28 (1980): 334-54, esp. 343ff.; A. F. Zamaleev and V. A. Zoc, *Mysliteli Kievskoj Rusi* (Kiev, 1981); A. F. Zamaleev, *Filosofskaja mysl' v srednovekovoj Rusi 11-16 vv.* (Leningrad, 1987); Ja. N. Ščapov, *Gosudarstvo i cerkov' Drevnej Rusi 10-13 vv.* (Moscow, 1989).

40. See Grumel and Darrouzès, *Les Regestes*, 1012; see also G. Podskalsky, "L'évêque Cyrille de Tourov (2e moitié du 12e siècle): Le Théologien le plus important de la Rus' de Kiev," *Irén.* 61 (1988): 517 (second speech by the monk). Even Symeon, the New Theologian, was not far from accepting this monopolistic claim on the part of the monks.

41. See G. Podskalsky, "Metr. Ioann II. von Kiev als Ökumeniker," *Ostkat. Stud.* 37 (1988): 178-84.

42. On Isaak Sebastokrator, see several fairly recent editions (with "emendations") of Proclus's text, and essays: I. J. Rizzo, ed., *Isaak Sebastokrator: Περὶ τῆς τῶν κακῶν ὑποστάσεως,* (Meisenheim and Glan, 1979); M. Erler, ed., *Isaak Sebastokrator: Über Vorsehung und Schicksal* (Meisenheim and Glan, 1979); idem, *Proklos Diadochos: über die Vorsehung, das Schicksal und den freien Willen an Theodoros den Ingenieur (Mechaniker)* (Meisenheim and Glan, 1980); C. Steel, "Un admirateur de S. Maxime à la cour des Comnènes: Isaac le Sébastocrator, in *Maximus Confessor: Actes du Symposium sur Maxime le Confesseur (1980)* (Freiburg, 1982), 365-372.

43. See R. Romano, "Sulla posslibie attribuzione del *Timarione* pseudoluciano a Nicola Callicle," *Giorn. ital. di filol.* n.s. 4 (1973): 309-15; idem, "In margine al problema della paternità del *Timarione*. Sull' anonimo *dux* di Tessalonica," *Vichiana* n.s. 2 (1973): 187-89; B. Baldwin, "The authorship of the *Timarion*," *Byz. Ztschr.* 77 (1984): 233-37.

44. See D. Stiernon, "Nicolas III Grammatikos, patr. de Constantinople de 1084 à 1111," in *Cath.* 9 (Paris, 1982): 1244-46.

45. J. Darrouzès, *Syméon le Nouveau Théologien; Chapitres théologiques, gnostiques et pratiques*, (Paris, 1957) (hereafter *Chapitres*); B. Krivochéine and J. Paramelle, *Syméon le Nouveau Théologien: Catéchèses 1-5* (Paris, 1963), *Catéchèses 6-22* (Paris, 1964), *Catéchèses 23-24* (Paris, 1965); J. Darrouzès, *Traités théologiques et éthiques*, vols. 1-2 (Paris, 1966/1967) (hereafter *Traités*); J. Koder and J. Paramelle, eds., *Hymnes 1-15* (Paris, 1969); Koder and L. Nyrand, eds., *Hymnes 16-40* (Paris, 1971), Koder et al., eds. *Hymnes 41-58* (Paris, 1973); A. Kambylis, *Symeon Neos Theologicos: Hymnen* (Berlin and New York, 1976) (hereafter *Symeon*).

46. A. P. Každan, "Predvaritel'nye zamečanija o mirovozzreii viz. mistika 10-11

vv. Simeona," *Byz.Slav* 28 (1967): 1–38; K. Deppe, "Der wahre Christ: Eine Untersuchung zum Frömmigkeitsverständnis Symeons des Neuen Theologen und zugleich ein Beitrag zum Verständnis des Messalianismus und Hesychasmus," Ph.D. diss., University of Göttingen, 1971; B. Krivochéine, "Essence créée et essence divine dans la théologie spirituelle de Syméon le Nouveau Théologien, " *Messager de l'Exarchat du Patr. Russe en Europe Occidentale* 75/76 (July–Dec. 1971): 151–70; D. Stathopulos, "The divine light in the poetry of Symeon the New Theologian (949–1025)," *The Greek Orth. Theol. Rev.* 19 (1974): 95–111; W. Völker, *Praxis und Theorie bei Symeon dem Neuen Theologen: Ein Beitrag zur byz. Mystik* (Wiesbaden, 1974) (reviewed by G. Podskalsky, in *Theol. und Philos.* 51 [1976]: 614–16); G. A. Maloney, *The mystic of fire and light: St. Symeon the New Theologian* (Deville, N.J., 1975); Sr. Sylvia Mary, "Simeon the New Theologian and the Way of Tears," in *One yet two: monastic tradition, East and West*, Orthodox-Cistercian Symposium, Oxford University, June 28–Sept. 1, 1973 (Kalamazoo, Mich., 1976), 95–119; J. van Rossum, "Priesthood and Confession in St. Symeon the New Theologian," *St. Vlad. Theol. Quart.* 20 (1976): 220–28; Ch. B. Christophorides, Ἡ πνευματικὴ πατρότης κατὰ Συμεὼν τὸν Νέον Θεολόγον, (Thessaloniki, 1977); R. Maisano, "La poesia religiosa di Simeone il Nuovo Teologo," *Riv. di storia e lett. relig.* 13 (1977): 35–45; Krivochéine, *Dans la lumière de Christ: Saint Syméon le Nouveau Théologien, 949–1022: Vie-Spiritualité-Doctrine* (Chevotogne, 1980) (hereafter *Dans la lumière*); idem, *Prepodobnyj Simeon Novyj Bogoslov, 949–1022* (Paris, 1980); A. de Halleux, "Syméon le Nouveau Théologien," in *L'expérience de la prière dans les grandes religions*, Actes du Colloque de Louvain-La-Neuve et Liège (Nov. 22–23, 1978) (Louvain-La-Neuve, 1980), 351–63; B. Fraigneau-Julien, *Les sens spirituels et la vision de Dieu selon Syméon le Nouveau Théologien* (Paris, 1980); C. Tsirpanlis, "The Trinitarian and Mystical Theology of St. Symeon the New Theologian," Ἐκκλησία καὶ Θεολογία 2 (1981): 507–44; M. Loos, "Courant mystique et courant hérétique dans la société byzantine," *Jahrbuch öst. Byz.* 32, 2 (1982): 237–46; A. J. van der Aalst, "Symeon de Nieuwe Theolog 949–1022: Politieke en Sociale Ideen van en Mysticus," 1–2, *Het Christel. Oosten* 37 (1985): 229–47, 38 (1986): 3–22; H. J. M. Turner, "St. Symeon the New Theologian and Dualist Heresies: Comparisons and Contrasts," *St. Vlad. Theol. Quart.* 32 (1988): 359–66.

47. See G. Cioffari, "Ricerca teologica e illuminazione dello Spirito nella teologia bizantina del secolo 11," *Nicolaus* 8 (1980): 341–50.

48 As by, e.g., I. Hausherr, in his introduction to Hausherr, *Un grand mystique byzantin: Vie de Syméon le Nouveau Théologien* (Rome, 1928), hereafter *Vie de Syméon*; J. Darrouzès (in the introduction and notes to his editions); Krivochéine, *Dans la lumière*, 188–93.

49. "Vita Symeonis," No. 146 (Hausherr, *Vie de Syméon*, 216). Symeon practiced theology "ἀμαθὴς τῶν θύραθεν ὢν μαθημάτων." See Niketas Stethatos's foreword to the Hymns of Simeon, who was said to be "τῆς θύραθεν ἐπιστήμης τῶν λόγων πάντῃ ἄγευστος" and yet "τῷ ὄντι σοφὸς καὶ θεολόγος δογματικώτατος": Koder and Paramelle, eds., *Hymnes 1–15*, 116, lines 114–18.

50. The question involves whether there is a real distinction, or merely a mental distinction [between Father and Son]: see "Vita Symeonis," 74f. (Hausherr, *Vie de Syméon*, 100–104); Symeon's "Theologica I" (Darrouzès, *Traités* 1:96–98); Hymn 21 (Koder and Nyrand, eds., *Hymnes 16–40*, 130–68.)

51. PG 154, 840 AB. Nephon refers primarily to the "Μέθοδος τῆς προσευχῆς" which probably cannot be ascribed to Symeon.

52 See Hausherr, *Vie de Syméon*, nos. 7–9.

53 See G. Podskalsky, *Griech. Theologie in der Zeit der Türkenherrschaft (1453–1821)* (Munich, 1988), 42.

54. See the recommendation (together with

Niketas Stethatos et al.) in Gregorios Senaites: PG 150, 1324D.

55. Symeon is hardly ever cited by Palamas himself. If one can trust the table of contents of the four volumes of Συγγράματα (Thessaloniki, 1962–1988) that have been published to date, then the only mention is of the Pseudo-Simeon "Μέθοδος τῆς προσευχῆς," in Vol. 1. Also, R. Sinkewicz's edition (*The One Hundred and Fifty Chapters* [Toronto, 1988]) does not offer a single citation of Symeon.

56. "Vita Symeonis," no. 72f. (Hausherr, *Vie de Syméon*, 98–100), no. 81 (ibid.,110), no. 92 (ibid., 126).

57. Hymn 19 (Koder and Neyrand, eds., *Hymnes 16–40*, 100, lines 79–81); Hymn 23 (ibid., 216, line 415).

58. "Vita Symeonis," no. 6 (Hausherr, *Vie de Syméon*, 12).

59. See the attempt to date some of the hymns in Kambylis, *Symeon*, hymns 26–30.

60. One catechism may be added, that for a long time was erroneously attributed to Diadochos of Photike: E. des Places, *Diadoque de Photicé: Oeuvres spirituelles* (Paris, 1955), 179–83.

61. See Beck, *Kirche*, 531f.

62. Ethic 4 (Darrouzès, *Traités*, 2:10, lines 21–29).

63. Ibid. (62, lines 755–60).

64. Hymn 4 (Koder and Paramell, eds., *Hymnes 1–15*, 196, lines 93–95).

65. Hymn 24 (Koder and Nyrand, eds., *Hymnes 16–40*, 246, lines 273–76.)

66. Hymn 31 (ibid., 384, lines 5–9); cf. Hymn 21 (see note 50).

67. Hymn 44 (Koder et al., eds., *Hymnes 41–58*, 76, lines 74–90).

68. Ethic 5 (Darrouzès, *Traités*, 2:78–118, esp. 78–80; 96–100).

69. Ethic 10 (ibid., 282–286).

70. Ethic 6 (ibid., 146–148).

71. Catechism 28 (Krivochéine and Paramelle, eds., *Catéchèses 23–34*, 142–62, esp. 142–46).

72. Century 1:4 (Darrouzès, *Chapitres*, 41) cf. Century 1:48 (ibid., 53).

73. Century 1:36, 3:45 (ibid. 50, 93).

74. Hymn 50 (Koder et al., eds., *Hymnes 41–58*, 168, lines 157–61).

75). Koder and Paramelle, eds., *Hymnes 1–15*, 106, lines 4–7.

76. Ethic 5 (Darrouzès, *Traités* 2:96–100), Ethic 9 (ibid., 218–256); Hymn 52 (Koder et al, eds., *Hymnes 41–58*, 198–210).

77. Hymn 44 (ibid., 88, lines 248–90 and line 292); Ethic 3 (Darrouzès, *Traités*, 1:396–400).

78. Catechism 14 (Krivochéine and Paramelle, eds., *Catéchèses 6–22*, 218, lines 198–220, esp. line 212).

79. Translation by the author from the German translation by H. G. Beck, *Vademecum des byz. Aristokraten: Das sogenannte Strategikon des Kekaumenos* (Graz, 1956), 94f. (no. 123). Cf. Darrouzès, *Traités*, 1:34.

80. See J. Gouillard, "Constantin Chrysomallos sous le masque de Syméon le Nouveau Théologien," *Trav. et Mém.* 5 (1973): 313–327 (also in idem, *La vie religieuse à Byzance* [London, 1981], vol. 11); idem, "Quatre procès de mystiques à Byzance (vers 960–1143)," *Rev. Et. Byz.* 36 (1978): 5–81.

81. See D. Wendebourg, *Geist oder Energien?* (Munich, 1980) (reviewed by G. Podskalsky in *Byz. Zeitschrift* 76 [1983]: 53f.).

82. Catechism 13 (Krivochéine and Paramelle, eds., *Catéchèses 6–22*, 198, lines 106–200, esp. line 124); Catechism 14 (ibid., 214, lines 142–216, esp. line 168). The indwelling by the three persons of God [the Trinity] is the subject of Century 1:7 (Darrouzès, *Chapitres*, 42). Whoever possesses the Holy Spirit possesses all three persons of God "unmingled and undivided": Hymn 21 (Koder and Neyrand, eds., *Hymnes 16–40*, 146, lines 200f.)

83. Catechism 14 (ibid., 212, lines 117–214, esp. line 128); Catechism 16 (ibid., 244, lines 82–246, esp. line 107). We see the symbol of the burning bush (Exodus 3:2), which is a symbol for Mary's virginity, used in this context also: Catechism 18 (ibid., 288, lines 293–298.)

84) Catechism 19 (ibid., 326, lines 153–160).

85. Catechism 20 (ibid., 336, lines 71–78); Hymn 49 (Koder et al., eds., Hymnes 41–58, 146, lines 1–10). Cf. Vita Symeonis, no. 36 (Hausherr, Vie de Syméon, 48).

86. Catechism 32 (Krivochéine and Paramelle, eds., Catéchèses 23–34, 244, line 80); Hymne 44 (Koder et al., eds., Hymnes 41–58, 94, lines 349f.).

87. Hymn 2 (Koder and Paramelle, eds., Hymnes 1–15, 182, lines 90–94). Cf. Hymn 33 (Koder and Nyrand, Hymnes 16–40, 412).

88. Hymn 54 (Koder et al., eds., Hymnes 41–58, 82, line 154).

89. Hymn 51 (ibid., 184, line 3). See also Niketas Stethatos's preface: Koder and Paremelle, eds., Hymnes 1–15, 112, line 64.

90. See Vita Symeonis, no. 23, 29f., 69f., 71, 113, 127 (Hausherr, Vie de Syméon, 32, 40, 92–96, 156f., 182).

91. A criterion which in a sense could be considered "objective" might be Symeon's sworn agreement with the fathers—were it not for the fact that he could state his agreement with the fathers on his own account, without reference to his position with the Church: Ethic 5 (Darrouzès, Traités 2:110, lines 418–435).

92. Catechism 30 (Krivochéine and Paramelle, eds., Catéchèses 23–34, 206); however, cf. Vita Symeonis, no. 5 (Hausherr, Vie de Syméon, 9).

93. Catechism 20 (Krivochéine and Paramelle, eds., Catéchèses 6–22, 344); Hymn 21 (Koder and Nyrand, eds., Hymnes 16–40, 142, lines 153–57).

94. Catechism 29 (Krivochéine and Paramelle, eds., Catéchèses 23–34, 176–78).

95. Ethic 1:1, (Darrouzès, Traités 1:180–82); Ethic 2:3 (ibid., 340–44); Hymn 58 (Koder et al., eds., Hymnes 41–58, 300, lines 306–309). See also G. Podskalsky, Byz. Reichseschatologie (Munich, 1972); idem, "Ruhestand oder Vollendung? Zur Symbolik des achten Tages in der griech.-byz. Theologie," in Fest und Alltag in Byzanz (Munich, 1990), 157–66 (text), 216–19 (notes).

96. See G. Podskalsky, "Marginalien zur Byz. Reichseschatologie," Byz. Zeitschrift 67 (1974), 351–38, esp. 357f.

97. Hymn 49 (Koder et al., eds., Hymnes 41–58, 154, lines 92–105); cf. Catechism 34 (Krivochéine and Paramelle, eds., Catéchèses 23–34, 290–92).

98. See A. Solignac, "Nicétas Stéthatos, moine byz., 11e siècle," in Dict. de Spir. 11 (Paris, 1981): 224–30; D. Stiernon, "Nicétas Stéthatos, hiéromoine byz., auteur spirituel et controversiste (11e siècle)," in Cath. 9 (Paris, 1982): 1217–19; see also D. G. Tsames, Ἡ τελείωσις τοῦ ἀνθρώπου κατὰ Νικήταν τὸν Στηθάτον, (Thessaloniki, 1971).

99. See J. Darrouzès, Nicétas Stéthatos: Opuscules et lettres (Paris, 1961) (hereafter Opuscules), 21.

100. PG 120, 852A–853A (chap. 1:1); 964 AC (chap. 3:20–22).

101. Letter 5:3 (to Gregorios Sophistes) (Darrouzès, Opuscules, 248).

102) Letter 7:5 (ibid., 276–78); Letter 8:2–3 (ibid., 282).

103. "De hierarchia," ibid. 340 (no. 37); see also J. van Rossum, "Reflections on Byzantine Ecclesiology: Nicetas Stethatos' 'On the Hierarchy'," St. Vlad. Theo. Quart. 25 (1981): 75–83.

104. "De hierarchia," (Darrouzès, Opuscules, 330–20, nos. 26, 28, 30); Περὶ ὅρων ζωῆς: ibid., 394–98 (nos. 32–35).

105. Περὶ ψυχῆς 66, ibid. 128, lines 12–21. The "Tabor event" has not yet been integrated: PG 120, 1000A (chap. 3:83).

106. See H. Kuss, "Byz. und lateinische Kultur in Süditalien: Studien zur Begegnung zwischen Byzanz und dem Abendland im

religiösen und geistigen leben Unteritaliens (900–1250)," Ph.D. diss., University of Göttingen, 1964; J. Gauss, *Zur Orientpolitik Gregors VII: Ost und West in der Kirchen- und Papstgeschichte des 11. Jahrhunderts* (Zürich, 1967); A. P. Kashdan (=Každan), *Byzanz und seine Kultur* (repr. Berlin, 1973) (this contains residual overtones of crude Marxism); I. Sorlin, "Publications soviétiques sur le 11e siècle," *Trav. et Mém.* 6 (1976): 367–98; B. M. Kaczinski, "Greek Learning in the Medieval West: A Study of St. Gall, 816–1022," Ph.D. diss., University of Michigan, Ann Arbor, 1976; *Le instituzioni ecclesistiche della "Societas christiana" dei secoli 11–12* (Milan, 1977); A. Guillou, *La civiltà bizantina del 9 all' 11 secolo: Aspetti e problemi* (Bari, 1978); M. Rentschler, "Griechische Kultur und Byzanz im Urteil westlicher Autoren des 11. Jahrhunderts," *Saeculum* 31 (1980): 112–56; E. Werner and M. Erbstösser, Ketzer und Heilige: *Das religiöse Leben im Hochmittelalter* (Vienna, 1986) (a class-oriented analysis of ideology). On the Arab world, see G. Troupeau, "La littérature arabe chrétienne du 10e au 12e siècle," *Cah. de civ. médiév.* 14 (1971): 1–20; c.f. ibid., 131–48, 239–55.

11
The Fall of an Intellectual: The Intellectual and Moral Atmosphere in Eleventh-Century Byzantium

Ja. Ljubarskij
Dumbarton Oaks

There are some things in history that can be understood in detail only by scholars with the good experience of living in a similar situation. One such thing is the peculiar ways of acting and behavior of intellectuals in autocratic and totalitarian Byzantium. It is generally assumed that the eleventh century is the period of intellectual climax, liberal and secular trends in culture, educational advancement, and toleration in morality.[1] That notion is correct provided we keep in mind its chronological and social limits. As a matter of fact what we have just said can be applied only to the middle of the eleventh century (I mean 1030s–1070s) and only to a very tiny circle of the educated people around Michael Psellos and some of his friends. (It is hardly possible to determine how numerous were the "educated class" and "literary public" capable of acquiring any ideas in Byzantium.)[2]

Even so, this "liberal," "secular," and "tolerant" climate of tiny, educated circles was of a very peculiar nature, and in order to illustrate it I would prefer not to plunge into general considerations but to take take one or two episodes as examples.

Educated and more or less independently thinking persons were constant targets of aggression in Byzantium. I will not discuss whether the aggression was initiated as is generally assumed by "illiterate monks," the fact is that we possess a lot of evidence of hatred directed against them.[3] Though different in nature, most of the offences concerned the attitude of the intellectuals toward pagan antiquity. As a rule this attitude played the role of litmus-paper indicating the state of mind of the Byzantines.[4] There is very little evidence of attempts by the "liberals" to defend themselves or even to launch a counteroffensive. The latter seem to remain defenceless and silent for centuries. Such attempts took place first in the eleventh century and their initiator was Michael Psellos.

Already in his youth Psellos directed a discourse against a certain Ofrida, who dared to attack his friend John Xiphilinos.[5] The young writer (the discourse was written in the forties) did not hesitate to use "strong words" describing the "dull and incapable" Ofrida, attacking the "intellectual and highly talented" Xiphilinos.

This quarrel appeared to be only a prelude to the much more serious and important combats of the future: polemics between Psellos and Michael Cerullarios and Psellos and John Xiphilinos, dating from a mature age of the writer. There is no need to retell once again the story of the relations between Psellos and Cerullarios.[6] I will mention only the two most important documents concerning these relations. I mean first of all Psellos's famous letter to Cerullarios, recently reedited with commentary and introduction by U. Criscuolo,[7] and the long accusation published but not delivered by Psellos after the death of the patriarch.[8]

In no way can the first-mentioned work be considered a private letter. The discourse was delivered in the presence of the emperor. Convincing evidence of it is the direct address to the emperor: ἀλλὰ οὐ θειόθαθε βασιλεύς (Epistola a Cerulario, 218). The phrase "Ἀλλ' ἐπανακτέον αὖθις ἡμῖν τὸν λόγον ἐπὶ τὸν οἰκεῖον εἱρμόν" (221-222) belongs to an oration, not to a letter. At any rate the letter was intended to be read publicly and turned out to be a sort of manifesto directed publicly to the patriarch.

Much has been said already about the contents of the letter, but one cannot help admiring the ability of the author, appropriate to a great thinker, to think through his ideas. The main idea of the writer is the total incongruence of two persons: Michael Cerullarios and himself. It is not the diversity and incongruence of different, separate traits but rather a difference and opposition in everything. "Do not you see by what mountains, what oceans, what continents we are separated from each other?" writes Psellos (Epistola a Cerulario, 69–71).

Very briefly one can define Psellos as a "liberal-minded," "secular," and "tolerant" type of person and Michael Cerullarios as "conservative," "spiritual," and "intolerant." Despite the diversity of "points of distinctions" there is in the letter one trait that can help differentiate, according to Psellos, between two kinds of persons: it is the attitude toward the "word" (λόγος), that is, rhetoric in the broadest sense of the word with special concern to its aesthetic value.

As becomes clear from the letter, Psellos at first wrote to Cerullarios trying to fascinate him with his lyre (θέλγειν), but Cerullarios remained the only one "not willing to hear" (ἀνήκοος) and "not willing to be bewitched" (ἀγοήτευτον). The metaphor of the "lyre" to which Cerullarios remains deaf occurs not just once in the letter. Willingness or unwillingness, capability or incapability to comprehend and appreciate "the word," especially in its aesthetic aspect, became for Psellos the main criteria for distinguishing persons as "ours" and "not ours." Appearance of such criteria meant a total break from the tradition of the Byzantine mentality of the previous centuries. This traditional Byzantine approach was most obviously represented in the preface by George the Monk to his chronicle. George fires there a broadside at all secular authors who write in a "lofty and verbose" manner.[9]

The letter mentioned is written in classical "ironic style": respect and even admiration for Cerullarios on the surface are nothing else but mere camouflage for inner contempt and hatred. One observation makes the wording of the letter sound not only ironic but even ominous. Until now scholars did not pay attention to the last part of the letter where Psellos says that he has just picked up the material regarding the life of Cerullarios and is now preparing a work (δέλτον) and will "adorn it with the flowers of rhythmical and beautiful diction" (λέξει ῥυθμοειδεῖ καὶ παγκάλῳ περιανθίσω τὸ σύγγραμμα). He hopes that his book will be enjoyed and praised all over the world (Epistola a Cerullario 263ff). What sort of δέλτον concerning Cerullarios was Psellos preparing at that time? It is reasonable to assume that Psellos hints at the work a little later edited as an "Accusation of Cerullarios." The interconnections between the two compositions are various but most obviously they reveal themselves in the use of the rare word συνκοριβαντιάω – "share in corybantic revels." In the letter (25–26) Psellos asks Cerullarios not to be angry with him for not being willing to συνκορυβαντίων with him. In the "Accusation" (253.22-24) Psellos fears that Cerullarios "will share celebrating secret rites and corybantic revels" (δέδοικα δὲ μή που καὶ συνωργίακε συνκορυβαντίων) with Dosithea (a fortune-teller from Chios). In the first case the word is used apparently in a good sense, but its "bad" connotation is apparent from the place cited in the "Accusation"!

"Praising" Cerullarios in the letter, Psellos was at the same time collecting material to be used later in his most severe accusation of the patriarch that had to bring him to dethronement and exile!

But before dealing with the "Accusation" I would like to make some remarks about another polemical work by Michael Psellos, his letter to John Xiphilinos.[10] In recent years this letter and the relation between Psellos and Xiphilinos as a whole has become an object of vivid discussion among scholars.[11]

Written approximately at the same time as the above-mentioned letter to Cerullarios, this discourse seems to be the result of the same "state of mind" of Psellos, but nevertheless differs very much from the previous letter. Like the letter to Cerullarios the discourse is a sort of counteroffensive, composed as a reply to the letter blaming Psellos for his secular inclinations.[12] But in contrast to that letter the discourse was directed to the old intimate friend of the author and has a certain personal and even intimate flavor not usually found in Psellos's epistolography. The author nostalgically and ironically mentions the "remnants of hair" on his head (55), affectionately appeals to books written by him as "children of his soul" (181), and sentimentally recollects their former common studies with Xiphilinos. The tone of the letter is extremely emotional and elevated. The "personal traits" are combined here with rhetorical figures and exaggerations.

But the strangest thing in the letter is its ending: the so-called repentance (μετάνοια) with thoughts expressed opposite to the previous ones. Psellos, who has just passionately defended his secular belief and convictions, is now full of Christian piety. "The whole Hellenic knowledge, that was in such esteem in former days [add here the Chaldaic, Egyptian and all other secret doctrines] is for me inferior to being a monk," asserts the former defender of secular knowledge.[13]

Such 180-degree turns were not alien to Byzantine writers in general, but nevertheless they are to be explained in each case separately. In our opinion the simplest explanation, mostly unexpected by Byzantine scholars used to seeing cliches everywhere, can work here: the intimate and "friendly" (not in the Byzantine "formal" sense of the word!) discourses do not need to be consistent and homogeneous. Just to the contrary, they can and even must be impulsive and spontaneous. The letter under review was written as an immediate response to the insulting letter of the former friend. Psellos loves Xiphilinos yet attacks him simultaneously, he blames him and repents of his blaming at the same time. Rhetorical figures and exaggeration in Byzantine epistolography do not preclude human feelings, as is generally assumed by scholars. In any case if they are not sincere human feelings expressed in this letter, it must be one of the most sophisticated and skillful imitations of them in Byzantine literature.

I would like to put aside the philosophical aspect of the letter that has been discussed recently. The main aim of Psellos is to defend "his Plato," Chrysippos, and ancient, secular scholarship in general from attacks by Xiphilinos and to prove their congruence with Christian dogma. The problem of "congruence or incongruence" of "outer," secular science (i.e, ancient scholarship) with Christian faith was actively discussed at this time and attitudes to the problem became also a sort of divide between "intellectuals" or "liberals" and so-called conservatives. Many times Psellos warns his audience not to make the Christian faith a pretext for ignorance and negligence of ancient scholarship.[14]

G. Weiss, commenting on one such passage, understood very well that the problem for Psellos's contemporaries was of much more importance than the mere contraposition of *Liebe zu Gott* and *Liebe zu den Wissenschaften* typical for western thought of this epoch.[15] In reality it had the same sense as in the letter to Cerullarios: the opposition of two human types: "liberal" and "conservative." There remained unchangeable in this letter and the first criterion of distinction the attitude to the "word" (λόγος) in its aesthetic aspect. Psellos's assertions sound a real challenge to the traditional Byzantine attitude: "I shall polish the roughness of my tongue with the elegance of language, easy style, good composition, harmony, so-called periods or figures; and I am sure it is not an obstacle towards virtue" (Epistola a Xifilino, 233ff.)

Although, as I have already stressed, both polemics were a sort of counteroffensive and the time of open warfare against the ignorance of the type of "Praise of Folly" by Erasmus Desiderius never did come to Byzantium, Psellos did not confine himself to "active defence" and in some cases launched a real offensive. But in the peculiar conditions of Byzantium this "offensive" took an extremely strange and unsuual form. Now we shall deal with such an example, the huge "Accusation against the patriarch Michael Cerullarios."

This discourse was written before January 1059 but was never delivered and was published by the vain author after the death of the patriarch. The incredibility and monstrosity of the accusations raised repeatedly puzzled modern scholars. But let us consider once more the situation, keeping in mind not only the "normal" condition of modern democratic society, but the peculiar circumstances of totalitarian Byzantium.

There is no doubt that the supposed trial of Cerullarios had been initiated by the emperor Isaakios Komnenos who suggested to Psellos that he play the role of prosecutor. The trial itself had an open political character and the supposed role of Psellos in it was comparable with that of Vishinsky in the notorious proceedings against the "enemies of the people" in the Soviet Union. But one point must be stressed here: Psellos really did not love Cerullarios for a very long time, and his hidden hostility can be detected even in his most flattering compositions devoted to Cerullarios.[16] To be sure, this hostility had little to do with the attitude expressed in the "Accusation," but at least Psellos had certain personal reasons not to reject the role of prosecutor. Moreover, in many places in the oration one can easily detect the remnants of Psellos's previous attitude toward Cerullarios: the patriarch, from the point of view of the prosecutor, is very austere, inflexible, and despises philosophy and "the word." But the main charges raised against Cerullarios in the letter quoted above reappear now as unimportant "secondary" reproaches. In the audience which Psellos had now, such arguments and accusations had not the slightest chance of success and Psellos therefore chose another way to achieve his goal, much more common and certain under the given circumstances: he accused the patriarch of deviation from orthodoxy.

The accusation contained five main points: a sort of corpus delicti or list of the supposed crimes of Cerullarios. The last of them (ἀδιαφορία) united many different misdeeds. The second, third, and fourth (τυραννίς–seizure of the power, φόνος–murder, ἱεροσυλία–sacrilege) include numerous incredible and fantastic crimes allegedly commited by Cerullarios. But the first and most serious charge (ἀσέβεια–impiety) was the very traditional and very dangerous accusation of devotion to ancient philosophers, especially Plato and Proclos ("Accusation," p. 240.8ff; p. 249.8ff.; p. 252.8ff., etc.), an extreme love for a different kind of ἑλλενισμοὶ and enthusiasm for almost every sort of heresy ("Accusation," p. 245.25ff., etc.). Such an accusation seems especially "strange" if we recall his letter to Xiphilinos written in defense of Plato. But these accusations fully conform to the main aim and general tone of the discourse!

Let us delay the discussion about the veracity of such accusations. It is of much more interest now to stress the sort of argumentation (very typical of totalitarian mentality) used by Psellos. There are two cornerstones to his reasoning. First, the dogma must be accepted as a whole. Every deviation from it turns the person into a defector and heretic, capable of committing every crime (p. 234.24 ff.). That is why it seemed reasonable for Psellos to ascribe to Cerullarios every sort of crime he could invent, not paying attention to their credibility.

The second "cornerstone" was of still greater importance. Psellos pretends to accuse not Cerullarios as a person, but the evil itself incarnated in him. The supreme aim of the discourse according to Psellos is the destruction of impiety (καθαιρεσία ἀσεβείας) and the demonstration of piety (ἐπίδειξις εὐσεβείας) (p. 232.11–12). That is why any compassion for Cerullarios according to Psellos was not only unreasonable but even criminal. The person sympathizing with him inevitably revealed his corruption and malice (anyone who feels sorry for Cerullarios offends God!).

As I have already mentioned, two compositions by Psellos devoted to Cerullarios (the letter and the "Accusation against the Patriarch") were closely connected with each other. Nevertheless the first appeared to be "a manifestation of Christian humanism," while the second was hardly more than an ordinary "witch-hunt." Such was the paradoxical logic imposed upon Psellos by the autocratic and totalitarian mentality of the Byzantines, a logic that turned the most liberal and most tolerant writer and thinker of the century into an extremely reactionary and severe prosecutor of Cerullarios.

The scenario mentioned above by no means seems to be fortuitous or accidental for the Byzantine writer. To confirm this statement it is now the best time to return to the interrupted story of the relationship between Psellos and John Xiphilinos. Its final lines are very expressive! After the death of Xiphilinos, Psellos composed a funeral oration devoted to his former friend.[17] This oration appears to be quite ordinary except for one point: its ending is totally opposed to the main content of the discourse. Psellos praises Xiphilinos as an educated and enlighted person in the first part and blames him for occupying himself with magic and sorcery and for a deviation from Christian doctrine in the second (p. 459.18 ff.).

It is not difficult to see that all these accusations in their essence are the same and made from a similar standpoint to those directed by Psellos against Michael Cerullarios in the "Accusation" discussed earlier. Psellos condemns Xiphilinos for impiety (ἀσέβεια) (p. 460.18), declares his principles to be opposite to that of his former friend ("I am laughing at the items you glorify and are proud of, they are for me instead a theatre or a scene" [p. 460.2 ff.]. The contrast between two parts of the oration is so great that it seemed reasonable for R. Anastasi to suppose that there had taken place a contamination of two different works.[18] Though very tempting, this suggestion can not be true because of a direct statement of the author that was not taken into consideration by the Italian scholar.[19] We cannot argue now how this little "accusation" was inserted in the epitaphios, but "the logic of events" seems here to be the same as in the case of Michael Cerullarios: Psellos defends the "liberal ideas" from the attacks of Xiphilinos and then turns at the end to become his prosecutor, a prosecutor of the most "reactionary" type. The "logic of events" we have just appealed to is nothing else but the sequence of the intellectual and moral climate of the century we are now speaking about. The paradox is that the "two faces" of Psellos appear to be combined now within the framework of a single composition!

But let us take another step. The epitaph of Xiphilinos was composed after 1075. Only a few years remained until 1082, the turning point in the intellectual history of Byzantium. In this year the trial of John Italos took place—the first in the long chain of similar legal proceedings throughout the twelfth century against persons deviating from the opinion of the church and state as regards the strict rules of orthodoxy.[20] Let us compare the accusation against Psellos' disciple and successor, John Italos, which was inspired by emperor Alexios I and the corpus delicti of Cerullarios and Xiphilinos. Of course they differ very much in details, but as a matter of fact they are similar in the core. In all three cases the persons are accused of impiety (ἀσέβεια) and devotion to pagan antiquity (ἑλλενισμός).

But what is the most striking thing common to all three accusations is that none of them had anything to do with reality. Neither the facts, nor the ideas by themselves had any value for prosecutors, once they served their purpose. The epoch of "enlightment" was succeeded by the time of "repressions," characteristic of the twelfth century.[21] Of importance for us is the fact that the middle of the eleventh century was the time of the highest intellectual upswing and "counteroffensive" of intellectuals, headed by the prominent writer, scholar and liberal Michael Psellos. But at the same time, the same Psellos turned out to be the first accuser and prosecutor of alleged dissidents. Unfortunately in the years to come such transformations and falls turned out to be typical enough for many intellectuals and sometimes for even the best.

Notes

1. See for instance P. Lemerle, *Cinq etudes sur le X1 siecle byzantin* (Paris, 1977); Ja. Ljubarskij, *Michail Psell. Licnost i tvorcestvo* (Moscow, 1978); L. Clucas, *The Trial of John Italos and the Crisis of Intellectual Values in Byzantium in the Eleventh Century* (Moscow, 1981); A. Kazhdan, *Change in Byzantine Culture in the Eleventh and Twelfth Centuries* (Berkeley, 1985).

2. See M. Mullet, "Aristocracy and Patronage in the Literary Circles of Comnenian Constantinople," in M. Angold, *The Byzantine Aristocracy IX to the XIII Centuries*, (1984), p. 73 ff.

3. See G. Weiss, "Die Leichenrede des Michael Psellos auf den Abt Nikolaos vom Kloster von der schonen Quelle," *Byzantina* 9 (1977), p. 292 ff; G. Podskalsky, *Theologie und Philosophie in Byzanz*, (Moscow 1977); L. Clucas, *The Trial*, p. 76 ff.

4. See B. Lourdas. "Intellectuals, Scholars, Bureaucrats in the Byzantine Society," *Kleronomia*, 2 (1970), p. 273 ff.

5. *Bibliotheca graeca medii aevi*, vol. 5, ed. C. Sathas, Athens-Paris, 1876, pp. 161–196.

6. I have done it already in Ja. Ljubarskij, *Michail Psell*, p. 79ff.

7. Michele Psello. *Epistola a Michele Cerulario. Testo critico, introducione, traducione e note a cura di Ugo Criscuolo* (Napoli, 1973).

8. Michaelis Psello. *Scripta minora, ed. Kurtz-Drexl* (Milano 1936), pp. 232–328.

9. *Georgii Monachi chronicon*, ed. de Boor, vol. I, 1904, p. 1.

10. Michele Psello. *Epistola a Giovanni Xifilino. Testo critico, introducione, traduzione e commentario a cura di U. Criscuolo* (Napoli, 1973).

11. See G. Weiss. *Die Leichenrede*, p. 296ff. Ja. Ljubarskij. *Michail Psell*, p.49ff; L Clucas. *The Trial*, p.133ff.

12. This obvious from the content of the letter (*Epistola a Xifilino*, 35ff a.o.)

13. *Epistola a Xifilino*, 229ff; especially 235–39.

14. See "The Praise of John Mauropous" in Sathas, *Bibl. gr. med. aevi*, 5, p. 151.28ff, cf. "Epitaph for the Abbot Nicolaus of the Monastery of the Fair Source" (published by P. Gautier in *Byzantina* 6 (1974), esp. chap. 9), the work was thoroughly analyzed by G. Weiss (*Eine Leichenrede*).

15. G. Weiss, *Eine Leichenrede*, p.291ff.

16. See Ja. Ljubarskij, *Michail Psell*, p. 81ff.

17. Sathas, *Bibl. gr. med. aevi*, vol.4, pp. 421-62.

18. R. Anastasi. "Sull' epitafio di Psello per Giovanni Xifilino," *Siculorum gymnasium* NS XIX, 1, 1966.

19. See Psellos's words: "I would like to have here the freedom to blame [Xiphilinos- J.L.], but the epitaph draws my speech away" (ἀνθέλκει δέ μοι τὸν λόγον ὁ ἐπιτάφιος). For the writer the last part of the work belongs to the epitaph as well!

20. The best accounts on the trial on Italos see P. Stephanou, *Jean Italos, philosophe et humaniste* (Rom, 1949); L. Clucas, *The Trial*.

21. See R. Browning, "Enlightment and Repression in Byzantium in Eleventh and Twelfth Centuries," *Past and Present* 69 (1975).

Index

Accusation of Cerullarios, 177, 179–180
Acheimastou-Potaminanou, M., 101, 102
Acta Sanctorum, 158
Adelung, F., 58–59
al-Adim, Ibn, 127, 132, 135
administrative system, Byzantine, 77–78
Admonitions of Kekaumenos, 111, 120
advent, of the messiah, 69–70
Akhbar, the, 127, 135
Albania, Slavic settlements in, 6
alps, Slavic settlements in, 5, 11, 12
Anastasi, R., 181
Anatolia
    monetary system of, 150
    topography of, 143–144
Antes, the, 1
apocalypse, 61, 68–69
Archaiologikon Delton, 15
Argos, Slavic pottery of, 26, 27
Arslan, Alp, 133, 134, 135, 136
art, Palaeologan, 91–92, 93, 98
art, post-Byzantine
    artists of, 97
    history of, 87–108
    patronage of, 93–94
    styles of, 98–107
al-Athir, Ibn, 127, 132, 133, 135
Attaleiates, Michael, 126, 128–131, 132, 134, 135, 136, 139, 156
Austria, Slavic settlements in, 8, 9, 11
Avars, domination of slavs by, 3, 4, 5
al-Azraq, Ibn, 127, 132, 135

Balkan peninsula. *See also* Byzantium
    art of, 87–107
    cities of, 78–79
    monetary system of, 150
    peasantry of, 77–78, 79–84
    Slavic migrations in, 1–12
    Slavic pottery of, 15–42
    topography of, 143–144
Baptism, 73–74, 160
Barlaam and Josaphat, 157
Barlaam of Seminara, 162
Barma and Postnik, 67
Beck, H.G., 154
Belić Aleksander, 8
Benakes, L.G., 155
Bezobrazov, Paul, 120–121
Boba, Imre, 11
Bogomils, the, 155
al-Bondari, 127, 132, 135
book illumination, Byzantine and post-Byzantine, 95, 97
Boschkov, A., 88
Botaniates, Emperor Nicephorus III, 130
Bowen, Harold, 78
Bowlus, Charles R., 11
Breaking the Code, 66
Bryennius, Nicephorus, 126, 128, 129, 130, 131, 134
Bulgaria
    art of, 90
    Slavic pottery of, 27
    Slavic settlements in, 2, 6, 9, 10
Bulgarian Church, reconstitution of, 157
Bulgars, domination of slavs by, 4
burial
    Christian, 27–28, 32
    Proto-Bulgar, 28

Slavic, 27–29, 32
Bury, John Bagnel, 111
Bushkovitch, Paul, 62, 70, 71, 74
Byzantine Agrimensors, 118
Byzantinische Zeitschrift, 153
Byzantinist texts, on battle of Mantzikert, 126–132
Byzantion, 125
Byzantium. *See also* Balkan peninsula
   civil war in, 45
   economy of, 141–150
   fall of, 43, 44, 51
   feudalism in, 115, 116–118, 119–120
   history of, 83
   iconoclasm in, 117
   intellectual activity in, 120–121, 175–181
   Islamization of, 81–82, 83
   land ownership in, 112, 114, 115–116, 118, 119
   legislation in, 112
   and Ottomans, 47
   political history of 11th century, 111–122
   population of, 144–145
   religion in, 153–163
   and Serbia, 43, 44–51
   societal structure of, 111–112, 116–117
   territory of, 143
   impact of Western civilizations on, 112, 119–120

Cahen, Claude, 125–126, 129–130, 131, 133–134, 135
Cantacuzenus, Emperor John VI, 45, 47
Carile, A., 126–127, 128, 129, 130–131
Carpathian basin, Slavic settlements in, 2, 3
Cathedral of Holy Sophia, 66, 71
cemeteries, Slavic, 27–29
Central Europe, Slavic settlements in, 11
Cerullarios, Michael, 176–177, 179–180
Charanis, Peter, 33
Chariskion, 114, 118, 119
Choniates, Niketas, 114–115
Christianity
   influence of on Byzantine art, 87, 93–95, 97, 103, 106–107
   in Byzantine Empire, 81–82, 90
   and Byzantine intellectuals, 178
   in Russia, 53–74
Christodulos of Patmos, Abbot, 156
Chronicle of Monemvasia, 33

Chrysippos, 178
Chrysomallos, Konstantin, 161
churches, post-Byzantine art of, 93–95
Cinq Etudes sur l'Onzième Siècle Byzantin, 142
cities, Byzantine
   changes in, 144
   decline of, 142
   influence of Ottomans on, 78–79
class structure, and Byzantine economy, 145–147
coins, Slavic, 32–33
Combefis, F., 158
Comnenos, Emperor Manuel I, 43
Constantinople, economy of, 145–146
Contarini, Ambrogio, 62
Continuator of Scylitzes, 126, 127, 128, 131
Corinth, Slavic pottery of, 26, 27
Čorović-Ljubinković, M., 26
cremation, 27–29, 32
Čremošnik, Irma, 26
Crete, art of, 96, 98, 99–103
Criscuolo, Ugo, 176
Croats, 9, 11
   origins of, 6–7
crusade movement, in Byzantium, 157

Damaskinos, Michael, 100, 101, 102
Dandolo, Enrico, 44
Danubian basin, Slavic settlements in, 2, 3, 10, 12
al-Dawadari, Ibn, 127, 132, 135
De Administrando Imperio, 6
Desiderius, Erasmus, 179
Dialects, Slavic, 7–11
Diehl, Charles, 111
Diogenes, Emperor Romanus IV, defeat of, 125, 127–128, 130, 131, 135, 136
Dionysus of Fourna, 106
Djedjevi Lozja, Slavic pottery of, 30
Dölger, Franz, 116
Donation of Constantine, 57, 60
Doncheva-Petkova, y., 23, 24, 27, 29–31
Dosithea, 177
Dragutin, King, 44
Duby, Georges, 146
Ducas, Emperor Michael VII, 130
Dumbarton Oaks Papers, 142
Dušan's Code, 4
Dušan, Emperor Stefan, 45–46, 47

Eastern Europe, Slavic settlements in, 11
Economic Expansion in the Byzantine Empire 900-1200, 142
economy, Byzantine, 141-150
    and class structure, 145-147
    differing theories on, 141-143
    monetary system of, 148-149
    and political factors, 146
    and expertise of ruling class, 149
    and trade, 147
    effects of transportation of, 143-144
ecumenical Patriarchate, role of in post-Byzantine art, 92-93
education, in Byzantium, 154-155
Epiphany ritual, in Russia, 53, 61-63
    description of ritual, 61
    history of, 62-63, 75
    Procession to the Jordan, 62
    as royal ritual, 63, 70-74
Ernstedt, Victor Karlovic, 120
Essays on History of Byzantine Education (Constantine IX), 121
Eulabes, Symeon, 159
Eustratios, 155
Exkousseia, 116-117, 118

Farmer's Law, the, 115
Fatihname, 133, 136
feudalism, in Byzantium, 115, 116-118, 119-120
Fine, John V.A. Jr., 6
fire, religious significance of, 73-74
Foss, Clive, 142
Fourth Crusade, the, 43

Garvan-Staretsa, Slavic pottery of, 30
Gautier, P., 126
George the Monk, 177
Georgia, art of, 93
Germany, Slavic settlements in, 4-5
Gestae Robertz Wiscardi, 126
Ghalib, Abu, 133
Gibb, H.A.R., 78
Giovio, Paulo, 62
Great Schism, the, 154, 158
Greece
    Slavic pottery of, 15-25, 26, 27
    Slavic settlements in, 2, 6, 10-11
Gregory, Timothy, 27
Grek, Maksim, 62

Grigoras, Nicephoros, 49

Harvey, Alan, 142
Helen of Anjou, 46, 51
Helen, Empress, 47
Helen, Princess, 44
heretical movements, in Byzantium, 155
Herrmann, Joachim, 5
History of the Byzantine Empire (F. I. Uspenskij), 114-115, 119, 121
Hlincha-type pottery, 30
Holy Scripture, the, 157
Holy Trinity, the, 161, 163, 171
"Humpty Dumpty" paradigm, the, 142
Hungary, Slavic settlements in, 8
Hunger, H., 126
Hussey, J.M., 154
Hymnus Acanthistus, 32
Hypopsephios, Monk Nephon, 158

icon
    in Byzantine art, 89, 98, 100
    religious ritual as manifestation of, 66, 71, 74, 75
iconoclasm, in Byzantium, 117
immunity, 116-117, 118
intellectual activity, in Byzantium, 175-181
    amid Christian dogma, 178
    hatred toward, 175
Isfahani, Imad al-Din, 133, 134
Islam
    in Byzantine Empire, 81-82, 83, 89-90, 155
Islamic texts, on battle of Mantzikert, 125-126, 127, 132-136
Italos, John, 120, 121, 154-155, 181
Italy, Slavic settlements in, 8, 9
Ivan the Terrible, and church ceremony, 63, 66-70, 72-73, 75
Ivić, Pavel, 4, 8

Jakovenko, Peter, 116-117, 118
al-Jauzi, Ibn, 127, 132, 135
al-Jauzi, Sibt ibn, 127, 132, 133, 135, 136
Jenkinson, Anthony, and Russian religious ritual, 56, 61, 64
John of Euchaita, 144
Justinian, Emperor, 1

Kajkavian dialect, 8-9

Kantorowicz, Ernst H., 69
Karsavin, Lev Platonovič, 121
Kazhdan, Alexander, 141-142
Kekaumenos, 160-161
Kerullarios, Michael, 154
Kirill, 157
Klaić, Nada, 5
Komnenos, Isaakios, 179
Komnenos, King Andronikos I, 120
Konomos, D., 105
Kontoglou, Fotis, 107
Korchak-Zhitomirksi type pottery, 25-26
Kosmas I, Patriarch, 155
Kremlin, layout of, 54-55, 73
Kronsteiner, Otto, 11
Krumbacher, Karl, 111
Kunstmann, H., 2, 4-5

Land ownership, in Byzantium, 112, 114, 115-116, 118, 119
languages, Slavic, 7-11
Lazarević, Prince Stefan, 47
Lefort, Jacques, 145
Legislation, in Byzantium 112
Lemerle, Paul, 142
Leon of Chalkedon, 155
Luke the Cypriot, 97
Lunt, Horace C., 4

Macedonia, art of, 90-91
Malingoudis, Phaedon, 10
Mango, Cyril, 145
Mantzikert, battle of, 125-136
    Byzantinist texts on, 126-132
    Islamic texts on, 125-126, 127, 132-136
    Turkish celebration of, 137
Materials for the Internal History of the Byzantine State (V. G. Vasil'evskij), 111, 112
Matthiae, Gugleilmo, 60
Maurice, Emperor, 1
Metochytes, Theodore, 45, 48-49
Millet, G. and Frolow, A., 89
Milutin, King, 44-45, 48-49
Mining, in Serbia, 44, 48, 49-50
Mitrofanović George, 103, 104
Monachism, in Byzantium, 156-157
monasteries
    in Byzantium, 114, 117-118
    post-Byzantine art of, 93-94
    in Serbia, 50
monetary system, in Byzantium, 148-149
Monotropos, Philippos, 157
Morrison, Cecile, 149
Mrnjavčević, Vukašin, 46
Muscovy. *See* Russia
mysticism, 158-163

Nemanya, Stevan, 43-44, 50
Nemanyid dynasty, 43-47, 51
Nestor, and Slavic pottery, 24
Niketas of Herakleia, 157
an-Ni'me, Ghars, 127, 133, 136
Nova Cherna, Slavic pottery of, 30
Novak, L'udovit, 3
Novel on the Law School (Constantine IX), 121

Obolensky, Dimitri, 77-78
Ofrida, 175-176
Olearius, Adam, 57
Olympia
    Slavic coins of, 32-33
    Slavic pottery of, 15-25, 26, 27, 31-33, 35-42
    Slavic tools of, 33
Ostrogorsky, George, 57, 64, 121-122, 142
Ottomans
    administrative system of, 77-78
    conquest of Balkan peninsula by, 84
    influence on Balkan cities, 78-79
    influence on Balkan peasantry, 77-78, 79-84
    influence on Byzantine art, 87, 89-93, 94-95, 98, 106-107
    and Serbia, 45, 46, 47-48
    timar (economic) system of, 78
Oxeites, Patriarch Johannes of Antiocheia, 156-157

Pachymeres, Georgios, 45, 48
Pakurianos, Gregorios, 156
Palaeologan art, 91-92, 93, 98
Palamas, Gregorios, 153, 161-162, 163
Paleologos, Emperor Andronicus II, 44-45
Paleologos, Emperor John V, 45, 46, 47
Palm Sunday ritual, in Russia, 53, 56-61
    description of ritual, 56
    history of, 56-57, 60-61, 75
    Procession on the Ass, 56, 57, 60, 64, 66, 68

as royal ritual, 63-70, 72, 74
Pančenko, Boris, 110
Pannonia, Slavic settlements in, 3
Patrut, Ion, 11
Paul, Apostle, 160
peasantry, Balkan
   family structure of, 80-81
   financial circumstances of, 79-80, 85
   influence of Ottomans on, 77-78, 79-84
   religion of, 81-82
Peira, the, 112, 113
Pelekanidis, S., 90
Penkova-type pottery, 25-26
Philotheus, Monk, 68
Podobedova, O.I., 72
politics, of 11th century Byzantium, 111-122
Polyviou, M., 94
Porphyrogenitus, Emperor Constantine VII, 6, 7, 11
pottery, Slavic, 15-42
   age of, 24-25, 30, 33
   characteristics of, 23-24, 29-30
   functions of, 24
   types of, 16-23, 25-26, 30-31
Prague-type pottery, 25-26, 30
Precarium/beneficium, 114
Primary Chronicle, 2
Pritsak, Omeyan, 4
Procession on the Ass, 56, 57, 60, 64, 66, 68
Procession to the Jordan, 62
Procopius, 1
Pronoia, 114, 115-116, 118, 119
Prosopographical studies, of Byzantium, 145
Proto-Indo-Europeans, as ancestors of Slavs, 2
Psellos, Michael, 113, 120-121, 126, 127, 128, 129, 131, 132, 136, 149, 154, 175-181
Ptochoprodromic poems, 145

al-Qalanisi, 127, 132, 135
Quantity Theory of Money, the, 149

Rastko/Sava (son of Nemanya, Stevan), 44
religion, in Byzantium, 153-163
   of Balkan peasantry, 81-82
   and classical education, 154-155
   and conflicts with state, 155-156
   and heretical movements, 155
   influence of Islam on, 155
   monachism, 156-157
   and mysticism, 158-163
   and the crusade movement, 157
   and the Great Schism, 154, 158
   and Rus', 157
religious celebration
   parallel between Christian and Jewish, 73
   as royal ritual, 63-74
   in Russia, 53-74
Rešetar, Milan, 8
Ritzos, Andreas, 99, 100
Romania
   art of, 93
   Slavic pottery of, 25
   Slavic settlements in, 4
Royal ritual, church ceremony as, 63-74
Rum Millet, the, 87, 92, 95, 98
Runciman, Steven, 81-82
Rus', 157
Rusanova, I.P., 25
Russia
   concept of Byzantine history in, 111-122
   religious celebration in, 53-74
   Slavic pottery of, 26

Sarata Monteoru, pottery of, 25
Scaveni, the, 1
Scytho-Sarmatians, domination of slavs by, 4
Sebastokrator, Isaak, 157
Seides, Niketas, 157
Serbia
   art of, 103
   and Byzantium, 43, 44-51
   church of, 44, 45-46, 50
   fall of, 51
   mining in, 44, 48, 49-50
   and Ottomans, 45, 46, 47-48
Serbo-Croatian dialects, 7-10
Serbs, 9
   origins of, 6-7
Sevim, A., 126, 134
Simonis, Princess, 44-45
Skabalanovič, Nicholas, 113-114, 120
Slavs
   types of burial, 27-29
   languages of, 7-11
   migrations of, 1-12

origins of, 2–4
pottery of, 15–42
settlements in Byzantium, 111, 113, 115, 119
tribes of, 1, 6–7, 9
Slawski, Franciszek, 7
Slovenes, 9
Slovenian dialect, 8–9
Smyrnaios, Theodoros, 155
Stefan of Nikomedeia, 153, 158, 159
Stethatos, Niketas, 153, 157, 158, 159, 160, 161, 162–163
Strategikon, 1
Strelitzas, Theophanes, 96, 98
Studenitsa, 50
Studites, Patriarch Alexios, 156
submission hypothesis, of church and state, 63–64, 70
Sumer, F., 126, 134
sviatki, 62
Sylvester, Pope, and Palm Sunday ritual 5, 57, 60
Symeon, 153, 158–163, 172
Synnada, Leo, 144

Themelis, 24
themes, Byzantine, 77–78
Theophylaktos of Ochrid, 112
Theophylaktos, Archbishop of Achrida, 157
Theotokopoulos, Domenikos, 106
timar system, Ottoman, 78
Timcrion, the, 157
tools, Slavic, 33
Torlak dialects, 7, 8
trade, in Byzantium, 147
Trubačev, O.N., 2–3, 7
tsar, performance of in religious ritual, 63–64, 66–70, 72–73, 74
Tsolakes, E. Th., 126

Tusculum Lexicon, 154
type I pottery, 16–18, 22, 23, 30
type II pottery, 19, 22–23, 30–31
Typika, the, 156
Tzangarolas, Stephanos, 103, 105

Udolph, J., 3
Uroš, King, 44, 46, 47, 48
Uspenskij, Constantine, 116, 117–118, 122
Uspenskij, F.I., 114–116, 118–120, 121, 122
van Wijk, Nicolaas, 7
Vana, Z., 25
vases, Slavic. See Pottery
Vasil'evskij, Basil, 111, 115, 118, 120, 121–122
Vasiliev, Alexander, 118
Vasmer, Max, 10
Vekos, John, 48
Vladimir, Saint, 72, 73
Voevods, patronage of art by, 93
von Rosen, R., 132
Vryonis-type pottery, 23
Vucinich, Wayne S., 77
Vyzharova, Zh. N., 24, 27–29, 32

Weiss, G., 178
Wolfram, Herwig, 11

Xiphilinos, John, 175–176, 177–178, 180–181

Yalouris, Nicholas, 15, 24, 26
Yugoslavia, Slavic settlements in, 1, 6, 8, 10

Zagruda, the, 80–81
Zakar, Sohil, 126
Zhitomirski-type pottery, 30
Zigabenos, Euthymios, 155